Performance Research

EDITORS:
Ric Allsopp Manchester Metropolitan University, UK
Richard Gough Artistic Director, Centre for Performance Research, Aberystwyth University, UK

GENERAL EDITOR: Richard Gough

CONSULTANT EDITORS:
Rachel Fensham University of Surrey, UK
Claire MacDonald University of the Arts London, UK
Alan Read King's College, University of London, UK
Heike Roms Aberystwyth University, UK
David Williams University College Falmouth: Dartington Campus, UK

Review Editors:
Karoline Gritzner, Aberystwyth University, UK
Daniel Watt, Loughborough University, UK

Administrator: Sandra Laureri, Aberystwyth University, UK

Associate Editor: Wayne Hill, Independent Producer and Writer

Performance Research is an independent, peer-reviewed journal published by Routledge Journals, Taylor & Francis Ltd for ARC, a division of the Centre for Performance Research Ltd, an educational charity limited by guarantee.

Performance Research was founded in 1995 by Ric Allsopp, Richard Gough and Claire MacDonald.

www.performance-research.net

EDITORIAL BOARD:
Philip Auslander, Georgia Institute of Technology, USA
Eugenio Barba, Director, Nordisk Teaterlaboratorium, Hostelbro, Denmark
Günter Berghaus, University of Bristol, UK
Rustom Bharucha, Independent Writer, Director and Cultural Critic, Kolkata, India
Johannes Birringer, Artistic Director, Alien Nation Co., Houston, USA
Paul Carter, University of Melbourne, Australia
Judie Christie, Centre for Performance Research, Aberystwyth, Wales
Toni Cots, Theatre Director and Researcher, Centre L'Animal a l'Esquena Girona, Catalunya
Enzo Cozzi, Royal Holloway, University of London, UK, and Universidad ARCIS, Santiago, Chile
Scott deLahunta, Independent Writer and Researcher, Amsterdam, Netherlands
Josette Féral, University of Quebec, Montreal, Canada
Norman Frisch, Independent, Performance Curator and Producer, New York, USA
John Hall, University College Falmouth: Dartington Campus, UK
Peter Holland, University of Notre Dame, USA
Marijke Hoogenboom, Amsterdam School of the Arts, Netherlands
Peter Hulton, Director, Arts Documentation Unit, Exeter, UK
Janez Janša, Independent Director and Dramaturg, Ljubljana, Slovenia
Adrian Kear, Aberystwyth University, UK
Bojana Kunst, Philosopher and Dramaturg, University of Ljubljana, Slovenia
Hans-Thies Lehmann, Johann Wolfgang Goethe-Universität, Frankfurt am Main, Germany
André Lepecki, New York University, USA
Alastair MacLennan, University of Ulster, UK
Susan Melrose, Middlesex University, UK
Patrice Pavis, University of Kent, UK
Andrea Phillips, Writer and Lecturer, Goldsmiths College, University of London, UK
Mike Phillips, Director, Institute of Digital Art & Technology, University of Plymouth, UK
Goran Sergej Pristaš, Dramaturg, Centre for Dramatic Arts, Zagreb, Croatia
Marian Pastor Roces, Independent Curator and Critic, Sydney, Australia
Paul Rae, National University of Singapore
Talia Rodgers, Routledge, UK
Valentina Valentini, University of Calabria, Italy
Mick Wallis, University of Leeds, UK
Tracey Warr, Independent Curator and Writer, UK
Daniel Watt, Loughborough University, UK

Forthcoming Issues

On Dramaturgy
Vol.14 No.3

Within a rapidly changing landscape of contemporary theatre and performance, the roles, functions and working conditions for dramaturgs are being redefined. This issue interrogates contemporary dramaturgy as an expanding field of tasks and skills, problems and strategies. It explores a wide range of dramaturgical practices in contemporary European theatre, dance, performance, and media art, and also draws attention to the pedagogical and institutional aspects of dramaturgy. In addition. 'On Dramaturgy' addresses the shared and collective nature of dramaturgical practice and proposes dramaturgy as a critical reflection on the politics of space and representation. The issue also considers the relationship between dramaturgical practice and the audience, exploring the emergence of new dramaturgies of/for the spectator.

Transplantations
Vol.14 No.4

The 50th issue of Performance Research raises a number of approaches to how we might consider the notion of transplantation traversing medical, biological, horticultural, socio-cultural, post-colonial, philosophical and linguistic perspectives and practices. It explores the borders and peripheries of performance, and the cultural, ethical and artistic implications of the uses and increasing prevalence of transplantation procedures. 'Transplantations' includes contributions on body transfers, foreign bodies, male pregnancy as strategic engagement, golems, poisoned arrows, disembodied geographies, trance and violence, bio-art, tattoos and identities, clown prosthetics, cultural transplantations, biomedical accidents, 'decisive transfusions', and skinned bodies, from theorists, scholars, practitioners, artists and a cartoonist. Our 50th issue celebrates and surveys the boundaries of performance research and its intersections with physical, fictive, virtual, and viral sites of transformation, translation and transplantation, as we move further into twenty-first century understandings, modes of being and ways of living together.

Submissions

Performance Research welcomes responses to the ideas and issues it raises. Submissions and proposals do not have to relate to issue themes. We actively seek submission in any area of performance research, practice and scholarship from artists, scholars, curators and critics. As well as substantial essays, interview, reviews and documentation we welcome proposals using visual, graphic and photographic forms, including photo essays and original artwork which extend possibilities for the visual page. We are also interested in proposals for collaborations between artists and critics. *Performance Research* welcomes submissions in other languages and encourages work which challenges boundaries between disciplines and media. Further information on submissions and the work of the journal is available at: http://www.performance-research.net or by e-mail from: performance-research@aber.ac.uk.

Published 2009 by Routledge
2 Park Square, Milton Park, Abingdon, Oxon OX14 4RN
52 Vanderbilt Avenue, New York, NY 10017

First issued in hardback 2018

Routledge is an imprint of the Taylor & Francis Group, an informa business

Copyright © 2009 Taylor & Francis.

All rights reserved. No part of this book may be reprinted or reproduced or utilised in any form or by any electronic, mechanical, or other means, now known or hereafter invented, including photocopying and recording, or in any information storage or retrieval system, without permission in writing from the publishers.

Notice:
Product or corporate names may be trademarks or registered trademarks, and are used only for identification and explanation without intent to infringe.

Typeset at The Design Stage, Cardiff Bay, Wales, UK

Abstracting & Indexing services: *Performance Research* is currently noted in *Arts and Humanities Citation Index*, *Current Contents/Arts & Humanities* and *ISI Alerting Services*.

ISSN 1352-8165
ISBN 13: 978-1-138-45877-2 (hbk)
ISBN 13: 978-0-415-55679-8 (pbk)

On Training

ISSUE EDITORS: RICHARD GOUGH & SIMON SHEPHERD

1	Editorial: On Training RICHARD GOUGH & SIMON SHEPHERD	96	On the Production of the Body Ideal VÉRONIQUE CHANCE
3, 4, 35, 53, 66, 113, 129, 134		103	Acting Freely JOHN MATTHEWS
	Pages from a Lost and Found Family Album RICHARD GOUGH & SIMON SHEPHERD	114	Partisan Warfare: Training, commitment and the politics of entertainment WOLF-DIETER ERNST
5	The Institution of Training SIMON SHEPHERD	119	In Permanent Process of Reinvention GUILLERMO GÓMEZ-PEÑA, ROBERTO SIFUENTES & KIMBERLEE PÉREZ
16	Did you say 'training'? JOSETTE FÉRAL		
26	Of Pounds of Flesh and Trojan Horses : Performer training in the twenty-first century FRANK CAMILLERI	130	Book Review: The Lifeworks of Tehching Hsieh DAVID WILLIAMS
		132	Notes on Contributors
36	Setting the Stage : Social-environmental and motivational predictors of optimal training engagement ELEANOR QUESTED & JOAN L. DUDA		
46	Movement, Training and Mind : Insights from the perspective of Motologie ULF HENRIK GÖHLE		
54	Wood and Waterfall : Puppetry training and its anthropology CARIAD ASTLES		
60	Psychological Training for the Actor: A question of plumbing or wiring? DICK McCAW		
67	Trained Performances of Love and Cruelty Between Species PETA TAIT		
74	When Train(ing) Derails BOJANA BAUER		
80	Repetition and the Birth of Language PIOTR WOYCICKI		
85	Spinal Snaps: Tracing a back-story of European actor training JONATHAN PITCHES		

Editorial
On Training

RICHARD GOUGH & SIMON SHEPHERD

The concept of training seems to have accumulated significance during the twentieth century and into the twenty-first. Once regarded, in general, as a natural, or automatic, first step towards a chosen career, training is now often seen as a potential solution to social and indeed personal problems. Unemployed young people are offered training programmes, those already employed are offered staff development, employers go on 'leadership' courses. Where training was the first step towards a chosen career, it knew where it was heading, the career was already established. Where training offers to solve problems or enhance individuals, it tends to invoke the possibility of something yet to be established – an end to youth alienation, personal enhancement, new ability in one's job, fulfilment. The promise offered by training is therefore not simply the transmission of skills and craft but also access to aspiration. And, in cultures where primary emphasis is placed on individuality, in promising to facilitate personal aspiration training also promises to make the world a better place.

Within this general trend there has been renewed interest in the specific area of training for theatrical and performance activities. Over the last three to four decades there have appeared numerous proposals for and descriptions of new and different training regimes. In their published forms these tend to combine descriptions of activities – both their rationale and practice – and arguments justifying the hypotheses and philosophy of the training.

Not all such publications assume that they are addressing those who want to perform. In the domain of 'applied' theatre the emphasis can fall instead on the skills of facilitation, on enabling others to take part in a creative project, where those taking part may not have the aim of performing in front of anyone else. Once again training comes to acquire a wider remit that no longer thinks of the trained individual simply in terms of their career but now also in terms of their general development as a person.

Connected with the issue of where training fits into the lives of people and their employment, where it fits into society, there is the question of what we think training is. While descriptions of training regimes by those that design and practise them are often passionate and eloquent, they tend to generate, often necessarily, their own terminologies. This raises the difficulty that, if we are to understand the activity of training in general, we need to have a general framework within which we can do so. Here we get into problematic territory. For specific regimes of training could argue that they require their specific languages in order to engage with, and step away from, assumed concepts and their emotional and physical embodiments. At the same time it is perhaps only within a meta-language that we can think about the relationships between these various trainings.

You will find that we have tried to foreground the matter of language in the range of essays in this volume. While the volume doesn't propose a meta-language as such, we hope that, in the dialectical relationship of specificity and generalised parallels, the contrasts between the essays offer a foundation for beginning on the work of developing a meta-language for training.

Alongside the matter of language, which continues throughout, the volume hopes also to produce reflection on training by organizing itself into four sections. The first group of essays tends to address the general nature of training and its various institutionalizations. This clearly has bearing on the sorts of chronological developments which this Editorial began by describing. From here a second group of essays looks at a range of training regimes and practices. None, however, is a straightforward 'practitioner' description. All seek to tease out some of the general questions and issues that are prompted by specific practices and their terminologies. They don't arrive at a generalized framework, but they do keep in play that tension between specificity and shared concerns.

Now so far it might be assumed that the languages and assumptions about training have to do with its practice and process, and indeed with the career or discipline for which it might claim to train. But, on the route towards a meta-language of training, it is worth asking what, if anything, is assumed in common about the thing which is being trained. In a culture which has proposed the multiple and divided subject, what, precisely, is the subject of training? To flag this issue, in the third group of essays the person of the author tends to become more prominent, as both the subject of the essay and the subject of training. These are essays which figure, in different ways, engagement with training. But there is a related, and much murkier, question that runs through the whole volume. The question is – what is the body that is trained? What do we assume this body to be? This in turn slides into a related question – what is the body of training? In a bid to formulate a framework, if not a meta-language, for thinking about training, it may be useful to start to describe, in any instance of training, the shape of its physical encounter across a group of bodies, to describe that material entity which consists of a set of bodies in organized and felt relation one to another: the body of training.

And of course for any such set of bodies there are the felt links to and differences from the bodies who are not 'in' the training, who are not similarly trained. Training is given, or finds for itself, an institutional place. Different trainings are differently institutionalized, but what they all have in common is a negotiation of the relationship between that thing which is called training and the wider, perhaps more amorphous, entity which is society. The final essays in the volume begin to move us into reflections on the relationships between different sorts of training and indeed the relationships between training and society. These too contribute part of the foundation for arriving at a meta-language of training, for one way of comparing trainings might be to ask what the material determinants on them are. Does it have special clothes, special equipment, a special place? What is provided by the trainers, and on what terms? What is bought by the trainees, and by what means? What is the precise relationship between training and the specific point in the trainee's life and career? How have that life and career adjusted to allow for the place of training? What, in short, is the cost of training?

This Editorial is much more full of questions than answers. The work of developing a general framework for reflecting on training, developing a meta-language, is, at the end, to be handed across to you, the reader. And there is, before we finish, one more bit of the foundation that has to be supplied. Going beyond the issue of the institution of training, there is the general question as to the social place of, and discourse around, the state of being 'trained'. Some people carry their trainings with them as charisma accessories – the gym-trained body, the person known to do martial arts. For others their particular training tends, in its functional or ethical nature, to subsume the individual to social imperatives. The off-duty doctor is differently positioned from the off-duty actor.

Editorial

There are, perhaps, expectations, often half-realized, about trainedness. These work not as a narrow assumption that, on- or off-duty, a trained person has the capacity to do what needs doing but perhaps instead as a more generalized assumption that the trained person has 'capacity' in general, as a quality. To be trained thus potentially becomes a discourse about personal capability and completeness. And in turn these feature within a discourse of personal, and indeed social, attractiveness. So in reflecting on the entity of training we might also like to meditate on its erotics. And with that thought we'll leave the reader to browse what follows.

Pages from a Lost and Found Family Album

In the autumn of 2007, CPR acquired the entire library and personal archive of Ram Gopal from Richard Booth of Booth's Books, Hay-on-Wye. In the remains of thirteenth-century Hay Castle, searching through tea-chests and banana boxes stuffed full of extraordinary manuscripts, correspondence, choreographic scores, theatrical ephemera and dance memorabilia, we found a box containing numerous photo albums; the top layer consisted mainly of albums of Ram's friends, dancers and colleagues; one was entirely of dogs and another of Greta Garbo. Among its leaves the desiccated body of a dead spider. Towards the bottom was a magnificent elephant-size folio of vellum pages wrapped in Thai silk that appeared to be the personal scrapbook of Anna Pavlova, which carefully entombed press cuttings, programmes and announcements of her tours and engagements. Under this lay an exquisite prospectus for the Chekhov Theatre Studio, Dartington Hall, the embossed gold lettering glistening like new on the terracotta-coloured boards. It seemed the booklet had never been opened. Cocooned in tissue, the thirty pages describe the course of training on offer, describe the Chekhov Studio and show pictures of Dartington Hall and its grounds.

At the very bottom of the box was a magnificent leather-bound album with brass clasps and a series of catches. As slowly we opened the book there emerged a sequence of pictures, curious in their subject matter. These were people training for some performance unknown, an unshaped sequence, those energized limbs now flat in our hands. Names tumbled from the pages, scribbled in different hands, Laban, Stanislavski, Meyerhold, Morris, Osterwa. Exotic names just-legible, scratchings of a pen with an old nib, Grotowski, Chekhov. Dimly realized places half-seen, Chinese acrobats, Indian dancers. All those bodies caught in moments of supreme expertise. And other bodies on their journey. And another dead spider.

The editors of the issue decided to insert a few pages from this lost and found album between the essays which follow. Not quite illustrations for those essays, the images offer their own account of the body-mind doing training. Real bodies at lost historical moments, inscrutable in their variety, organized by some obscure principle, they haunt the interstices of this work.

And as for the magnificent leather-bound album, clues to its provenance can be found at the end of this issue.

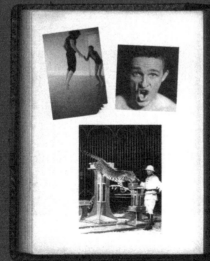

The Institution of Training

SIMON SHEPHERD

By 1911 Elsie Fogerty had developed her chorus of students to a point where they could dance in unison to the rhythm of their own speaking. It was, Fogerty felt, a new encounter with the ancient Greek Dionysiac art.

Fogerty appears at the top of this narrative because she was working at a time when training was at its most institutionally glamorous. She herself founded one of the new centres for theatre training, the Central School of Speech-Training and Dramatic Art. In Britain, with which this essay is mainly concerned, these centres were modelled on conservatoires for musical training, the earliest of which included the Royal Academy of Music (1822) and the London Academy of Music (1861). In putting together their proposal for a National Theatre in 1904 William Archer and Harley Granville Barker said that the theatre should have attached to it a training school. It would function not merely to supply trained actors but also to keep the theatre's practices in touch with the modern world: 'by providing for it recruits strong in the vital principles of their art, instead of assisting it mechanically to hand on an academic tradition (however worthy) from one artistic generation to another' (Archer and Barker 1907: 100).

They saw this school as an agent of modernity because they defined training itself as a new sort of approach both to art and to work. It would break with the dilettante flirtation with theatre as an art. And, crucially for the story that will develop here, it promised an end to the casualization of theatrical labour. It was thus, potentially, a tool for professionalization of the acting career, and modern in its conspicuous departure from the previous model that governed entry to the theatrical profession. That model consisted of joining a company, or, more effectively, being born into the family, and learning on the job, where knowledge was transmitted from the experienced to the inexperienced, a domesticated version of the relationship between master and apprentice. These arrangements had obtained for centuries and carried within them an explicit conservatism, whereby one learns what already exists. By contrast, Fogerty's chorus took forward their training by discovering something that had never before existed in British theatre art.

Fogerty, Archer, Barker and their contemporaries saw themselves as a consciously modern movement, facing a need to renew British theatre. But this application to theatre and music came pretty late in the history of training itself. Driven by more urgent life-and-death necessities various armies in the sixteenth and seventeenth centuries discovered a need to train their soldiers, to ensure they obeyed orders and kept discipline. Maurice of Nassau led the way in the early 1560s when he revived and re-applied Roman methods of drill. This did more than make soldiers obedient and efficient. It turned a heterogeneous collection of men into a coherent military group: 'when a group of men move their arm and leg muscles in unison for prolonged periods of time, a primitive and very powerful social bond wells up among them'

(McNeill 1982: 131). This work was continued by Gustavus Adolphus and Frederick the Great.

The word 'training' only started to become associated with the activity of education in the early to middle sixteenth century. The Oxford English Dictionary shows the dominant meaning applied metaphorically to bringing up youth, leading them forward by persuasion, and from here to teaching them. The word is specifically used in relation to bodily activity in the mid-century as in 'trayned and exercysed' in - significantly - 'the feictes of Warre'. That association was popularized in an initiative of Elizabeth I that established a new measure for defence of the realm, a citizen army, where men were drilled into coherent units. These were known to contemporaries as 'trained bands', as in the Elizabethan State Papers Domestic for 1592: 'One of their trained bands, under Sir Harry Coningsby, has been a year without a captain and officers; Sir Jno. Cutts's band is in much the same case … In spring their bands ought to be viewed and trained' (EMLS 2008). While the development and activity of trained bands led to jokes in the theatre, later on came evidence of the powerful impact of training at a level very different from physical skills. The trained bands became, in the early 1640s, the vanguard of the Parliamentary opposition to the crown. They had developed political analysis and commitment.

The task of getting a young man to drill in unison with other members of a military company is clearly a very different form of education from the experience on the job where the apprentice supposedly learns from the master, going on to qualify in his own right by making his master-piece. In one respect there is a similarity - learning by copying. In another it is radically different: the apprentice attached to a small household manufactory and a craft guild is placed within a hierarchy of mastery as extended family, paternalism underpinned by the legal relationship of indenture. The craft guilds were second only to family as a traditional, ancient, structure of personal relationships. By contrast, the man in a band of soldiers is committing part-time to a group of peers not structured as a craft hierarchy.

This relationship between 'training' and a more ancient-feeling 'craft apprenticeship' becomes polemically explicit in the early decades of the eighteenth century. The preparation for the profession of surgeon was jealously guarded by two traditional groups, the College of Physicians and the Company of Barber-Surgeons. They taught through methods of disputation. Against this a new practice was developed by the hospitals of St Bartholomew, St George and St Thomas. They introduced training of surgeons based on practice and empirical evidence, the demonstration of dissection (Linebaugh 1977). These were not just new methods but a challenge to old institutions. Before it reaches theatre, then, training has been associated not only with transmitting skill and technique but also with creating coherent group entities that are outside the traditional structure of relationships. Insofar as those structures of relationships felt 'natural' - extending outwards from master/father - then training denaturalizes.

2.

That denaturalizing aspect haunts training through its general twentieth-century history. A rough sketch of this history shows that in about the first third of the century, sport, politics and theatre expressed an interest in bodies made fit and efficient. This ran parallel to the projects of artists and architects such as Léger and Le Corbusier who were striving for 'standardization' and purism of form. The bodily ideal was available, however, for both positive and negative appropriations, with, in the latter case, projects of labour efficiency and military discipline moving towards de-humanizing ends, as articulated most notoriously in the fascist regimes (Segel 1998). But we should be wary of simplifying the narrative. Hillel Schwartz suggests the new kinaesthetic, which inhabited graphics as well as bodies, produced gestures that did not signal conformity but gave 'true expression to a private impulse':

> the technology of the image colluded with modern dancers and corporeal mimes (as it was colluding with industrial time-and-motion experts and scientific physiologists) to redefine the nature of physical grace and the manner by which we expect our bodies to tell the truth about our innermost selves. (Schwartz 1992: 91, 101)

So too Mark Franko reminds us that for the masses to be 'organized' emotionally, 'This could not happen without emotional self-recognition, for organization signified a readiness for action' (2002: 23). The implication is that the fit body is a natural part of a larger political project.

For those in theatre, training pointed towards ways of revitalizing theatre art. This manifested in various practices across Europe, including the work of Meyerhold, Laban, Wigman, Dalcroze, Copeau and Saint-Denis. In Britain Fogerty was scathing about the performer who relies on feeling without having access to 'technical principles' (1932: 16, 20). Her views chime with T. S. Eliot's 1928 remarks about the ballet in his 'Dialogue on Dramatic Poetry':

> You all approve of the ballet because it is a system of physical training, of traditional, symbolical and highly skilled movements. It is a liturgy of very wide adaptability, and you seem to laud the liturgy rather than the variations. Very well ... I say that the consummation of the drama, the perfect and ideal drama, is to be found in the ceremony of the Mass. (Eliot 1999: 47)

Originally a Greek word for public service, liturgy became associated with the explicitly public rites, as against private devotions, associated with religious worship. Thus Eliot suggesting a drama modelled on the Mass parallels Fogerty discovering the Dionysiac roots of theatre. For both, training provided a traditional, yet abstracted, practice, not bound by the needs of realist representation and as such gestured to something beyond daily stuff, a 'liturgy'.

By mid-century, however, training was losing its associations with radical artistic purism. As the left-leaning journal *New Theatre* saw it in its survey of London institutions in the mid-1940s, only one school trained actors for the future – namely Saint-Denis's Old Vic Theatre School; the rest merely trained for 'today' (Jenner 1948). Training regimes now deferred not only to commercialism and realist art but also to a dominant class order. Joan Littlewood famously opined that theatre training schools, and the Royal Academy of Dramatic Art in particular, taught 'poise, propriety and "tricks of the trade"'. This 'poise' combined upper-class behaviour – 'cup-and-saucer, French-window stuff' - with artificiality: 'curiously affected speech and the lack of anything resembling normal activity in the movements and gestures.' (in Holdsworth 2006: 45-7) Littlewood's view thus sees theatre training as a supplement to the learning of manners, where the training makes that class style into an aesthetic value. This production of

• **Karfreitag Fürbitten.**
photo Melchio2006

photos Glen Arkadieff

class aesthetics by theatre training was underpinned, as the director André van Gyseghem saw it, by an economic reality. Writing in 1947 he noted the increasing numbers of people trying for a career in theatre. To service the demand there sprang up new private training schools, which only the rich could afford, with the effect that entry was restricted 'to children of such parents as can afford to keep them on two years after they leave school or college ... and this means that children of working-class families are for the most part barred training'. The 'dramatic academies' are, in summary, 'as much finishing schools for young ladies and gentlemen as anything else' (van Gyseghem 1947: 16).

In the year after, at a national conference - the so-called 'Parliament of the British Theatre' - there were calls for a more widespread drama education, including the establishment of drama in universities. This institutional commitment to a more inclusive, democratized, theatre practice was part of the cultural outlook specific to immediately post-war Labour Britain. A decade later the backlash against upper-class theatre became more narrowly focused, and indeed itself aestheticized, in the fashion for actors with working-class and regional voices delivering, of course, appropriately earnest lines in appropriately abstemious scenographies. But this love-affair with the working-class and regional (the adjectives being symptomatically interchangeable) amounted simply to a continuation by other means of dominant realism underpinned by the uniform production of Stanislavskian individuality. It was explicitly a repudiation of the more radical experimentalism pioneered a decade before by Michel Saint-Denis and his colleagues at the Old Vic Theatre School.

The blow to theatre training as such was struck not by an apparently new modern class doing old things in new voices but by a whole set of differently new practices. The early- to mid-1960s saw the arrival of Happenings and improvisation. Then around the seminal period called '1968', the art and design people and the political activists began to make theatre, declaring, simultaneously, their lack of training for it. Indeed in the climate of the times it was important to reject not simply theatre training but any training. '1968' was the period of political unrest, major challenges to state organization and the doctrine of personal liberation, which enjoined that you 'do your own thing'. There was an interest in what one fashionable book called 'de-schooling' society, where schools are conceived as institutions preparing their subjects for submission to discipline, order, organization and capitalist values. A radicalized education put creativity, personal fulfilment and - a key term of the period - play at the centre of its activity. This was exemplified in Albert Hunt's work in Bradford, at a college not of theatre but of art, a subject seen at the time as rebellious, both creatively and socially. If the trained body and mind were prepared for submission and orderliness, the untrained body and mind could be creative and free ...

Put that way, the binary logic looks, rightly, absurd. By the early 1970s many of the free and creative - and politically committed - theatre workers were making shows that repeated very similar formulae. The repudiation of training had not, of itself, guaranteed new theatre forms. Indeed it's arguable that, when the new forms of physical theatre later emerged, they were developed by those who trained seriously. But in the mid- to late-1970s that was not the dominant discourse. If in the early century training was a means of challenging stale art and tradition, seven decades later political and artistic radicalism were demonstrated by staging the absence of training. The early punk bands assumed the rhetorical position of being 'garage bands' and 'three-chord wonders'. But while the artists and thinkers had attacked training for its complicity with capitalist values, in the mid-1980s capitalism's government continued this assault by other means. On one hand dismantling productive industry and its craft apprenticeships and on the other maintaining a highly trained military and a militarized police force, it discursively severed training's relationship with productivity. In its place came a society of amateurism in high places, advancement on the basis of ruthlessness and greed, and an expansion of service industries: a culture where the only valued skills were 'interpersonal' ones, charm without respect.

By the last decade of the twentieth century, training was positioned again in a new place. It no longer sat in subservient relationship to organization and institution and Party. Training was now in a market-place of those who had learned to call themselves consumers, where the cult of celebrity had produced the collective fantasy of life-change through make-over. It was a mark of a healthy life, and a life healthily in the control of an individual, to have a 'Personal Trainer'. The well-heeled acquired muscular legs.

For those with an interest in theatre, training once again offered the promise of returning to the seriousness of the art. In part, the relatively isolated experiments from a decade or so before were becoming more widely known in the institutional canonization of such as Grotowski and Barba. But so too it became popular to select classes, courses, residencies, 'workshops' - a whole package of trainings put together by individuals for themselves, the menu for a theatre arts make-over. Its influence was felt even among those who were the inheritors of the 1970s tradition of radical de-institutionalization: performance artists themselves took a position on training, as an issue of *Performance* magazine from 1986 records:

> For a long time it has been considered that technique was something which must be discarded in order for it not to form a barrier between the maker and perceiver. Leaning not to fabricate, to act purely from instinct, has been the first step on the path to true creation and innovation. But slowly, from that standpoint of pure instinct, it can be possible to train the body and mind to frame the creative impulse in such a way that it can be said to be amplified by technique. (La Frenais 1986: 18)

The issue features artists who opted to undergo new and apparently alien forms of training. While clearly a specialized minority activity, this is an interesting testimony to a desire to engage

• Marianne Noack. Zentralbild Wendorf 7.12.69 Berlin: DDR – Turnmeisterschaften der Frauen im olympischen Achtkampf in der Dynamo-Sporthalle – Marianne Noack (SC Empor Rostock) bei ihrer Pflichtkür am Schwebebalken

with 'training' even by those most institutionally distant from it.

The performers Marty St James and Anne Wilson describe their lessons in ballroom dancing, and Ian Munro talks about becoming a deep-sea diver. For the dancers there was the thrill of learning the technique, of discovering they could not fudge what they had to do, and of being shouted at when they got it wrong: 'after having gone through art college, become artists ... to be placed in a position that's absolutely skill-based'. Here is the turn from the 1970s' ethos, but there's more to it: 'I had to stop being a wimp, as she [the instructor] said - pick my back up, stand up straight and stride out ... There's no right to fail.' Similarly the diver found that things could not be fudged, and the need to learn skills for survival in a situation of real risk had its effect:

> I went into it expecting to be a passive observer to something very interesting. What I was actually confronted with was the necessity to stop being a baby ... An awful lot of artists are only artists because they have always been babies. They are very, very, self-indulgent. (La Frenais 1986, 22, 27)

While the training was undertaken as an extension of, or even challenge to, their art, it seems that the most significant part was a sense of personal toughening - not being a wimp or baby. After the 1970s' approach to artist education, this was growing up, properly entering the real world ... as the Thatcher government might have described it. Training here seems to be rehabilitated as part of a backlash against the 'liberal' 1970s, and, while for the early-century modernists it involved submission to that which was higher or beyond, in the performance-art world of the mid-1980s it finds its significance in the strengthening of the individual.

And with that strengthening comes a feeling of access to something beyond familiar daily practice: 'getting into the great Mare, the great sea, the great ocean, the female element' (La Frenais 1986: 28). While a sense of training's access to something larger has always been there, the definition, and the promise, of that larger entity have changed. At one time the trained voice and a demonstrable set of 'good' manners signalled the presence in the person of a class position, much as a soldier's disciplined movement signalled the presence in the soldier of the army, or the presence in the efficient worker of the factory. A few decades later the body and mind that put themselves through martial arts training and workshops in oriental theatre modes were apparently not only gaining access to but opening themselves to penetration by alternative and explicitly 'non-Western' philosophies of living. The gym-trained body signals that it has been impressed, as it were, by a life-style that values health, organizes leisure and affords sunshine. Training becomes attractive because of its capacity to enhance, as they say, the individual. While all sorts of professions and activities still require specific skills, from driving to surgery, the work-related training has spawned a glamorous alter-ego called personal development. And that alter-ego promises not so much a structured engagement with skills as a visionary projection of enhanced individuals all glowing in the radiance of uncompromising blandeur.

3.
Beneath this rough narrative of training, can we discern any defining characteristics of that specific thing which is training for performance?

The trained bands aimed by drilling to produce orderliness and coherence in a previously disparate group. The training of the early-eighteenth-century hospitals aimed by practical demonstration to produce skills of a high quality. Theatre training replicates the dual processes of developing group coherence and transmitting individual skills. The difference of actor training from the other two may be said to lie, however, in a sense of abiding unnaturalness. This derives from two intractable contradictions. The first of these has to do with the function of actor training.

Archer and Barker thought training would put

an end to dilettante engagement with theatre and would thereby professionalize the art form. This problem persisted, however. When post-war Britain was beginning to rebuild itself, there was a discussion in New Theatre prompted by Equity's restriction of entry to the acting profession to those who had either worked in rep or attained a diploma. The Principal of RADA warned in the October 1946 issue about the 'danger' of the illusions that those coming out of the armed forces may have held about actor training, namely that it offers an 'escape' from military routine and a 'direct means' for 'self-expression' frustrated by war service, 'in effect, a freedom from unpleasant discipline'. But, he says, there is 'no profession that demands a higher degree of discipline' (Barnes 1946: 19). The view of the General Manager of the Q Theatre at Kew Bridge was even sterner. He recommended that RADA be reorganized 'with the idea of providing a professional status somewhat similar to that in law and medicine. The door would then be closed to the young man or woman who at present enters the profession under the cloak of influence or the magnet of glamour' (Stevens 1947: 19). Note in both the insistence that training has specific function, the distancing from mystique and, in Stevens's case, the explicit link to other, clearly functional, professions. So too note the repudiation of self-expression and personal glamour.

But despite this attempt to make the training functional, there was still a problem. It was articulated by André van Gyseghem in 1947 when he observed that there were ever more people wanting to become actors, and attending training, while there were not sufficient jobs for them to get. In 1973 Hayman made the same point. In effect, while training may have worked to end the dilettantism associated with theatre, it could not guarantee progression into professional careers. With more trainees than jobs, training seemed to offer something beyond what was needed, to be in excess.

This sense of it also underlies an antipathy to the award of qualifications. Fogerty wanted her

• **Three card monte.**
photo ZioDave

training school to take students through a range of subjects and lead towards a university diploma. By contrast when drama schools later in the century began to turn into higher education (HE) colleges, some of those already in the 'industry' poured scorn on the idea that actors or designers needed degrees, suggesting instead that all they need is the experience on the job, a line that appears to have been trotted out afresh most recently (March 2009) by the director of the British National Theatre.

Against the idea that training is unnecessarily formalized, in excess of what is needed, indeed 'unnatural', there is a model that promises genuine organicity, and feels, hence, natural. This too has a long history, and it will take us into the second contradiction in theatre training.

The promise of organicity derives from the invocation of a supposedly ancient model of apprenticeship, where the relationship between master and pupil is a 'personal' one. It was this that Fogerty attacked in 1932: 'The defect of the Conservatoire method was to give the impression that there was a certain secret of style and interpretation which was handed on by a teacher and impressed upon a pupil' (Fogerty 1932: 22). Similarly the Principal of RADA kicked it into touch when he warned that training was not about expression of the self. Both of them, characteristically for their time, believed in a standardized technique that was larger than, went beyond, the individual. The problem was that, in a world where not all trainees got jobs, those who did often got them because of their individual features. In the casting of actors, personal appearance and manner play a part. Even at Saint-Denis's Old Vic Theatre School, which battered student egos with its fierce and poetic rigours, the institution 'started acknowledging the market value of good looks' (Wardle 1979: 111). Thus, despite the strictures against those who confused the discipline of training with glamour, the professional operation of the theatre industry had glamour structurally, and commercially, written into it.

This was a contradiction at the heart of the work of those who were trying, in the early decades of the century, to use training to raise the status of theatre as a whole. But that contradiction seemed to be avoidable by the development of a form of training that sought to create a theatre that was alternative to that which was commercially dominant. In the later decades of the twentieth century a range of different training initiatives emerged, which had in common with each other their antipathy to standardized technique and personal glamour.

• Rev. George. H. Clements giving Holy Communion, Chicago, 1973.
photo John H White

These initiatives, associated with the names of such people as Barba, Grotowski, Lecoq, Littlewood, Suzuki, were often predicated not on teaching so much as enabling and releasing the actor, therapeutically assisting in their self-realization. Hostile to the commercial and the glamorous as they might have been, they had at their heart the production of the expressive individual.

Often this expressivity was found at the cost of hard work, punishing exercises, even psychic turmoil. These were the markers, indeed perhaps guarantors, of the distance from commercialism. And they pointed the way, offered a language, to a variety of artists who saw themselves as outside the mainstream. As we saw above, a number of performance artists in the early 1980s came to think that the radical challenge to the dominant lay not in the by now outworn formula of creative freedom but in the project of personal training. Among them Anne Seagrave explicitly embraced the concept of apprenticeship, calling herself a 'Dance Apprentice' – because nobody else was using the phrase. This 'apprenticeship' consisted of an interest in different dance techniques, as a foundation for something else: 'learn different techniques, and then perform something that was individual and from yourself at the other end' (La Frenais 1986: 31). And we arrive to discover, after all, safe and sound, the untrammelled self.

Contrast this with Elsie Fogerty and her Greek chorus some seventy or so years before. Her training turned individual students into a group, and as a group they discovered something not available to individuals, the energy of the group as entity. Fogerty called this state Dionysiac 'Ecstasy'. That ecstasy and the whole exercise may be seen as typical of its time, a modernist interest in subsuming individuals into a group and into a higher force. For Seagrave in the mid-1980s the apprenticeship model culminated in a foregrounding of the individual, and, of course, by this time ecstasy was something you could buy in clubs.

4.

While Seagrave's apprenticeship is something very different in manner from the work of Grotowski or Suzuki, we have run into a larger, more fundamental, contrast. Between the modernist trainers of the early decades and the later versions of training and apprenticeship, the difference was in the emphasis placed on the individual in relation to standardized technique. And behind this lie differences of emphasis in the relationship between person and group.

Some of the shapes of that relationship can be exemplified in a couple of more or less contemporary instances from late modernist dance theatre. In the chorus-line movies made around the early-middle part of the twentieth century, a simple opposition is proposed: the fictional - and actual - stars have individualized interactions within the drama of the story, while as it were behind them undifferentiated individuals move in unison, almost as part of the scenery, what Kracauer in 1927 called 'mass ornament'. Cast, initially, as a member of such an undifferentiated line, a star actor will, we know, emerge from that line into individual distinctiveness, or, as the fiction has it, natural-born talent will declare itself. In short, while drilling may produce sufficient competence to do the work required of a chorus line, it will not, of itself, guarantee individual prominence. Where that individuality is at its most charismatic, and powerful, its skills will be established as that which is natural rather than taught. In the world where van Gyseghem noted the insufficiency of jobs for performers, these cinematic stories were turning the inadequacy of training into romance.

But, contemporary with the practice of chorus-line drilling, there was another model of dance performer training. This was mass dance. Mark Franko describes it as an 'improvisational exercise for anywhere from twenty to fifty untrained performers'. In it dancers learned both to express themselves physically and to value the potency of a group. Franko quotes the dancer Ruth Allerhand describing the experience through which 'they found themselves and each other, and which has awakened in them a strong feeling of respect and responsibility for others' (Franko 2002: 24, 26). Within performer training mass dance is significant because it offers a programme for reconciling group and individual that begins by explicitly valuing group. This was informed by shared ideals, a political vision committed to the importance of group activity. It was within this ideological framework that individual development took place. As Ruth Allerhand put it in 1935,

> Through union with others, in adjusting himself to the group, he comes to an active discovery of a real solidarity. From the individual to the mass! The individual no longer feels that he is the whole, he sees that he represents the substance. He is not so much a link in the chain, a cog in the machine, as a very alive, very productive cell within a body.
> (Allerhand 1995:137)

While the Hollywood story has individuals emerging from the mass of identical bodies, the mass dance experiment has individuals returning to the mass.

Allerhand's neat switch of metaphor - from cog in machine to cell in body - is more than a figurative invocation of organicity. Behind it, and perhaps unknown to Allerhand, there was a model that had been tried out successfully, yet again, by the military. In the First World War the German commander Ludendorff developed a system of distributed command. Obedient to an overall structure, the storm troopers of 1918 were equipped to take control of a unit within that structure and make their own decisions on the battlefield. In preparations of a newer German army in 1936, this model inhabited the call for 'independently thinking and acting warriors - from the youngest soldier upward, the independent commitment of all spiritual, intellectual and physical faculties is demanded' (in van Creveld 1985: 306). The storm-trooper model suggests people can be trained, in a standard way, to promote group efficiency by functioning as an individual: not simply expressing themselves but making conscious group-informed personal decisions.

The exchange between 'personal' skills and group imperatives flows in both directions.

Because of its context, the storm-trooper model seems to have application to material necessities that are a long way distant from the practices of theatre. But another model from somewhere beyond theatre, also of this period, was dragged into a theatrical context, with some interesting implications. We have met this before in T. S. Eliot's 'dialogue' about the ballet. One of his speakers claims that the ballet 'is valuable because it has, unconsciously, concerned itself with a permanent form'. Its strength is 'in a tradition, a training, an askesis' which functions like 'a moral training', and distinguishes ballet dancers from actors. Askesis, a Greek word, has to do with practising self-discipline, with a form of improvement through exercise of the body and, at the same time, of that which is inside body, inner being, 'soul'.

The ballet dancer's technique, unlike that of the contemporary actor, did not have reference outside itself in, for example, its functional capacity accurately to represent a recognizable reality. Its reference point was only to the established technique of ballet. Nor did the technique work to establish the external distinction between one individual and another. In its external appearance it functioned as 'liturgy', the non-individualized rites of dedication to an entity greater than the individual.

5.
While in some respects the self-discipline of *askesis* may appear to have similarities to the later-century regimes that develop the expressivity of the individual, it differs insofar as it is to do with improvement rather than expression, not releasing but disciplining. More important than its shape as a training process, however, is the proposition it makes about the institution of training itself. By way of getting at this, and leading towards my concluding observation, let's draw in one of Eliot's contemporaries, albeit one on a very different side of the fence.

Ewan MacColl tells a story of how, when working with amateurs in order to stage the agitational sketch *Meerut* (1933), 'we had to drill ourselves' as if for 'an athletic event' (Samuel 1985: 230-1). Here the rigours of bodily training are necessitated by an already-existing political commitment. The training, we might say, is undertaken as part of a project of engagement with the world. This project of engagement may be motivated by political aims, aims to do with the betterment of the social group, as in the case of MacColl or Allerhand and the mass dancers. Or it may, as in other of my examples, be driven by a commitment to enhance one's individual performance. Even those late-century training regimes are arguably trying to find a way of performing that has a commitment to being alternative to the commercial theatre at the narrowest and the alienations of modern society at the widest. The assumption in all cases is not only that training happens as part of a larger project but, more crucially, that it is also under the control of that project. Training is conceived as something that is shaped by requirements external to it.

And here is where the *askesis* model makes its dislocation. For it invites us to emphasize the extent to which the training process works on the individual and group irrespective of the external requirements. It is a project in itself. What happens in this project is that, in developing skills for the ballet, the dancer has a 'moral training'. This formula defines training as a mechanism that prepares both body and subjectivity to absorb and embody value and to practise its liturgy. Any liturgy: *askesis* is the same process in a Christian seminary as in an Islamic terrorist training camp. Training can be used to support the dominant and to oppose the dominant, to sustain those values that seem 'natural' and to promote that which deviates from the 'natural'. There is something deeper here than the transmission of skills or the organization of group coherence. Training is a mechanism that is as much *moral* as instrumental. In other words, its distinctive power is that it can prepare individuals and groups to embrace value, any value - without necessarily being concerned about, or seeking legitimacy from, questions of function, rightness, naturalness. It is this capacity that makes the institution of training most troublingly unnatural.

With thanks to Simon Donger and Richard Gough for their comments and Sandra Laureri for sourcing the images.

REFERENCES

Allerhand, Ruth (1995) 'The Lay Dance', in M. Franko, *Dancing Modernism / Performing Politics*, Bloomington: Indiana University Press.

Archer, William and Barker, H. Granville (1907) *A National Theatre: Scheme and estimates*, London: Duckworth.

Barnes, Kenneth (1946) 'What Makes an Actor', *New Theatre* 3(5): 18-19.

Cole, Marion (ed.) (1967) *Fogie: The life of Elsie Fogerty, CBE*, London: Peter Davies.

Creveld, Martin van (1985) *Command in War*, Cambridge, Massachusetts: Harvard University Press.

Eliot, T. S. (1999) 'A Dialogue on Dramatic Poetry', *Selected Essays*, London: Faber and Faber.

EMLS (2008) Early Modern Literary Studies, <http://extra.shu.ac.uk/emls/iemls/statepapers/1591-94/Scan0200.pdf> (viewed 10 March 2009)

Fogerty, Elsie (1932) 'Translator's introduction', in C. Coquelin *The Art of the Actor*, London: George Allen and Unwin.

Franko, Mark (2002) *The Work of Dance: Labor, movement, and identity in the 1930s*, Middletown, Connecticut: Wesleyan University Press.

Gyseghem, André van (1947) *Theatre Old and New*, vol. 44, London: Bureau of Current Affairs.

Hayman, Ronald (1973) 'The Actor Prepares - for What?', *Theatre Quarterly* 3(11): 49-57.

Holdsworth, Nadine (2006) *Joan Littlewood*, London and New York: Routledge.

Jenner, Caryl (1948) 'Training Schools in London', *New Theatre* 5(3): 19-21.

La Frenais, Rob (1986) 'Learning to Fly', *Performance* 40: 18-31.

Linebaugh, Peter (1977) 'The Tyburn Riot Against the Surgeons', in *Albion's Fatal Tree: Crime and society in eighteenth-century England*, Harmondsworth: Penguin.

McNeill, William H. (1982) *The Pursuit of Power: Technology, armed force and society since AD1000*, Chicago: University of Chicago Press.

Samuel, Raphael, MacColl, Ewan and Cosgrove, Stuart (1985) *Theatres of the Left 1880-1935: Workers' theatre movements in Britain and America*. London: Routledge & Kegan Paul.

Schwartz, Hillel (1992) 'Torque: The New Kinaesthetic of the Twentieth Century', in J. Crary and S. Kwinter (eds) *Incorporations*, New York: Zone.

Segel, Harold B. (1998) *Body Ascendant: Modernism and the physical imperative*, Baltimore and London: Johns Hopkins University Press

Stevens, Robert (1947) correspondence in 'What the Readers Say', *New Theatre* 3(9): 19.

Wardle, Irving (1979) *The Theatres of George Devine*, London: Eyre Methuen.

Did you say 'training'?

JOSETTE FÉRAL

This article first appeared in French (2000). To avoid confusing readers of English, the French word entraînement *(usually translated as 'training' in English) has been translated here as 'preparation', except where using the French term is the point. When the new French word* training *is discussed, we render it into English in italics. All translations of quotations are ours. Text translated by Leslie Wickes.*

For some time now, two words have shared the acting field between them: *training* and *entraînement*. Present in the texts, coexisting in discourses, evoked by artists and researchers over the years, they seem to maintain a peaceful existence that gives the impression that they are synonyms and can be used interchangeably. In this manner, they comprise a single and sole reality: that of actors' efforts to perfect their art before mounting the stage.

This is not a false impression, and yet ... this state of balance is in fact an illusion. In effect, for those who attentively observe the literature on the subject, as well as certain texts and speculations of current practitioners, it is apparent that this equilibrium is in the process of rupturing. The word *training* seems, at least in France, to inscribe the concept in particular contexts. Far from being a trend, a preference for an easy 'anglicism', this shift tends to bring to light some profound transformations that have been affecting the preparation of actors for the past thirty years.

As it was first documented in 1440, the English word *training* originally signified 'drawing, trailing; drawing out, protracting' (OED s.v. 'training'). It is borrowed from the Old French word *trainer* and does not acquire the sense of 'instruction, discipline, education' until 1548 (Barnhart 1988: 1157). At this point it refers to a 'systematic instruction and exercise in some art, profession or occupation, with a view to proficiency in it' (OED). Indifferently used in the artistic, sports and military fields, and even in the training of animals, it evokes 'the process of developing the bodily vigour and endurance by systematic ... exercise, so as to fit for some athletic feat' (OED). It is therefore intimately linked from its first appearance to the notions of exercise and perfecting.

This English word, which was not found in French dictionaries until the 1980s, soon made its appearance in the 1990s under the influence of sports and studies in psychology and psychoanalysis ('*training autogène*', '*training group*'). At this point it designates a 'preparation through repeated exercises' or 'a psychotherapeutic method of relaxation through autosuggestion (*training autogène*).' The dictionaries do not document the use it is put to in the theatrical world. They insist on the notions of exercise and methodical repetition that are the foundation of sports as well as psychoanalysis. Researchers then began to refer back to its earlier connotations.

Thus in his 1854 book, *Guide du Sportsman ou Traité de l'Entraînement et des Courses de Chevaux*, E. Gayot defines the word *training* as a 'preparation for physical activity.' In 1895, Paul

Bourget notes in his book *Outre-Mer*: 'almost all devoted themselves to physical exercises done in the American style, that is to say, like a *training*, a mathematical and reasoned physical preparation.' This reference to the American model is interesting because it links the word to a sport (gymnastics) which was moving across the Atlantic. In 1872, in his *Notes sur l'Angleterre*, Taine evokes the '*training* of the attention'. The use of the word spread so widely and so thoroughly that, in 1976, an August 12th Arrêté recommends the use of the term *entraînement* instead of *training* to signify 'the action of perfecting and staying in shape in a given field' (Quemada 1994: 472).

Despite these measures, the use of the word *training*[1] nevertheless becomes common practice and seems to become a valid synonym for the word *entraînement*[2], though the latter remains more common in texts.

When it is applied to theatre in the Anglophone world, the word *training* is used systematically to designate all aspects of an actor's preparation. Thus it indiscriminately refers to the instruction given at acting schools, in acting classes, on stages and in workshops, and also to the practical exercises that actors may undertake *before* a production, as well as to the work carried out by actors who wish to perfect their art without a specific production in view. This absence of distinction between three different aspects of preparation (formation, production and the development of the actor's art) makes training a quasi-generic term in the Anglophone world. It is a convenient, all-purpose word that encompasses all forms of exercises, techniques and methods employed by actors attempting to acquire the basics of their vocation.

In France, the use of the word *training* as applied to theatre is a recent arrival ... [3] At the earliest, it dates from the middle of the 1980s. Predominantly used in spoken language, it appears fairly late in written texts. For example, the works of Grotowski (1971, 1974), as well as the

[1] Defined as 'a preparation through repeated exercises' (Quemada 1994: 472).

[2] Defined as 'preparation for a physical or intellectual activity; learning through methodical repetition' (Imbs 1979: 1228).

[3] France seems to be the only country in the French world to have thus generalized the use of the word *training*, at least in oral language, about fifteen years ago.

• Odin Teatret & CTLS archives - Work demonstration: *Moon and darkness* with Iben Nagel Rasmussen
Photo: Torben Huss.

4 Lectoure: Bouffonneries. English version (1979) *The Floating Islands*, Graasten: Drama.

5 Lectoure: Bouffonneries. English version (1991) *The Secret Art of the Performer*, London: Centre for Performance Research and Routledge. Latest edition (2005) *A Dictionary of Theatre Anthropology: The secret art of the performer*, London: Routledge.

6 Saussan: *L'entretemps*. English version (1999) *Theatre: Solitude, craft, revolt*, Aberystwyth: Black Mountain Press.

7 It is interesting to analyse the variety of theatrical learning institutes that existed at the beginning of the century. When Copeau founded his school in 1920, the panorama of the period in France included numerous schools, classes and workshops. The Conservatoire National Supérieur d'Art Dramatique had already long been in existence. (It was created in 1784 as L'Ecole Royale de Chant et de Déclamation and became the Conservatoire in 1808.) The situation is the same elsewhere in Europe. In Belgium, the Conservatoire de Bruxelles et d'Anvers had been in existence since 1860. In Finland, the Finnish National Theatre offered courses to its actors from 1906 to 1920, and the Swedish Theatre did the same between 1910 and 1973. The Finnish School of Drama was created in 1920. In Germany, important schools had been in place for several years in Berlin, Frankfurt and Munich. In Italy, the Academia Nazionale d'Arte Drammatica Silvio d'Amico was founded in Rome in 1930. However,

first of Barba's books (1982), make no mention of it and favour *entraînement* instead. The same is true of works by Brook (1991, 1992), Vitez (1991, 1994) and Yoshi Oida (1999), which all speak of *entraînement*, not *training*.

However, from 1982 to 1985 a change occurs that can be traced through the various works of Barba. In effect, *L'Archipel du Théâtre*, published in 1982[4], uses the word *entraînement* to designate the work of the actor. The text reads: 'preparation (*l'entraînement*) does not teach how to act, how to be clever, does not prepare one for creation' (Barba 1979: 73). This usage is confirmed in the chapter that follows, entitled '*Questions sur l'entraînement*'. Nevertheless, by 1985, with the *Anatomie de l'Acteur*[5], things have changed. The word *entraînement* has given way to *training* even though it continues to designate the same work by the actor. The texts of Nicola Savarese ('*Training et point de départ*') and Eugenio Barba himself ('*Training: de 'apprendre' à 'apprendre à apprendre'*') explicitly refer to the word to evoke the actor's preparatory work. This usage becomes systematic in Barba's *Théâtre: solitude, métier, révolte*[6], which appeared in 1999. The book is proof that, from this point forward, the word *training* has definitively entered common practice, even supplanting the word *entraînement* completely in certain texts. This evolution of a typically French use is even more evident in light of the fact that Barba himself affirms that he initially privileged the more intercultural word *training*, which permits the use of a single concept that supercedes [goes beyond] geographic and linguistic borders while avoiding the reductive sports connotations that too often evoke an actor's gymnastics.

We might investigate such an evolution. Is it simply a case of a lexical fluctuation in favour of a word whose English timbre conveys a more vital and dynamic image of the actor's work? Is it rather an ideological shift betraying another concept of what an actor's preparation should be? The multiple and highly diverse uses of the word to express the different methods of training actors do not permit any one answer. It is

nevertheless apparent that, aside from the distinctively French predilection for English words, the decision may have been motivated by the need to import a word with specifically theatrical connotations into the theatrical vocabulary. It would thus represent an effort to escape sports and military references that sometimes continue to inform its French counterpart *entraînement*. With regard to a direct cross-Atlantic influence, the matter cannot be clearly proven, as the methods of preparing actors in the United States and in the English world in general (Lee Strasberg, Viola Spolin, Uta Hagen, Stanford Meisner, Stella Adler, Kristin Linklater, Cicely Berry) have few echoes in France.

However, this evolution of words coincides with an evolution in practice that I would now like to analyse.

ENTRAÎNEMENT, NOT TEACHING

The notion of an actor's *entraînement*, and more importantly, the practices that this notion encompasses, date at the very earliest from the beginning of the twentieth century in Europe and North America. As tributaries of the evolution of theatrical practice over the years, they are inseparable from the transformations that have affected theatrical representation and the growing place occupied by the actor, a 'complete' actor, whose formation is not only physical but also intellectual and moral, with the aim of conferring a new 'poetic' (Copeau 1974: 115) on him or her. In France, Copeau, Dullin and Jouvet were among the first to emphasize the necessity for a systematic preparation of the actor as a reaction to the instruction that was then practised in most schools of theatrical learning.[7] They created the theatre-schools, the theatre-laboratories, of which Grotowski, Barba and, without a doubt, Mnouchkine and Brook are the direct heirs.

It seems therefore that the notion of preparation must first be dissociated from that of education, which is left to schools. These schools, many of which emerged in the nineteenth and twentieth centuries, initially promoted a vision of formation distinguished [defined] by the preeminence of the text on stage and by the necessity for actors to prepare themselves first and foremost to take on a role, to hold a 'job' (classes in diction and vocal development were strongly emphasized). Copeau and Dullin forcefully express the distrust of the instruction given in these schools:

> What is the current state of an actor's technical formation? It is almost non-existent. Either the artist attends the Conservatory, and will have a great deal of difficulty in correcting the defects he acquires there, or he takes a few random classes and begins to work immediately, using nothing but his natural gifts and without really learning his trade. (Dullin 1969: 57)

Barba reiterates Dullin's criticism today. In this instance he denounces the insufficiencies of the formation offered in schools not because of the nature of the courses offered but because of the pedagogical approach they adopt (a plurality of professors for each student) which cannot permit a real apprenticeship in the trade.

> Theatre schools have always made me feel uneasy ... They are organized just like schools, placing pupils in contact with various teachers who may be very able, efficient and eager to pass on the best of their experience, but whom the context labels as teachers of this or that subject. I believe that, in theatre, apprenticeship cannot be carried out by teachers. I am convinced it needs masters. (Barba 1999: 95)

These criticisms - that numerous directors repeat today in their turn (see Féral 1997/1998)[8] - emphasize that, from the turn of the century, the unavoidable necessity for actors to learn their craft through other pedagogical bases has been evident. From Stanislavski to Grotowski, moving through Jaques-Dalcroze, Meyerhold, Vakhtangov, Tairov, Appia, Craig, Reinhardt, Copeau, Dullin, Jouvet, Decroux and Lecoq, a new pedagogy emerges that aims not only at the physical preparation of actors - which became necessary as soon as the body was placed at centre-stage - but also at a 'complete education that harmoniously develops their bodies, their

without a doubt, the tradition of theatrical formation is strongest in the United Kingdom. The country already had numerous schools, of which the most important were the Royal Academy of Dramatic Art (RADA) (1904), the Central School of Speech Training and Dramatic Art (1906), and later, in the 1930s, the London Academy of Music and Dramatic Art and Guildhall School, to mention only a few.

[8] When questioned about the ideal formation for a performer, most directors deplore the insufficiency of the formation offered in schools, while recognizing that this instruction has improved over the course of the years.

• Suzuki Method of Actors' Training by Suzuki Company of Toga, *SCOT Archive*

spirits and their characters as men' (Copeau 1974: 134).

If the ultimate goal of preparation is often expressed in identical terms by the various reformers - that is, to permit actors to find themselves in a state of creativity on stage - the modalities of this preparation that they advocate, the forms that it must take (exercises, techniques, methods), differ.

For example, it is interesting to note that Copeau eagerly speaks of the actor's work, of physical conditioning, of gymnastics, all founded on exercises that create a physical discipline (Copeau 1984: 509). Dullin evokes the necessity of perfecting the actor based on a technique and exercises that establish the bases of a method (Dullin 1985). Max Reinhardt touches on the question of exercises, pointing out the need for an actor to function well both physically and intellectually (1950: 9). Etienne Decroux speaks instead of gymnastics and technique (1985: 128). Closer to home, Jacques Lecoq prefers the notion of physical preparation, dramatic gymnastics, corporeal education, to that of preparation. For his part, Vitez continually returns to the 'actor's work'. Finally, from an American perspective, Michael Chekhov speaks more readily of exercises than preparation.

Of course, methods of preparation differ. They all establish the necessary foundations of the actor's performance, the flexibility of the body and voice work, but also work on the actor's interiority, with the objective of facilitating the actor's passage from one to the other, of putting him or her into a state of creativity. According to the schools of thought and the methods of preparation advocated, this interiority bears different names: impulsions (Grotowski), reactions (Barba), emotions (Dullin), sensations (Copeau), as well as sensibility (Jouvet). Most frequently, it is through the means of exercises that the actor learns how to make interiority and exteriority coincide, how to express one through the other. The body thus effectively becomes the vehicle of 'thought' (Grotowski 1968: 16).

To attain this harmony, it is not a question of giving actors recipes or know-how, though it is evident that they must possess certain techniques of relaxation, breathing and concentration, as well as improvisation and visualization … These bases, which are necessary in order to give the performer ease and flexibility, remain the preliminaries to a much deeper work that forces actors (simultaneously in body and in spirit) to work on themselves.

The great reforms of preparation (for example, those of Copeau, Appia, Grotowski and Barba) aim primarily at making the actor's body a sensitive instrument, but they also - one might even say above all - endeavour to teach the actor the laws of movement (Jaques-Dalcroze calls them the laws of rhythm, while Barba calls them the laws of balance and imbalance, the contrary forces at work in all movement). More than pedagogy intended simply to add skills, most of the pedagogies that are now being established progressively aim for a certain denuding of the actor. Grotowski would bring this to its ultimate expression by inciting the actor to follow a *via negativa* - advice that seems to echo the precepts of Copeau, who does not hesitate to declare the exigency of washing the actor clean of 'all the stains of the theatre', of 'denuding him of all his habits' (1974: 124).

OF A FEW PRINCIPLES

These new actor's pedagogies, which distinctively mark the twentieth century, thus establish the foundations of a good preparation. These foundations are reiterated throughout various texts:

1. The multiplication of methods of preparation, deplored by Copeau in the 1920s, is a sort of vast patchwork to which actors, eager to develop skills quickly, devote themselves in the hope of responding to the diversity of the market. However, it is far from allowing a coherent formation. All those who have examined the pedagogy of actors come to this conclusion.

To avoid this explosion caused by preparation under several professors, the formation of actors must pass into the hands of a master. Grotowski has forcefully defended this idea, as has Vitez. The idea of a master is directly borrowed from the Orient, the techniques of which have been a powerful inspiration for most theatre reformers. Copeau defended it from its very inception, much as Barba defends it today, hence the emphasis on the theatre-schools (le Vieux Colombier) and theatre-laboratories (Grotowski), which are the only structures where a continuing and in-depth preparation can occur. The actor has time to develop within the group, to achieve deep personal progress[9]. The idea of the theatre as school, the company as a place of formation, the school as inextricably linked to the theatre, is one that incessantly haunts theatre practitioners (Dullin 1969: 57-8).

2. At the heart of these school-laboratories the preparation works to confer particular skills on the actor, but these skills are never considered to be the sole objective. Though they are a necessary part of learning the craft, they must also be counterbalanced so that the actor is not so seduced by technique as to become an 'athlete' of the stage.

In opposition to Decroux, who affirms that 'technique immunizes the man who possesses it against two arbitrary tyrannies: that of fashion and that of the teacher; [it] eliminates the mediocre, ... makes good use of the average talent and exalts the genius' (Decroux 1985: 135). Copeau reminds that, when poorly understood, it can, on the contrary, make the actor mechanical and damage the art.

> One must ... forbid [the actor] to specialize, to become mechanical through the abuse of technique. (Copeau 1974: 125).

We might ask ourselves what technique has to offer. For Jaques-Dalcroze, who bases preparation on rhythmic gymnastics, technique facilitates actors' awareness of the strengths and limits of their own bodies. It allows the actor 'to unfetter [his or her] motions', to have an entire mastery of the body, 'free and spontaneous' (Ansermet 1983: 17).

For Tadashi Suzuki, it develops the actor's capacity for physical expression and nurtures the actor's tenacity and concentration (Suzuki 1995: 155). For Peter Brook, it allows one to develop the body's sensitivity:

> When we are performing acrobatic exercises, it is not to achieve virtuosity, nor to become gifted acrobats (though this can sometimes be both useful and marvellous), but to become sensitive.
> (Brook 1991: 31)

As Yoshi Oida reminds us, technique should never be an end in itself: 'It doesn't really matter which style or technique you learn' (Oida 1997: 112).

[9] Vitez would speak of the school of the group, as opposed to that of the individual.

• Odin Teatret & CTLS archives.
Photo: Roald Pay.

• Suzuki Method of Actors' Training by Suzuki Company of Toga, *SCOT Archive*

3. What does one learn beyond technique? Actors discover it for themselves. Actors acquire a more thorough knowledge of their own bodies and their particular obstacles, explore the laws of movement (balance, tension, rhythm) and try always to extend their own limits. Grotowski says 'the theatre and acting are for us a kind of vehicle allowing us to emerge from ourselves, to fulfill ourselves' (1968: 220). This learning is, of course, attained through knowledge of one's own body and the attempt to push its limits, but it is also attained - perhaps even primarily attained - through the actor's work on the self. On this subject, Barba speaks of the acquisition of an ethos, a notion that is central to all those who seek to reform preparation: 'Ethos as a scenic behaviour, that is, physical and mental technique, and ethos as a work ethic, that is, a mentality modelled by the environment, the human setting in which the apprenticeship develops' (Barba 2005: 278).

In order for preparation to be a lifelong process, it must be inscribed in the duration of a career. There is no quick preparation. Any preparation for a particular production of the moment that does not also have the deeper and more universal goal of improving the actor's abilities is doomed to have little effect.

'Do not progress too quickly. Do not rush to achieve your final completed form. Give yourself time,' observed Copeau in 1917 (1974: 127).

The actor must take the time necessary. Begun when the actor was a student, true preparation must continue throughout life. It is only when it is considered as a 'continual formation' that preparation truly allows actors, like musicians or dancers, to maintain their instrument in peak condition, or in other words, in a state of creativity.

When viewed this way, the ultimate goal of preparation cannot necessarily be linked to a performance. Preparation must not be viewed as utilitarian or pragmatic, as a process that provides the actor with skills that can be instantly employed. It does not necessarily have a direct and immediate application in performance. Without a doubt, it bestows upon the actor that indispensable quality of stage presence, yet the majority of the exercises, gestures and movements found in preparation courses cannot be directly transposed onto the stage. The process of preparation is far more important than the result. On this subject, Barba speaks of the temperature of the process as more important than even the process itself (2005: 281).

4. It is useful to distinguish precisely between different phases in the exercises over the course of preparation. For the actor, the first phase consists of the attempt to accomplish and then perfectly master a set of given exercises. During this phase, each exercise has a definite purpose (working on balance, breathing, concentration, flexibility etc.) and it is important for the actor to succeed in performing these exercises to perfection. Once this objective is attained, the second phase begins. During the second phase, the actor, while continuing to practise the exercises already mastered, must take on greater challenges by putting 'one's energies to the test ... . The performer can model, measure, explode and control their energies' (Barba 2005: 278). At least, this is Grotowski's and Barba's response. In this work, actors learn to push back the limits of their own bodies and to attain a particular stage-presence. 'Using the training exercises, the performer tests his or her ability to achieve a condition of total presence, a condition that he or she will have to find again in the creative moment of improvisation and performance' (Barba 2005: 278).

But what are these exercises? What exercises should the actor choose? What place should they hold? What aspect of an actor's formation should they develop? Meyerhold, Appia, Craig, Reinhardt, Copeau, Dullin, Decroux, Lecoq, Vitez and Brook have all tried to devise appropriate exercises to give the actor a formation of both body and spirit.

If one were to compare the types of exercises each advocates, it would not be difficult to perceive that the approaches differ radically from one to another. These differences are justified by the personal approaches of the artists themselves and by the genre of theatrical performance that they prefer, but also by the ultimate goal - each exercise is devised to a specific end.

Beyond the diversity of approaches, however, it often seems that the nature of the exercise is not the most important aspect of the preparation. In effect, what is more important for the actor than the choice of exercise are the powers, the energy, the rhythms, the tensions, the obstacles and the surfeits that these exercises authorize [give weight to / make possible / foreground]; so much so that, when taken to their limits, the nature of the chosen exercises is of very little importance. As Grotowski notes on the work of his actors:

> The exercises have now become a pretext for working out a personal form of training (entraînement). The actor must discover those resistances and obstacles which hinder him in his creative task ... By a personal adaptation of the exercises, a solution must be found for the elimination of these obstacles which vary for each individual actor. (1968: 133)

5. Consequently, it is no surprise that collective preparation gives way to individual preparation, the only way that the actor is allowed to achieve in-depth progress. Actors will thus learn to choose for themselves the exercises that are most useful to them. They will pursue them for their own profit. Having now become individual, preparation should help actors to self-define, to control their powers, to surmount their hesitations and fear, and to extend their own limits. It is only

at this price that they will succeed in creating Barba's *corps décidé*, the exceptional body that allows performance to happen.

With regard to the level of investment that that actor must make in these exercises, it must be total. As Yoshi Oida reminds us:

> Whenever you practise, imagine that you are doing your exercises in front of an audience. It suddenly becomes important that you engage fully, and avoid sloppiness. In this way, the quality of your work will improve, and the *entraînement* will be genuinely useful. If you think that you are 'only doing an exercise', the work will be of little value, irrespective of how well you perform it' (1997: 18).

This approach cannot be used if it is not accompanied by the quest for a form, for the outline of a structure (the composition of the role, the construction of form, the expression of signs). As Grotowski reminds us, all of these movements must not be for nothing. The quest for form is important, because is it only through the quest that one escapes a repetitive preparation and enters art itself. 'We find that artificial composition not only does not limit the spiritual but actually leads to it' (Grotowski 1968: 17). Only at this cost can preparation allow the actor to transcend technique to arrive at art.

*

Confronted with such an evolution, it is evident that preparation has disentangled itself from the pedagogical method. It has become a way of life. It no longer necessarily teaches how to perform, how to be a good actor, it does not even prepare one to create but it allows the actor to rediscover, as Grotowski notes, 'his possibilities to the utmost ... This is not the instruction of a pupil but utter opening to another person ... The actor is reborn - not only as an actor but as a man'(Grotowski 1968: 25). From this perspective, preparation has become an ethical, almost metaphysical, process. The actor's private life is

• **Odin Teatret & CTLS archives - Training, Holstebro 1984.**
Photo: Torben Huss.

seamlessly connected to his or her artistic life (Copeau 1974: 134).

This project, which Copeau elaborated at the turn of the century, endures today, and each theatrical reformer continues it in his or her turn.

With respect to the etymological question that I raised at the beginning of this article, and to the distinction that I make between the words *training* and *entraînement*, the dualism/ambivalence has lost its power in the sense that the differences of meaning that I emphasized, and which the two notions conveyed, have lost their pertinence. In effect, today these notions cover much more distinct realities. The use of the English (*training*) seems to prevail in the case of a structured preparation done within the formative framework of a specific method (Suzuki, Barba), while the notion of *entraînement* seems to dominate in artists' daily practices when they devote themselves to exercises in order to prepare for a performance: stretches, physical work-outs, even 'warming up'.]¹⁰ What is important to notice in this long evolution is the slow loss of a reality that held sway in the 1970s when actors received their formation in companies or under the tutelage of masters.

REFERENCES

Ansermet, Ernest (1983) 'Qu'est-ce que la rythmique?' in Adolphe Appia *Œuvres Complètes III*, Lausanne: L'Age d'Homme, pp. 16-19.

Barba, Eugenio (1979) *The Floating Islands*, Graasten: Drama.

Barba, Eugenio (2005) *A Dictionary of Theatre Anthropology : The secret art of the performer*, London and New York: Routledge.

Barba, Eugenio (1999) *Theatre: Solitude, craft, revolt*, Aberystwyth: Black Mountain Press.

Barnhart, Robert K. (ed.) (1988) *The Barnhart Dictionary of Etymology*, New York: H. W. Wilson.

Brook, Peter (1991) *Le Diable c'est l'Ennui*, Arles: Actes Sud.

Chekhov, Michael (1980[1953]) *Être Acteur, Technique du Comédien*, Paris: Pygmalion Gérard Watelet.

Copeau, Jacques (1974) *Registres 1: Appels*, Paris: Gallimard.

Copeau, Jacques (1984) *Les Registres du Vieux Colombier II*, Paris: Gallimard.

Decroux, Étienne (1985) *Words on Mime*, Claremont: Mime Journal.

Dullin, Charles (1969) *Ce Sont les Dieux qu'il Nous Faut*, Paris: Gallimard.

Dullin, Charles (1985 [1946]) *Souvenirs et Notes de Travail d'un Acteur*, Paris: Librairie Théâtrale.

Féral, Josette (1997/1998) *Mise en Scène et Jeu de l'Acteur*, Montréal/Carnières: Jeu/Lansman.

Féral, Josette (2000) 'Did You Say "Training"?' in Carol Müller (dir.) *Le Training de l'Acteur*, Arles: Actes Sud, pp 7-27.

Grotowski, Jerzy (1968) *Towards a Poor Theatre*, New York: Simon and Schuster.

Imbs, Paul (dir.) (1979) *Trésor de la Langue Française : Dictionnaire de la langue du XIXe et du XXe siècle (1789-1960), vol. VII*, Paris: Centre National de la Recherche Scientifique, Nancy: Institut National de la Langue Française.

Oida, Yoshi (1997) *The Invisible Actor*, London and New York: Routledge.

Quemada, Bernard (dir.) (1994) *Trésor de la Langue Française : Dictionnaire de la langue du XIXe et du XXe siècle (1789-1960), vol. XVI*, Paris: Gallimard and Centre National de la Recherche Scientifique, Nancy: Institut National de la Langue Française.

Reinhardt, Max (1950) 'Discours sur l'Acteur', *La Revue Théâtrale* 13: pp. 7-12.

The Oxford English Dictionary (1989) eds John Andrew Simpson and Edmund S. C. Weiner, eds, 2nd edn, vol. 18, Oxford: Clarendon Press.

Suzuki, Tadashi (1995) 'Culture is the Body', in Phillip B. Zarilli (ed.) *Acting (Re)considered: Theories and practices*, London: Routledge, pp. 155-60.

[10] Interestingly, today the *Petit Robert* lists the two words as synonyms. The word *training* has now entered common use.

Of Pounds of Flesh and Trojan Horses
Performer training in the twenty-first century

FRANK CAMILLERI

Performer training in the West has been increasingly commodified in the course of the last two decades by having its most tangible and transmittable aspect (i.e., training techniques) severed from the wider contexts that had initially given it impetus. This situation indicates the strong possibility of a paradigm shift that is currently still underway: *performer training in the twenty-first century seems to have outgrown the twentieth-century need of a formative ethical dimension as it becomes increasingly implicated in the processes and procedures of institutionalization.* I consider this a 'fundamental' shift precisely because it concerns the very foundations of performer training, i.e., it concerns not technique per se but the manner in which technique is approached and treated. Furthermore, the widespread extent of this movement, which is fuelled by heavy institutional intervention in the educational and cultural industries, assures its paradigmatic status rather than being merely a 'tendency' or a 'trend'. Though the full effects of this shift still need to filter upwards to become more clearly manifest in performance and pedagogical practices, there is ample evidence of its activity in the inter-century decades (1990s and 2000s). The current article deals with this activity.

Ian Watson voices one aspect of this fundamental change under the section 'Some Contemporary Shifts' (2001: 7). The contrast he highlights, between 'individual' work aimed at holistic and creative formation and 'systematized training' aimed at the sophistication of technique, indicates the most immediate aspect of the distinction I will draw between ethical and ideological approaches to training, i.e., which I see between technique conceived as process rather than as product. Following other scholars and practitioners who have already applied the term to laboratory contexts (see Stanislavsky 2008: 552-78; Camilleri 2008: 254), I refer to 'ethical approaches to training' to indicate the latent and more holistic dimension that accompanied the pursuit of Western theatre-makers in the twentieth century. As Fabrizio Cruciani observes, 'the history of twentieth-century theatre is the history of individuals who find their fulfilment in the setting up of groups, of micro-societies which live the utopia of *an ethical project* in the arts' (1995: 239, my translation and emphasis). In this context, training is not an end in itself but part of a bigger project. I will contrast this with what I call 'ideological approaches to training' that characterize the compartmentalization and marketing procedures that involve technique training at the end of the first decade of the twenty-first century. 'Ideological' is my preferred term instead of 'institutional' or 'systematized' because it provides a more complex dimension that is sensitive to the relations between the political, economic and cultural elements in specific societies. This same web of socio-cultural relations also serves to implicate ethical approaches in that no material phenomenon is conceivable outside these relations as a practice. What sets the two apart is their relationship to the socio-cultural forces around them that also informs the way they approach training: ethical laboratories are resistant to dominant paradigms in their displaced and interrogative practices, whereas ideological approaches tend to support dominant structures in terms of institutional allegiances.

ETHICAL APPROACHES

Part of the difficulty of defining ethics rests in the fact that to do so would constitute a categorical subversion in promoting one account at the expense of others. Peter Singer's practical approach argues that ethics is neither 'a set of prohibitions' nor 'an ideal system', neither is it 'something intelligible only in the context of religion' nor is it 'relative or subjective' (1993: 2-4). The problems with pinning down ethics are apparent even in such a utilitarian perspective, for we can immediately detect challenging tensions between something that is not a system or set of prescribed rules, and something that is not relative or subjective. Geoffrey Galt Harpham prefers to describe ethics in spatial terms where sensitivity to the other prevails: it is thus 'the locus of otherness' and 'the arena in which the claims of others ... are articulated and negotiated' (1995: 404, 394). Harpham identifies a constitutional problem at the core of ethics: 'As the locus of otherness, ethics seems to lack integrity "in itself", and perhaps ought to be considered a matrix, a hub from which various discourses, concepts, terms, energies, fan out, and at which they meet, crossing out of themselves to encounter the other, all the others' (404). In this perspective, ethical choice is never a matter of selecting the right over the wrong because a choice is 'ethical' only insofar as all available options embody worthy principles. Ethical choice is thus always 'a choice between ethics' (396). It is this complex and porous quality of the term that makes it appropriate to describe a paradigmatic approach to actor-training in the twentieth century.

The compelling paradoxes that constitute ethics can serve as a stem upon which we can graft what has been identified as 'a central paradox within performer training', i.e., that 'discipline and rigorous techniques ... help the performer find spontaneity and freedom' (Allain and Harvie 2006: 212). This paradox lies at the heart of the distinction between ethical and ideological approaches to training. The main endeavours of practitioners such as Stanislavsky, Meyerhold, Copeau, Decroux, Grotowski, Lecoq and Barba were directed at liberating the performer from all sorts of blocks: the ways they found vary but their 'discipline and rigour' to training was not subject to an institutionalized curriculum or a set of regulations but to 'an ethical framework ... open to the exigencies of research and discovery' (Camilleri 2008: 254).

An 'ethical approach' is thus a *modus operandi* that is also a *modus vivendi*. In other words, a committed form of training that is integral to a performer's life to such a degree that the principles and techniques investigated and practised in the laboratory shape one's life. This sentiment, or rather a variation of it due to the different historical and cultural circumstances, is voiced by Stanislavsky himself in a chapter called 'Ethics and Discipline':

> Actors ... have a duty to be bearers of beauty, even in ordinary life. Otherwise they will create with one hand and destroy with the other. Remember this as you serve art in your early years and prepare yourself for this mission. Develop the necessary self-control, the ethics, the discipline of a public figure who takes the beautiful, the elevated, the noble into the world.   (2008: 577)

Later practitioners, ranging from Grotowski to Lecoq (Murray 2003: 43-4), blurred Stanislavsky's boundary between the 'public figure' and the 'private person', often as a result of an external displacement that made it possible to live theatre in addition to doing it, which in turn impacted on the way training is approached.[1] An ethical approach thus marks a way of training where sensitivity and commitment to the otherness of technique assures that it is not a fixed or

[1] Without going into the specificities of each case, but without trying to conflate individual histories into a unified narrative, it is possible to recognize a red line of spatial or geographical displacement among theatre practitioners that led to a corollary shift in training techniques in the twentieth century, e.g., Stanislavsky's self-financed Theatre Studio, Meyerhold's laboratory studios, Copeau's retreat to the countryside, Grotowski's workspace in Brzezinka and his Workcenter in Pontedera, Barba's theatre in Holstebro, Decroux's tiny basement studio in his house, even Lecoq's school (Murray 2003: 49, 56) and Brook's three-month meanderings in Africa and his relocation from the UK to France in 1970.

determined end in itself but rather is alive and adaptable according to the development of the performer. If technique is considered like language, it is then like enabling speakers to change language itself and not simply improve their proficiency. In this way of working, a stage is reached where *modus operandi* and *modus vivendi* mutually inform each other, not only on the superficial level of technique but more so on the ethical level: *technical principles* (such as the consideration of context, spatial and psychophysical awareness, the responsibility to act, decisiveness, and precision as an inner process of discovery) *become ethical principles*.[2]

All this does not mean that laboratory practitioners are the paragon of ethical behaviour. Indeed, considered from without, certain actions and decisions taken by *individual* practitioners appear to be ethically questionable. These range from the sometimes inexplicably 'austere' treatment of apprentices, to the 'abandonment' of performers once an objective has been achieved, and even to the extent of sexual 'openness' that occurs been older practitioners and younger apprentices. Conversely, it might be claimed that committed performers who follow the ideological approach also combine *modus operandi* with *modus vivendi* in an integral way. However, it is the *context* that provides the crucial distinction. A displaced and open-ended context, which cultivates sensitivity to the otherness of technique and performance, is very difficult to obtain within the rationalized practices of institutional structures. If the ethical approach is informed and characterized by *displacement*, the ideological approach is geared towards technical *placement* meant as subject formation.

IDEOLOGICAL APPROACHES

Though it is hardly possible to escape from the conventional and narrow sense of ideology as some kind of rigidly held system of political beliefs, I use the term mostly as it is informed by Louis Althusser's reworking in the light of the complex Lacanian notion of subject-formation (see Althusser 1971: 160-5; 135-41). According to the Althusserian narrative, the formation of performers in a highly institutionalized landscape occurs in the image of the dominant socio-economic conditions. To this effect, by 'ideological approach' I denote a predetermined and predetermining way of operating that defines the parameters of the real and the self in a way that is conditioned by the socio-economic structures of the historical moment. An ideological approach to training is thus, in this account, a training that already knows where it is going, where the point of arrival is already predicated, where exercises and techniques are all in function of something already known, where the approach is packaged. And this predication and packaging is, ultimately, at the service of the industries that surround the phenomenon of performer training today: mainly the academic, publishing and funding industries, which in turn form part of the rarefied realms of 'education', 'culture', 'economy' and 'politics'.

Althusser's critique sounds dated and crude forty years down the line, but it is still possible to extract the principles and mechanisms of ideological practice. Althusser's analysis takes on a prophetic quality when we consider that at the time of its composition in the late 1960s, performer training was just about to take its first steps in a process that was to lead it into becoming part of the so-called educational ideological apparatus. In the late 1960s, Eugenio Barba was conducting laboratory research in Holstebro at the same time as making films and documentaries, publishing books and organising events that would bring laboratory practice to the attention of academia. Contemporaneously, other practitioners whose work is now entrenched in institutional education programmes were also investigating the nature of performer training, e.g., Grotowski in Poland and Decroux in France. These were the spearheads of a movement that included other research practices such as Ingemar Lindh's Institutet för Scenkonst in Sweden and Mike Pearson's and Richard Gough's

[2] See my discussion of Ingemar Lindh's investigation of collective improvisation which is permeated by the mechanics of encounter and sensitivity to the other in the context of the performer's technical work upon oneself, the relationship with space and text, the role of the spectator, and the discipline of the work (Camilleri 2008: 252).

Cardiff Laboratory Theatre in Wales. The seeds of the current inter-century paradigm shift towards institutionalization were sown forty years ago, paradoxically at a time when institutions were under siege by such alternative cultures.

The ideological 'packaging' of training takes various forms. The packaging process actually begins with the nomenclature of the practitioners themselves, e.g., the term 'biomechanics' and the individual *étude* of, say, 'Throwing the Stone', imply a body of training and a specific technique that as such refer to a content. It is this 'content' that then lends itself as 'knowledge' that can be curriculumized and modularized in academia, and which is then subjected to the various regulatory entities (including health and safety, assessment criteria etc.) that come with conservatoires, performing arts schools and universities. The whole package is then further processed as a promise by marketing strategies aimed at attracting paying customers.

An objection might be raised at this point that 'this is the way of things, how things develop and progress'. My riposte is that such 'naturalness' and 'obviousness' is precisely the effect of the ideological phenomenon described by Althusser: that ideology interpellates us as subjects and 'naturalizes' a process that is essentially a construct (1971: 161). The fact that this construct was not a natural process at all is evidenced by the theatre practitioners themselves who, in the first instance, had to forge these techniques as an unknown quantity rather than as a known or natural experience. The aspect of the above objection that is more difficult to rebut concerns the fundamental (thus arguably 'natural') process that marks codification, because the moment a technique or an exercise is formulated, it immediately lends itself to packaging, reproduction and placement. In this sense it is indeed 'natural' for things to be cut down to size in any process of development and transmission, but then that is also why our only hope lies in the strategic resistance of constant questioning and reworking announced by an ethical framework (cf. Derrida 1999: 72-3). The ethical approach is just as ideological in being a specific material practice and in defining the parameters of the real and the self, but its constitutive nature of *displacement* (geographic, architectural, technical etc.) makes it resistant to the dominant ideology of the socio-cultural moment whose material practices are aimed at *placement* and sameness. This is the resistance implied in the original sense of the 'avant-garde' before this term was appropriated and commodified into a style and a practice.

SHARED TERRITORY: THE ETHICS OF RESPONSIBILITY AND THE MORALITY OF REGULATIONS

The crucial aspect I am trying to highlight here is not so much a rigid distinction between two paradigms but the extent of the territory shared by both. Indeed, the success of the ethical approach is partially measured by its ideological application, in the sense that 'packaging' is initially due to the laboratories themselves, which necessarily present knowledge in coherent logical components that are transmittable in a more efficient and less time-consuming manner. The separability of exercises, which is an important aspect of laboratory training processes, is at the centre of what makes codified technique prone to commodification. When these repeatable components are transposed into the wider context of commodities, technique takes on a different dimension and marketability informs and structures its logic. One argument that Simon Murray proposes in his contextualization of the rise of various types of physical theatre is precisely the marketability and commodification of the body (2003: 38-9). In such a market, exercises and techniques are choice products, but the ethical context that had initially brought them about is obscured. In an ethical approach, everything from choice of space to way of life is in function of the work. In an ideological approach, the work is in function of the myriad structures and regulations that surround it.

The ideological contact with technique follows the *dynamics of appropriation* as distinct from the *dynamics of encounter* that characterize ethical endeavours. The ideological packaging of technique already presupposes an end and a known process. The results of ideological and ethical approaches might be superficially similar (e.g., a trained body and engaging performances), but their processes and less tangible dimensions are not. If the ideological impulse to codify lies at the heart of the ethical approach, that impulse becomes *self-negating* – because in the ethical approach points of arrival are not institutionalized as practice but are transformed into points of departure. Ingemar Lindh observes how in the process that led to the performance 'To Whom It May Concern' (1985) the initial task of the Institutet för Scenkonst was to work against the techniques that had emerged in their previous performance, i.e., the work on active immobility inspired by frescos in 'Fresker' (1979-82) was interrupted by the new work on explosive 'super energy' (Lindh 1998: 109). It is this kind of constitutive displacement that renders such practices resistant to the ideological impulse of fixing and placing.

Another instance of shared territory between ethical and ideological approaches concerns the locus of responsibility. In an ideological approach, the ethical framework of laboratory principles and guidelines is replaced by regulations. A good example of this involves the institutionalization of health and safety issues. In an ethical outlook these matters are integral to the work in forming part of a wider framework of respect, responsibility, commitment and discipline. There is often no need to name this invisible dimension, but these elements are manifest in the way that work is conducted in a studio. Simple mundane procedures, such as cleaning the floor, take on a quasi-ritualistic function and are the result of a practical necessity that also serves as a warm-up or point of entry into the work. A clean and uncluttered environment is an essential issue for laboratory practitioners intent on cultivating psychophysical awareness. It is also a sign of discipline as well as of respect and responsibility to keep the space clean. In most institutions, cleaning the space or a clean space is not considered an integral part of the work; it is divorced from the training process and allotted to 'cleaning service providers' with the result that students abdicate the responsibility of cleaning the space.

In an institutionalized context, a private empirical process is not possible: you have a group or professional ethos that is really an instituted compilation of rules (usually set up to protect the institution from legal culpability) to which you are expected to adhere, regardless of your aesthetic and ethical views on the matter. A case in point is health and safety regulations which are aimed at complementing such professional work practices. A typical example of the way that the ethos of these regulations contrasts a laboratory ethic is the common prohibition of naked flames (even of a single candle) in studio and performance spaces. Practitioners in an institutional context are expected *to work with a substitute rather than with the thing itself*. This is perhaps an insignificant example, which nonetheless stands at the core of the paradigm shift from ethical to ideological approaches. In an ideological approach the onus of responsibility is placed not on the individual but on regulations which were initially set up to compensate for the lack of responsibility that occurs during the transplantation of technique from an ethical context to an ideological one. The terms 'responsibility' and 'respect' are used in the widest possible sense, i.e., not as forms of imposed responsibility or respect but ones that are ingrained in an integral way (such as the cleaning of the space and the responsibility of using a naked flame) that does not distinguish between my responsibilities as a human being and my responsibilities as a performer.

In an institutional context, regulations come to

function as morality rather than ethics. The distinction between morality and ethics is a fine one, and these two terms are often used interchangeably (Singer 1993: 1). However, it is important to tease out a working difference between the two in order to illuminate the distinction between ethical parameters and ideological regulations. Harpham argues that morality represents 'a particular moment of ethics, when all but one of the available alternatives are excluded, chosen against, regardless of their claims' (1995: 397). Viewed from this angle, morality is the endpoint of ethics. The relationship between the two is complex, because despite announcing different moments, morality and ethics are dependent on each other. Without morality, ethics would be inconsequential: 'without decision, ethics would be condemned to dithering. It is morality that realizes ethics, making it ethical. At the same time, however, morality negates ethics, and needs ethics in order to be moral' (397). The dynamic at work in the relationship between ethics and morality is reminiscent of the view that at the heart of the ethical approach to training is a self-negating ideological impulse. The morality announced by regulations, which determines what is right and wrong in an institutionalized process of formation, functions as a point of arrival and a closure. On its part, the ethical framework that sustains laboratory practice makes sure that points of arrival are not transmogrified into a dead shell but transformed into creative possibilities.

The relationship between ethics and morality provides a further twist in the context of performer training. If morality is ethics-in-action and the actor is concerned with action, then the responsibility of the actor is necessarily moral. The implicit suggestion here is that the moment of performance is the moral instant of an ethical process. This is perhaps why practitioners such as Grotowski, Lindh and Barba have resisted and rethought the moment of performance in spatial and other terms, and why for Decroux, Lecoq and again Lindh performance was intimately related to pedagogical contexts. In both cases the moment of finality announced by the morality of performance is subjected to the dynamics of displacement.

OF POUNDS OF FLESH
AND TROJAN HORSES

Paul Allain's articulation of the challenges faced by Gardzience Theatre Association in the 1990s is symptomatic of those confronted by other ethical approaches to training in the current paradigm shift.

> The economic regulation which Western models of funding demand, in terms of rationalising expenses, do not co-exist comfortably next to Gardzienice's open structures. An era seems to have drawn to a close: a period which began with the protests and student expression of the 1960s and 1970s and which led to the openness of paratheatre, which gave a broader theoretical base for theatre. The roots of Gardzienice grew in a distant time of self-trained, marginal groups, shaped by paratheatre. Now different attitudes to culture and money are being established, which threaten to undermine these traditions. (Allain 1997: 57)

The paradigm shift in performer training at the turn of the twenty-first century coincides with a shift in funding cultures. A combination of sheer necessity and funding opportunities from the 1990s onwards has increasingly pushed laboratories towards ideological perspectives. In order to survive in the current climate, theatre laboratories have to adapt to changing circumstances by adopting something akin to a split personality that allows them to follow the ethical way at the same time as catering for the ideological demands of their sponsors.[3]

A case in point is the three-year EU-funded Tracing Roads Across Project (2003-6) of the Workcenter of Jerzy Grotowski and Thomas Richards. Perhaps the epitome of secluded and displaced laboratory practice up till Grotowski's death in 1999, the Workcenter under Thomas Richards and Mario Biagini was granted Culture 2000 funding with the objectives to 'foster an

[3] Nicole Bugeja's discussion of the 'economic strategies and mechanisms' applied to safeguard contemporary research theatre practice has been inspirational for this section of the article (2007: 75-112).

intense cultural dialogue between the participating nationalities; strengthen and enlarge an existing transnational network of cultural operators; promote the emergence of new networks of young artists/theatre groups; foster international coproductions' (European Commission 2009: 6). Beyond the trappings of bureaucratic language, the project was aimed at providing the Workcenter with financial security that would allow it to continue its research for a stipulated period. It was also obliged to open its doors for three years with a packed schedule of events all over Europe. Tracing Roads Across has served to give the post-Grotowski work of the Workcenter substantial exposure and currency in various academic and publishing contexts. A number of publications, including a recent issue of *TDR* (T198 summer 2008), have followed in the wake of the project. It has also had the effect of fuelling an already existing tendency to reproduce a Workcenter 'style' or 'technique' that has been copied and reproduced in various contexts: from the singing of traditional songs (complete with the mannerisms of Richards or Biagini) and recurrent performance images of persons being born (by appearing from between other people's legs), to women all dressed in red and the predictable use of candles.

It was evident during the project that the Workcenter leaders were trying to protect the identity and nature of their work by retaining strict control on its exposure. But the moment doors are open, a practice becomes amenable to commodification. During the project, the split personality dynamic I mentioned earlier could be sensed in some of the events. For example, in the closing conference of the Impulse in Bulgaria (Varna, June 2004) there were various moments of unease and tension in the manner that sections of the panel and audience were addressed by Richards and Biagini: answering questions by means of other questions such as 'Why do you ask us these questions?' and by remarks like 'Read the books that have been published', seemed to go against the spirit of 'Opening Doors' (Camilleri 2004). Such behaviour, which was not restricted to the Bulgaria conference, can be ascribed to the institutional and contractual tensions that push Richards and Biagini in a direction different from the ethical practice to which they had been accustomed. The problem is symptomatic of the paradigm shift in the early twenty-first century: one cannot wholly resist commodification while accepting to partake of its fruit – there is always a pound of flesh to be paid.

The European Commission document I quote in the preceding paragraphs also includes details of another project that was awarded Culture 2000 funding: 'European Theatre Laboratories as Cultural Innovators' under the leadership of Eugenio Barba's Odin Teatret. The contractual objectives of the project state:

> Further exchange and presentation of performances in the future, extending similar activities ['performances, festivals', 'cultural barters', 'symposiums'] into European countries; support the qualified pedagogical process parallel to the education given in schools ['universities and cultural centres']; to develop training programmes with immediate connection to concrete work within the companies, groups and projects; movement of artists; the documentation of the project.
> (European Commission 2009: 1)

These are practically the same objectives that Barba has been following since the 1960s, including the prominent roles that pedagogy and training play in his practice. This Culture 2000 project marks the latest evolutionary stage that laboratory practices as a general phenomenon have experienced in the twentieth century. Barba is once again at the forefront when it comes to adapting to the socio-economic conditions of the times. From a very early stage in his practice Barba has sought and managed a relationship with institutional bodies, in the process allowing him to fulfil his 'ethical project in the arts'. 2002 marked an important point in his dealings with academia: Odin Teatret established the Centre for Theatre Laboratory Studies (CTLS) in conjunction with Aarhus University. This means that a branch of Odin Teatret is now officially part of a university; it is highly likely that this step will lead to further joint ventures.[4] Barba is too much of an old hand and a master at institutional contact to suffer from any form of split-personality tension. However, something, somewhere, must always give. The Symposium of the International School of Theatre Anthropology on 'Improvisation', which was held in Wrocław in April 2005 with the assistance of Culture 2000 funding did feel like it was following a tried and tested formula and like this was one big show that has been rehearsed and performed countless times before. In this sense it was definitely an 'ideological' event that packaged and marketed training and performance practices for consumption. But that is, presumably, the particular pound of flesh that Barba has to pay. The open secret of his success lies in the fact that, apparently and strategically, he pays his dues willingly without begrudging anything to Caesar. This appears to be a wiser strategy than direct resistance to the forces of commodification: it becomes a Trojan horse that spells the survival and continuation of a theatre practice.

Big multi-year projects are not the only means that mark the crossroads of ethical and ideological positions in twenty-first-century performer training. The commercial wing that research-oriented practices have been obliged to develop alongside their laboratory work is now a requisite. A glance at the websites of these practitioners, which in themselves are symptomatic of the endeavour to bestow visibility on their work, is enough to indicate how theatre-makers are categorizing and rationalizing their practice in terms of performances, training, projects, current events, documentation and contact. The website links are a veritable trail, packaged at attracting students and sponsors alike because, as Alison Hodge observes, 'in the present economic climate of Western theatre practice ... sustained training and ensemble work are becoming scarce. It may be that the "total" model of Grotowski's practice is difficult to absorb within the commercial environment of Western capitalism' (2005: 62). Due to the open-ended and long term nature of their work, research-based practices cannot depend on the presentation of performances for revenue, and so they offer all sorts of pedagogical services from short workshops to longer residencies. Of particular note is the MA programme in Acting Techniques established by Teatr Pieśń Kozła (Song of the Goat Theatre) with Manchester Metropolitan University. In this case, the packaging entails the promise of an authentic experience of working with these practitioners at their own base in Wrocław. It also entails collusion with the forces of commodification in the way that the revolutionary 'avant-garde' spirit has been reduced to a recognizable aesthetic (a 'tradition') that is curriculumized and made teachable (Teatr Pieśń Kozła 2009). A university degree of this kind would have been inconceivable in the 1990s. It has been brought about by a combination of factors that includes the appeal of 'physical theatre' as a performance practice worthy of academic study. The recognition of practice as research has also put a premium on the research work of laboratory theatre whose practitioners have found a home in academia.

This is where the author of this article enters the picture in the guise of the hybrid practitioner-scholar that has increasingly characterized university drama and theatre departments since the 1990s. As a laboratory practitioner since 1989 I have found a permanent home in academia since 2004: working at a university allows me to continue my research practice within certain parameters. The institutional obligations that come with this security include adherence to rules and regulations (administrative as well as pedagogical) and high expectations of publications and funding grants acquisition. The time and energy this adherence and these expectations demand is the pound of flesh practitioner-scholars have to pay. In this sense, the author of this article and the article itself are both complicit with the ideological shift I have

[4] The development of the Cardiff Laboratory Theatre into the Centre for Performance Research (CPR) in 1988 and the subsequent close association with Aberystwyth University (which has been used in 2008 as an implicit excuse by the Arts Council of Wales to cut revenue grants to CPR) is also characteristic of the paradigmatic movements discussed in this article.

identified. The challenge is to find a way of working within the institution that acknowledges the esoteric dimension of our exoteric practice.

IN FIFTY YEARS' TIME

When a new technique is discovered, it is only a question of time before it is incorporated within the ideological circle of educational institutions, publishing industries and funding agencies. A stage has been reached where, encouraged by funding strategies and research grants, 'techniques' are invented to feed demand rather than to serve a practical need. Indeed, a substantial number of presentations at practice-as-research conferences are visible witness to the fetishization of technique and to the habit of putting the cart of results in front of the horse of process. The saturation bubble of demand and supply can never burst in an ideological framework: it can only move sideways, just as it has moved in the direction of the body as a locus of intervention and speculation in the second half of the twentieth century (Murray 2003: 38-9). The seeds of a *future* paradigm shift, which have been sown in the final decade of the twentieth century, are already sprouting: the increasing application of new technology and new media will inevitably impact the way preparing for performance is conceived. As the potential of cyborg possibilities become widespread realities in the new century, laboratory training will most probably revert to its ethically informed and utopian beginnings.

REFERENCES

Allain, Paul (1997) *Gardzienice: Polish theatre in transition*, London: Harwood Academic Publishers.

Allain, Paul and Harvie, Jen (2006) *The Routledge Companion to Theatre and Performance*, London: Routledge.

Althusser, Louis (1971) *Lenin and Philosophy and Other Essays*, trans. Ben Brewster, London: NLB.

Bugeja, Nicole (2007) 'Research Theatre in Contemporary Europe: An analysis of the means of continuation', unpublished MA dissertation, Malta: University of Malta.

Camilleri, Frank (2004) Personal notes.

Camilleri, Frank (2008) 'Hospitality and the Ethics of Improvisation in the Work of Ingemar Lindh', *New Theatre Quarterly* 24(3): 246-59.

Cruciani, Fabrizio (1995) *Registi Pedagoghi e Comunità Teatrali nel Novecento*, rev. ed., Rome: Editori and Associati.

Derrida, Jacques (1999) 'Hospitality, Justice and Responsibility: A dialogue with Jacques Derrida', in Richard Kearney and Mark Dooley (eds) *Questioning Ethics: Contemporary debates in philosophy*, London: Routledge, pp. 65-83.

European Commission (2009), 'Culture 2000 - Implementation 2003' <http://ec.europa.eu/culture/archive/culture2000/pdf/projets2003/perform_artsA2.pdf> [accessed 12 March 2009].

Harpham, Geoffrey Galt (1995) 'Ethics', in Frank Lentricchia and Thomas McLaughlin (eds) *Critical Terms for Literary Study*, 2nd edn, Chicago: University of Chicago Press, pp. 387-405.

Hodge, Alison (2005) 'Gardzienice's Influence in the West', *Contemporary Theatre Review* 15(1): 59-68.

Lindh, Ingemar (1998) *Pietre di Guado*, Pontedera: Bandecchi and Vivaldi.

Murray, Simon (2003) *Jacques Lecoq*, London: Routledge.

Singer, Peter (1993) *Practical Ethics*, 2nd edn, Cambridge: Cambridge University Press.

Stanislavsky, Konstantin (2008) *An Actor's Work: A student's diary*, trans. Jean Benedetti, London: Routledge.

Teatr Pieśń Kozła (2009) 'MA Course in Acting Techniques' <http://www.piesnkozla.pl/ma_course_in_acting_techniques,en.html> [accessed 12 March 2009].

Watson, Ian (2001) 'Introduction', in Ian Watson (ed.) *Performer Training: Developments across cultures*, London: Harwood Academic Publishers.

Setting the Stage
Social-environmental and motivational predictors of optimal training engagement

ELEANOR QUESTED & JOAN L. DUDA

From the stadium to the stage, time investment is a recognized prerequisite for proficient performance. According to Ericsson, expert performers typically accumulate 10,000 hours of practice to become exceptional in their performance arenas (Ericsson et al. 1993). However quantity represents only one facet of training that might encourage maximal performance gains. 'Going through the motions' for 10,000 hours may not be sufficient to guarantee expertise. The *quality* of engagement in training also holds significance for the development of proficiency, as well as for the longevity of the performer's career. Performers can only train at their best when they are 'firing on all cylinders' and feeling well. Thus, to get the most from one's training, the experience should also contribute towards the performer's physical and psychological welfare. These often-overlooked requisites to optimal engagement in training may be primary determinants of whether performers realize and sustain their full potential.

Theories of motivation have frequently been employed as frameworks within which to explore antecedents of sustained, healthful and optimal engagement in physical and scholarly pursuits. 'Motivation' is one of the most widely examined psychological constructs in achievement domains. Yet in performance contexts, the term remains vague and often inadequately understood (Roberts 1992). Early theories construed motivation as a quantitative entity synonymous with the degree of energy and effort directed towards the targeted behaviour. This conceptualization does not take into account *why* the behaviour was initiated or how it was regulated (Roberts 1992). From a qualitative perspective, 'motivation' refers to the meaning and value of the behaviour for the individual as well as the cognitive processes that underscore interpretation of the reason to act (Ames and Ames 1984).

According to this latter conceptualization, the *type* of motivation driving the behaviour is considered to be the primary determinant of performance and training quality and also relevant to the degree to which the performer experiences well- and ill-being. Research undertaken in academic and sport contexts indicates that features of training environments (i.e., teacher/coach behaviours) play a fundamental role in promoting adaptive motivational processes. In turn, these have been associated with desirable consequences, in and beyond the training forum. Much of this work has been grounded in the self-determination theory (SDT) framework (Deci and Ryan 1985, Deci and Ryan 2000).

In this paper, we will firstly explore the central tenets of SDT. Research that has examined the social-environmental and motivation-related correlates of optimal training, performance and health-related engagement through the theoretical lens of SDT will be reviewed. Drawing from SDT-driven work undertaken in educational, sport and dance settings, we will draw conclusions and suggest future directions from a research and applied perspective.

A MOTIVATIONAL CONTINUUM AND PSYCHOLOGICAL NEED SATISFACTION

Individuals engage in training for a variety of reasons. The term 'motivation regulations' refers to this range of motives for actions in all domains of life; in essence, the 'why' of behaviour. Differentiating between types of motivation regulations is a central feature of SDT (Deci and Ryan 1985, Deci and Ryan 2000). Two types of motivation were originally distinguished: intrinsic (i.e., from within) and extrinsic (i.e., from something, or someone else). SDT extended this somewhat simplistic conceptualization and posits motivation regulations for behaviour engagement to lie on a continuum with varying degrees of autonomy (Deci and Ryan 2000). According to SDT, intrinsic motivation represents the most self-determined or autonomous behaviour regulation. When intrinsically motivated, individuals engage in activities for reasons underpinned by inherent interest, enjoyment and satisfaction. Integrated regulation refers to behavioural engagement for reasons that are in congruence with the individual's overall aspirations and lifestyle; the behaviour is both volitional and anchored to the individual's identity. Identified regulation lies next on the continuum and also represents autonomous reasons for behavioural engagement, but in this case, one recognizes the underlying purpose and potential value of the behaviour for themselves and therefore freely participates. When one partakes in an activity on account of internal or external contingencies (e.g., appeasement or avoidance of guilt, desire to exhibit ability or averting demonstration of failure) the regulation can be described as introjected. External regulations are considered to be highly controlled and underpin engagement in behaviours for reasons that are externally defined. Typical examples of external motivators include praise, rewards and punishment avoidance. At the far end of the continuum lies amotivation, representing a lack of any impetus driving behaviour. A burgeoning collection of SDT-driven investigations indicate that the level of self-determination undergirding engagement in achievement-related activities is a critical determinant of a performer's cognitive, behavioural and emotional responses in those settings.

FACILITATING NEED SATISFACTION AND AUTONOMOUS BEHAVIOUR REGULATION: THE ROLE OF COACHES, TEACHERS AND INSTRUCTORS

SDT assumes the satisfaction of three psychological needs (namely competence, autonomy and relatedness) to be essential for self-initiated actions, and subsequent

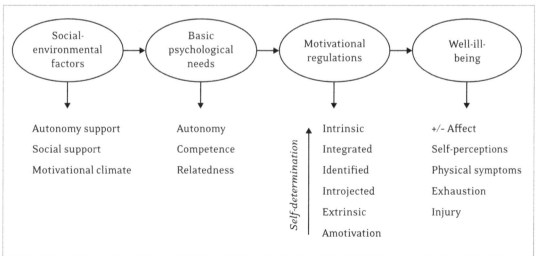

• Figure 1. Schematic representation of Self-Determination Theory.

psychological development and well-being (Deci and Ryan 2000). Competence represents the feeling that one is effective and efficient in the pursuits undertaken. Feeling connected, cared for and that one belongs in a social setting is captured by the construct relatedness. Satisfaction of the need for autonomy occurs when actions are perceived as self-governed, volitional and reflective of personal values. SDT hypothesizes that individuals seek out and persist in endeavours that are optimally challenging (Deci and Ryan 2000). Essentially, the desire to feel efficacious and self-determined as well as cared for provides the fuel to energize more intrinsic behavioural engagement. Thus, when participation in training is autonomously regulated, persistent and effective engagement, as well as corresponding performance and health-related benefits, are considered to be the likely consequences.

SDT proposes that the social environment can support or impede need satisfaction and subsequent self-determined behavioural engagement. Coaches and teachers are ideally placed with this regard. The organization and delivery of training as well as the interpersonal approach adopted by the leader are fundamental to whether performers in the context at hand feel autonomous, competent and connected.

REWARDS AND REINFORCEMENT

In the 1970s and 1980s, Deci and colleagues undertook a series of experiments examining the motivational impact of rewards and verbal feedback. Findings indicated that social-contextual cues (such as praise and rewards) that fostered feelings of competence benefited intrinsic motivation (Deci et al. 1999). Positive verbal feedback augmented, whereas negative responses thwarted intrinsic motivation for the activity in question. However, when rewards were contingent on performance, task completion or merely task engagement, studies found intrinsic motivation to be consistently undermined (Deci et al. 1999). This was attributed to the controlling nature of rewards; when behavioural engagement is conditional on incentives then the impetus for self-regulation is considered to be forestalled.

In the past thirty years, a plethora of studies have supported the fundamental tenets undergirding these early findings. A recent experimental study undertaken in a Physical Education (PE) context re-illustrates the potential benefits of using reinforcements (Mouratidis et al. 2008). In line with the early work of Deci and colleagues, positive competence feedback enhanced intrinsic motivation for a shuttle-run task, via the reinforcement of the need for competence. A negative association between competence feedback and amotivation was also revealed. This suggests that when feedback is pitched in a way that supports basic needs, learners tend to feel more autonomous and less helpless and amotivated during the task in hand. Collectively, this line of research highlights the importance of careful and calculated use of rewards, feedback and praise. It is important that these responses support, rather than destabilize the performer's psychological needs.

AUTONOMY SUPPORT

'Autonomy support' is the dimension of interpersonal style that has attracted the majority of SDT research attention in achievement settings. Teachers who support the learner's autonomy encourage choice, use of initiative and self-directed behaviours. More-controlling teachers tend to adopt a more authoritarian style, set specific agendas and endeavour to control and/or coerce the learner's goals and behaviours towards a pre-determined outcome (Pelletier et al. 2001). A substantial body of research undertaken in sport settings indicates that leader's attempts to exercise control (by imposing rules, deadlines or coercion via rewards/punishments) undermines participants' self-determined behaviour (Amorose 2007). On the contrary, more autonomously motivated actions are more likely when leaders support autonomy by offering choice and considering the other's perspective (Pelletier et al. 2001). More specifically, studies show that need satisfaction, autonomous motivation and subsequent desirable outcomes are more likely in autonomy-supportive sport settings (Amorose 2007). In our own work undertaken in vocational dance settings (Quested and Duda in press-b), perceptions of the dance teachers as autonomy-supportive predicted dance students' intrinsic motivation and amotivation (positively and negatively, respectively).[1]

SOCIAL SUPPORT

Social support in training is evident when teachers and coaches exhibit signs of respect, care and consideration and proffer emotional support. Socially-supportive teaching is expected to facilitate the performer's need satisfaction (in particular, feelings of relatedness), autonomous behaviour regulations and quality of engagement in the achievement setting (Amorose 2007). In sport settings, the expected link between social support provided by coaches and athletes' reported feelings of relatedness has been empirically substantiated (Reinboth et al. 2004). Less conclusive is the evidence *vis-à-vis* the link between perceived social support and motivation regulations in achievement contexts. Previous studies have failed to support an association between perceptions of social support in the training setting and athletes' autonomous motivation for their sport participation (Amorose and Horn 2000). Perhaps even more surprisingly, longitudinal studies have indicated that when coaches are perceived as providing social support, intrinsic motivation is subsequently undermined (Amorose and Horn 2001). This theoretical anomaly may be attributable to an increase in desire (and therefore internal pressure) to please the individual who is exhibiting care and concern (Amorose 2007). As a consequence, engagement in the targeted behaviour becomes controlled by these contingencies. Nevertheless, it seems that social support has the propensity to afford motivation-related benefits. In the future researchers and practitioners might consider the quality and nature of social support (e.g., instrumental and/or expressive, conditional or non-contingent) offered when examining the potential impact upon self-determined behaviour of performers.

MOTIVATIONAL CLIMATE

The way that competence and success are defined and recognized in training holds implications for the behavioural and affective patterns exhibited by performers. This premise is a defining feature of achievement goal theory (AGT) (Ames 1992, Nicholls 1989). Contextual cues are held to shape individuals' interpretations of their achievement goals and views about success (Ames 1992, Nicholls 1989). AGT-driven research in sport indicates that perceptions of the motivational climate can influence an array of motivational, behavioural and health-related responses among athletes (Duda 2001). Motivational climates that encourage self-referenced judgments of competence have been labelled as task-involving (Ames 1992). In such settings there is an emphasis on personal development and co-operative learning and a focus on individual effort and improvement. In ego-involving climates a normative conception of competence is emphasized and so personal performance accomplishments and ability level are assessed relative to others. Thus, performers are always 'looking over their shoulder' with the end goal being the demonstration of superiority. Ego-involving climates are characterized by a dearth in participant decision-making, competition and intra-individual rivalry, reprimand following error, and marked by a hierarchy tied to the ability level of the performer; the more able receive more attention (Duda 2001). An array of advantageous performance and health-related responses has been attributed to higher task-involving motivational learning climates such as persistence, enjoyment and physical and psychological well-being. On the contrary,

[1] In this study, perceived autonomy support did not significantly and negatively predict extrinsic regulation. This theoretical anomaly was explained by the fact that the latent variable representing 'extrinsic motivation' incorporated the three extrinsic regulations that vary in their degree of autonomy (identified, introjected, external).

ego-involving environments have been linked with less desirable health and performance related consequences including unhealthy eating, diminished self-esteem and dropout from the activity in question (Duda 2001).

Recent investigations have considered perceptions of the motivational climate as a relevant social-contextual variable within the SDT framework. Features of social environments such as *the* opportunities for self-selected tasks and competence enhancing activities, as well as self-referenced achievement judgments) might be expected to help one feel more connected, efficacious and able. On the contrary, engagement in an ego-focused training context might link to the thwarting of the basic needs as the climates are inherently competitive and comparative. Research in sport (Reinboth and Duda 2004, Reinboth and Duda 2006) and dance (Quested and Duda 2009-a, Quested and Duda 2007a, Quested and Duda 2009-b, Quested and Duda in press-a) is largely supportive of the hypotheses with regard to perceptions of task-involving climates. However empirical support for the expected associations between perceptions of ego-involving climates and undermined needs is less consistent. In vocational dance contexts, dancers' perceptions of ego-involving cues negatively predicted satisfaction of the needs for competence and relatedness (Quested and Duda in press-a). However other studies in sport, as well as hip hop company training settings (Quested and Duda 2009-a, Reinboth and Duda 2006) have failed to support an association between perceptions of ego-involving learning climates and need satisfaction. Perhaps other situational characteristics and individual differences moderate this link. For example, in the vocational dance context, dancers are training full-time. In the latter mentioned studies, behavioural engagement in the relevant setting was part-time. Thus, time spent in an ego-involving climate could be a moderating variable in the association between perceptions of an ego-involving learning context and need satisfaction.

WHY WE NEED NEEDS AND WHY 'WHY' MATTERS: OUTCOMES ASSOCIATED WITH THE 'SOCIAL-ENVIRONMENTAL—NEEDS—MOTIVATION REGULATIONS' SEQUENCE

The application of SDT in education, sport and (more recently) dance research has witnessed considerable growth. This is perhaps attributable to the value of the framework as a means to understand the personal, environmental and motivational antecedents of human behaviours, cognitions and responses. A number of outcomes have been considered in this regard.

ADHERENCE AND PERSISTENCE

If expertise takes ten years to nurture (Ericsson et al. 1993), then sustained engagement in performance-related training is imperative. Research in elite sport settings has examined the motivation-related predictors of sustained engagement in athletic activities (Pelletier et al. 2001). In a 22-month study involving competitive swimmers, amotivated swimmers at the beginning of the season (time one) had the highest rates of dropout at the two later time points (ten and twenty-two months). However there were noteworthy differences in the patterns of persistence predicted by the different forms of non-autonomous motivation. Introjected regulation at time one significantly predicted training persistence ten months later, but not twenty-two months on. This indicates that introjected regulations can coerce behavioural engagement, but this does not sustain behaviour in the long term. External regulation at the start of the season did not predict dropout from training at time two (ten months later), but drop-out by time three (twenty two months later) was positively predicted by externally regulated swimming training reported at the beginning of the season. On the contrary the more self-determined athletes (i.e., high intrinsic/identified regulations) were more likely to persist after ten and twenty-two months. In line with the expectations of SDT, Pelletier and colleagues found swimmers who perceived their coaches to be controlling were more likely to adopt non-self-determined (i.e., external and amotivated) behavioural regulations. When coaches were perceived as autonomy-supportive, the swimmers were more likely to adopt autonomous behaviour regulations.

A 21-month study involving female handballers corroborated and extended these findings (Sarrazin et al. 2002). These authors found perceptions of less task-involving and more ego-involving coach behaviours as well as low reported competence, autonomy and relatedness satisfaction to be shared characteristics among those players who eventually dropped out. The study also revealed that intention significantly mediated the associations between motivation regulations and subsequent training persistence. However this effect was only moderate, suggesting that intentions might have changed over the 21-month time period and/or the athletes' withdrawal was sometimes for reasons outside of their own control (e.g., injury, relocation).

Taken as a whole, these studies reinforce the utility of understanding motivational processes, not only for interpreting optimal functioning in 'the here and now' but also in the future. In particular, the extent to which coaches and teachers can foster self-determination for engagement in training activities appears critical for the promotion of long term engagement.

'DOING WELL': MOTIVATIONAL AND SOCIAL PREDICTORS OF TRAINING AND PERFORMANCE QUALITY

Regardless of the nature of the activity, quality engagement and learning are usually considered to be prerequisites for expertise development. SDT-based studies undertaken in educational settings have found autonomous motivation for learning to equate with persistence, better learning, higher grades and more satisfaction with the learning experience (Guay et al. 2008). Thus, taking pleasure in and identifying with the benefits associated with educational pursuits can make personal investment in training more worthwhile. Autonomy-supportive and structured learning environments are held to facilitate autonomous behaviour and enhanced learning in education contexts (Guay et al. 2008). Research supports the role of need satisfaction as an inherent mediator in the association between social influences and adaptive approaches to learning. For example, when students' needs for competence and autonomy are nurtured, then academic aptitude has been shown to be improved (Grolnick and Ryan 1989, Grolnick et al. 1991). Specifically, in these studies academic grades and teacher ratings of students' capability were significantly predicted by the students' reported degree of autonomy and competence satisfaction. Like teachers, parents are a prominent socializing influence in the lives of children. Accordingly, these studies also examined parental autonomy support. In line with SDT, provision of parental autonomy support directly predicted academic outcomes and these associations were mediated by need satisfaction.

It may seem intuitive that autonomy and competence would emerge as the more salient needs in learning environments. However satisfaction of the need for relatedness has also been recognized as an important predictor of positive academic experiences. In a classroom-based study, Furrer and Skinner (2003) found that feeling 'connected' to peers, parents and teachers linked to significant changes in students' engagement in the classroom over the course of the school year. The relative contribution of the children's relatedness satisfaction exceeded that predicted by perceived control of learning (Furrer and Skinner 2003). Hence, it is important for teachers and parents to create a caring, trusting and emotionally supportive environment to help foster young performers' vigour and investment in training. Research concerning the motivational correlates of optimal learning in physical activity or other non-academic training environments is warranted. Predictors of optimal learning and performance have been considered to a lesser extent in these contexts.

'FEELING WELL': WELL- AND ILL-BEING

Deci and Ryan (2000) define well-being as more than personal experiences of positive affect but refer to 'an organismic function in which the person detects the presence or absence of vitality, psychological flexibility and a deep inner sense of wellness' (2000: 243). In essence, performers exhibiting a high degree of well-being are fully functioning and experiencing personal growth alongside desire fulfilment in their achievement endeavours. The multifaceted nature of well-being dictates that the state could be operationalized in numerous ways. Accordingly, a variety of assessments has been employed to gauge the degree of well-being experienced by performers. Self-esteem, vitality, affective states/traits, happiness and satisfaction are among the more common indictors of well-being applied in research undertaken in sport, as well as other domains. In line with Deci and Ryan's definition, it is important to recognize that well- and ill-being are not polar opposites. The absence of physical or psychological ill-health does not necessarily equate to optimal functioning. Thus, examinations of the antecedents of thriving well-being are just as important and may point to different contributors when contrasted to investigations of the determinants of compromised welfare (e.g., burnout, physique anxiety, illness).

The proposition that coach behaviours can impact upon the health status (degree of well- and ill-being) and performance potential of athletes is well corroborated in the literature (Amorose 2007). Moreover, the hypothesized mediating roles of need satisfaction and motivation regulations in this relationship have been supported in recent sport and dance investigations. For example, in a series of studies Reinboth and colleagues (2004, 2006) found perceptions of the coach-created motivational climate to be predictive of athletes' degree of need satisfaction and reported well-/ill-being (i.e., vitality, physical symptoms, emotional and physical exhaustion). In a longitudinal study spanning an athletic season, these authors found an increase in perceptions of a task-involving training environment to positively predict changes in the athletes' autonomy, competence and relatedness. Increases in need satisfaction corresponded with increased subjective vitality reported by the athletes. The former findings were largely replicated in our recent investigations in vocational and company dance settings (Quested and Duda 2009-a, Quested and Duda 2009-b, Quested and Duda in press-a).

In achievement settings, displays and tests of competence are customary. When pitted against the needs for autonomy and relatedness, it might be logical to expect competence to hold the most functional significance for the performers' psychological and emotional welfare. Previous investigations including those undertaken in sport (Reinboth and Duda 2006) and in the case of company-based hip hop dancers (Quested and Duda 2009-a) have substantiated this hypothesis. In these studies, competence was the most salient predictor of the athletes' and dancers' reports of positive and negative affect. On the contrary, in the case of vocational dancers, relatedness emerged as the strongest predictor of dancers' emotional states (Quested and Duda in press-a). Perceptions of the task- and ego-involving cues in the dance schools also had quite a striking impact upon relatedness satisfaction. The strength of these paths exceeded those between perceptions of task- and ego-involving motivational climates and both autonomy and competence. Thus, although satisfying one's desire to feel competent is clearly important in the case of performers in achievement contexts, feeling connected to others is also highly relevant to the performer's welfare.

In the view of SDT theorists, relatedness is often considered to be a subsidiary need, fulfilling a more distal role than autonomy and competence in the nurturing of well-being (Deci and Ryan 2000). Thus, the discrepancy between the most functionally significant need in the competitive sport and vocational dance studies is intriguing. Perhaps there are moderating features inherent to vocational dance contexts that might accentuate the relevance of relatedness. For instance, incongruent with the athletes and the company-based hip hop dancers, vocational dancers are engaged in their dance training fulltime. Often they will have left home for the first time to train in another city or country. Thus, it is conceivable that feeling that one 'belongs' in the dance school and holds a meaningful connection with other students, staff members etc. could have a more pronounced impact upon the affective states the dancers experienced. The disparity in the findings of the aforementioned studies highlights the need for further research, particularly in other full-time, non-obligatory achievement contexts (e.g., companies on tour, summer schools, sport academies). In such domains feeling connected to peers and teachers may be particularly salient to healthful engagement.

The hypothesized links between motivation regulations and reported dimensions of well-being have also been empirically substantiated. Research undertaken with young gymnasts revealed motivation regulations to predict variability in the day-to-day well-being experienced by the athletes (Gagne et al. 2003). Specifically, using a daily diary-style methodology, Gagne and colleagues found that increases in autonomous motivation increased pre-practice feelings of positive affect, self-esteem and vitality, and decreased negative affect reported by the gymnasts. In our recent work with fulltime student dancers (Quested and Duda in press-b), we examined the extent to which motivation regulations for dance engagement contributed towards dancers' self-evaluations and concerns (social physique anxiety, self-esteem, body dissatisfaction). Heightened social physique anxiety, greater dissatisfaction with one's body and low levels of self-esteem have been linked to disordered eating tendencies, behaviours that are known to be more prevalent among dancers (Smolak et al. 2000). We found that when dancers engage in their training for extrinsic reasons they are more likely to report higher social physique anxiety.[2] This suggests that when dancers' participation is driven by internal or external pressures they are more likely to be emotionally susceptible to judgements of observers. Amotivation also positively predicted heightened anxiety associated with others viewing the dancers' physique, as well as greater body dissatisfaction and compromised self-esteem. Perceptions of autonomy support in the dance environment directly predicted the dancers' self-evaluations and concerns, and these associations were mediated by amotivation. These findings highlight the importance of promoting more autonomous motivation for dance training. Future research adopting longitudinal designs as well as the application of diary-style methodologies (Gagne et al. 2003) would serve to delineate the antecedents of adaptive as well as negative self-perceptions of dancers as well as among other performing artists.

Taken in their totality, the studies briefly reviewed support the SDT-based proposition that a) social-contextual features impact upon athletes' and dancers' degree of well- and ill-being experienced and b) that need satisfaction and motivation regulations serve as mediators of these relationships.

FOSTERING OPTIMAL FUNCTIONING IN ACHIEVEMENT SETTINGS: CONCLUSIONS AND PRACTICAL APPLICATIONS

Research undertaken in sport, dance and education contexts demonstrates that SDT is an applicable framework for understanding predictors of adaptive behaviours and optimal emotional and training-related responses. This literature base provides a sound conceptual grounding from which recommendations for teachers and trainers can be derived. The endorsement of autonomy-supportive, task-involving approaches to teaching would appear to be essential in the development of sustained, constructive and healthful engagement in training settings.

[2] In this study, the three extrinsic regulations (identified, introjected, external) were captured in one latent variable.

The TARGET framework (Epstein 1989) is a schema representing the central achievement structures in learning settings. Specific dimensions of the training environment (e.g., the Task, Authority, Recognition, Grouping, Evaluation and Timing) can be targeted with a view to enhancing the task-involving and autonomy-supportive, and tempering the ego-derived features of the context at hand. Modifications of the social environment created by coaches and teachers can be tailored in such a way to promote need satisfaction and autonomous behaviour regulations in the case of the performers involved. For example, with respect to the 'task' facet, provision of opportunities for performers to undertake diverse, challenging and self-selected tasks in training would create a learning environment supportive of autonomy need satisfaction. If recognition and reward are more private, and founded on personal progress, feelings of competence may be enhanced. A reduction in public, normative comparisons may reduce intra-individual rivalry and competition, and as a consequence a sense of greater relatedness between performers may result. The submission of authority to the learners by actively endorsing self-monitoring, enabling learners to take leadership roles and encouraging peer-learning could serve to enhance autonomy and competence as well as relatedness need satisfaction.

This review set out to introduce self-determination theory (Deci and Ryan 2000) and highlight the relevance and application of the central theoretical principles in training environments. There is much insight to be gleaned from the existent research undertaken in sport, education and dance. However, from a relative perspective, lines of research undertaken in dance and especially other performing arts are in their infancy. The stage is now set for future SDT-driven research in other performance domains. The application of the SDT framework in musical and theatrical contexts could contribute towards maximizing the training experience and welfare of performing artists.

REFERENCES

Ames, C. (1992) 'Achievement goals and the classroom motivational climate', in J. Meece and D. Schunk (eds) *Students' Perceptions in the Classroom: Causes and consequences*, Hillsdale, New Jersey: Erlbaum, pp. 327-48.

Ames, C. and Ames, R. (1984) 'Systems of student and teacher motivation: Toward a qualitative definition', *Journal of Educational Psychology* 76: 535-56.

Amorose, A. J. (2007) 'Coaching effectiveness', in M. S. Hagger and N. L. D. Chatzisarantis (eds) *Intrinsic Motivation and Self-Determination in Exercise and Sport*, Leeds: Human Kinetics, pp. 209-27.

Amorose, A. J. and Horn, T. S. (2000) 'Intrinsic motivation: Relationships with collegiate athletes' gender, scholarship status and perceptions of their coaches' behavior', *Journal of Sport and Exercise Psychology* 22: 63-84.

Amorose, A. J. and Horn, T. S. (2001) 'Pre- to post-season changes in the intrinsic motivation of first year college athletes: Relationships with coaching behavior and scholarship status', *Journal of Applied Psychology* 13: 355-73.

Deci, E. L., Koestner, R. and Ryan, R. M. (1999) 'A meta-analytic review of experiments examining the effects of extrinsic rewards on intrinsic motivation', *Psychological Bulletin* 125: 627-68.

Deci, E. L. and Ryan, R. M. (1985) *Intrinsic Motivation and Self-Determination in Human Behavior*, New York: Plenum.

Deci, E. L. and Ryan, R. M. (2000) 'The "what" and "why" of goal pursuits: Human needs and the self-determination of behavior', *Psychological Inquiry* 11: 227-68.

Duda, J. L. (2001) 'Achievement goal research in sport: Pushing the boundaries and clarifying some misunderstandings', in G. C. Roberts (ed.) *Advances in Motivation in Sport and Exercise*, Leeds: Human Kinetics, pp. 129-82.

Epstein, J. L. (1989) 'Family structures and student motivation: A developmental perspective', in C. Ames and R. Ames (eds) *Research on Motivation in Education*, New York: Academic Press, pp. 259-95.

Ericsson, K. A., Krampe, R. T. and Teschromer, C. (1993) 'The role of deliberate practice in the acquisition of expert performance', *Psychological Review* 100: 363-406.

Furrer, C. and Skinner, E. (2003) 'Sense of relatedness as a factor in children's academic engagement and performance', *Journal of Educational Psychology* 95: 148-62.

Gagne, M., Ryan, R. M. and Bargmann, K. (2003) 'Autonomy support and need satisfaction in the motivation and well-being of gymnasts', *Journal of Applied Sport Psychology* 15: 372-90.

Grolnick, W. S. and Ryan, R. M. (1989) 'Parent styles associated with children's self-regulation and competence in school', *Journal of Educational Psychology* 81: 143-54.

Grolnick, W. S., Ryan, R. M. and Deci, E. L. (1991) 'Inner resources for school achievement: Motivational mediators of children's perceptions of their parents', *Journal of Educational Psychology* 83: 508-17.

Guay, F., Ratelle, C. F. and Chanal, J. (2008) 'The role of self-determination in education', *Canadian Psychology* 49: 233-40.

Mouratidis, A., Vansteenkiste, M., Lens, W. and Sideridis, G. (2008) 'The motivating role of positive feedback in sport and physical education: Evidence for a motivational model', *Journal of Sport and Exercise Psychology* 30: 240-68.

Nicholls, J. G. (1989) *The Competitive Ethos and Democratic Education*, London: Harvard University Press.

Pelletier, L. G., Fortier, M. S., Vallerand, R. J. and Briere, N. M. (2001) 'Associations among perceived autonomy support, forms of self-regulation, and persistence: A prospective study', *Motivation and Emotion* 25: 279-306.

Quested, E. and Duda, J. L. (In press-a). Exploring the social-environmental determinants of well- and ill-being in dancers: A test of Basic Needs Theory. *Journal of Sport & Exercise Psychology*.

Quested, E., & Duda, J. L. (In press-b). A self-determination theory approach to understanding the antecedents of dancers' self-evaluative tendencies. *Journal of Dance Medicine and Science*.

Quested, E. and Duda, J. L. (2009-a) 'Perceptions of the motivational climate, need satisfaction, and indices of well- and ill-being among hip hop dancers', *Journal of Dance Medicine and Science* 13: 10-19.

Quested, E. and Duda, J. L. (2009-b) 'The experience of well- and ill-being among elite dancers: A test of basic needs theory, *Journal of Sport Sciences, 26*(S2), S41.

Reinboth, M. and Duda, J. L. (2004) 'The motivational climate, perceived ability, and athletes' psychological and physical well-being', *Sport Psychologist* 18: 237-51.

Reinboth, M. and Duda, J. L. (2006) 'Perceived motivational climate, need satisfaction and indices of well-being in team sports: A longitudinal perspective', *Psychology of Sport and Exercise* 7: 269-86.

Reinboth, M., Duda, J. L. and Ntoumanis, N. (2004) 'Dimensions of coaching behavior, need satisfaction and the psychological and physical welfare of young athletes', *Motivation and Emotion* 28: 297-313.

Roberts, G. C. (1992) 'Understanding the dynamics of motivation in physical activity', in G. C. Roberts (ed.) *Advances in Motivation in Sport and Exercise*, Champaign, Illinois: Human Kinetics, pp. 1-51.

Sarrazin, P., Vallerand, R., Guillet, E., Pelletier, L. and Cury, F. (2002) 'Motivation and dropout in female handballers: A 21-month prospective study', *European Journal of Social Psychology* 32: 395-418.

Smolak, L., Murnen, S. K. and Ruble, A. E. (2000) 'Female athletes and eating problems: A meta-analysis', *International Journal of Eating Disorders* 27: 371-80.

Movement, Training and Mind
Insights from the perspective of Motologie

ULF HENRIK GÖHLE

This text will use the issue of training to look at its bodily dimension: movement. I intend to depict the central role movement plays in the shaping and structuring of the self. The understanding of this role could be new groundwork for further research into movement-based training. The topic of training has been extensively looked at by various scientific disciplines. However they have, in the main, studied functional aspects. Here I intend to shed light on a neglected dimension of training, suggesting that training corresponds and mediates with the cognitive as well as emotional inner structures of the self.

To begin with some definitions, training is a process which induces, alters and maintains a development. Training is associated with skills. Differentiating training from learning we could say that learning can be situated and often happens unconsciously as well as consciously. Training objectifies and singles out practices and skills to be learned with a specific goal in mind. A good example would be the learning to walk of a young child: the child learns to balance on two feet and step forward while keeping this balance - this would be a new skill learned; from now onwards the child will start to try this out over and over again in various situations and with many variations - this is training. Training succeeds initial learning. Differentiating training from practice, we could state that practice is the actual application of a skill, a customary and expected use of it. Once a skill is well trained, we practice it. Training seems to be a transitional phenomenon that stands between the initial learning and the habitual practice.

Training enables further learning since advanced skills build on well-established basic skills. Training is hence an integral part of any developmental process. That is why an extended developmental/psychological perspective developed by the scientific discipline of Motologie can aid further inquiry into training. Infants and small children train constantly, rehearsing and refining what they have learned and discovered, and as they do so they change themselves continually. For adults this change is somewhat more subtle, however a look into the beginnings of our human development opens new understandings of how infants transform movement into something processed and stored mentally. This could be a key to understanding how we adults transform something from this mental world into actual movement and hence create training.

As adults we might, for example, learn about communication including theoretical aspects and scientific models. We might refer to empirical data too and make sense out of all this information. Through this our communicative behaviour might become more enlightened but most probably the practice will not change significantly. Only when we engage in communication training do we start to change the actual behaviour of communication because we put our rational understanding into practice. Training utilizes analysis to subject practises to change. Training can consist of exercises, tasks, games or role play, with or without partners, all designed to put knowledge into action. At its most effective the new practices acquired through training may become internalized enough to once again become unconsciously employed as embodied knowledge. Here it becomes clear that training activates us humans differently to other processes of learning which do not consciously subject our bodily practices to analysis and change. The scientific discipline of Motologie addresses directly processes of conscious and unconscious physical learning and development. The connection between body and psyche forms the core topic of the discipline.

MOTOLOGIE: SCIENCE CONCERNED WITH THE CONNECTION BETWEEN PSYCHE AND MOVEMENT

The scientific discipline of 'Motologie' was founded at the University of Marburg, Germany, in 1983 and researches the connection between psyche and movement. Motologie grew out of the discipline of 'Psychomotorik' of the 1950s to 1970s and sees itself as its academic and scientific continuation. In France, Denmark and Switzerland there are still university courses under titles like 'Psychomotorik' or 'Psychomotricité' with similar scientific discourses. Phenomena observed in the practice of psychomotricity were the impulses for further scientific inquiry into the connection between movement and psyche. Children show their character and their state of development in exercise, play and mutual action and interaction. Through observation of these processes therapists have been able to observe and provide support for developmental difficulties. Over the years, Motologie has developed a meta-theoretical perspective that draws from diverse scientific discourses including sport-science, psychology, medicine, neuroscience, anthropology and pedagogy. These models along with their gathered empirical data on the relationship between bodily movement and psyche have been analysed and brought together with their own scientific findings.

EXPLAINING MOVEMENT

In the early phase of development of Motologie as a discipline, empirical proof about the connection of motor-development and mental-development were published. (Eggert and Kiphard 1971; Schilling 1973). In an effort to gain scientific recognition, quantitative diagnostic methods and precise qualitative methods of movement observation were foregrounded as methodologies. This, it should be noted, occurred at a time when cognitive psychology had little interest in research into the bodily dimension of our psyche. The further development of Motologie can be described as a steady broadening of its perspective, to include greater emphasis on the contexts of the bodily dimensions of human development. An example, for an early detailed view, is Friedhelm Schilling's (1985) publications on hand movement and writing-development. Later Seewald and Prohl (1998) provided more contextualized studies on developmental support for children in kindergarden.

Today's senior Professor of Motologie, Jürgen Seewald, describes the two poles Motologie uses to interpret the phenomena of movement and psyche as between the terms of 'explaining' (erklären) versus 'understanding' (verstehen) of movement (Seewald 2001). Explaining movement can be characterized as developing the diagnostic tools to trace the connection between psyche and movement. Motologie has constructed its own tests and also adapted tests from other disciplines. The 'Körperkoordinationstest für Kinder' (KTK) (Kiphard and Schilling 1974) or the 'MOT 4-6' (Zimmer & Volkamer 1987) are quantitative tests of motor skills for children, and results can be compared to assessments of other skills like language and cognitive understanding. These tests are still used to trace developmental problems. Other methods like the Kestenberg Movement Profile (KMP) (Kestenberg-Amighi et al. 1999) try to use a more qualitative descriptive approach to establish a link between movement and psyche. The KMP postulates body rhythms, which are deduced from psychoanalytical phases and structure the way we conduct movement: the oral sucking rhythm, the anal pressing rhythm and many more that structure the play of muscle agonist and antagonist and hence the manner in which movement is executed. This muscular pattern results in a more or less tensed manner of movement flow and reflects the largely unconscious emotional quality of movements. The KMP claims to visually fix this pattern in a diagram (profile) and bring an objective dimension to this subjective assessment of bodily movement. However, this method of diagnostic reasoning marks the transition from the explaining to the understanding of movement.

UNDERSTANDING MOVEMENT

The scientific dimension of understanding (verstehen) was introduced to Motologie by Seewald (1992). Theoretically grounded in phenomenology and hermeneutic understanding, the understanding of movement is a spiral process of engaging in a situation of movement dialogue in play and mutual action, then followed by a reflective distance of the therapist in order to view the experience from a bird's eye perspective.

Some of this derives from psychoanalytic practice. In psychoanalysis the examiner uses his or her inner world and feelings to gauge the dimension of what he or she sees. Transfer and counter-transfer phenomena between examiner and examinee are terms that try to describe the bodily dialogue that happens between two people. In this dialogue emotions are mutually felt.

In understanding movement we cannot talk about diagnostic in its strict sense, it is more about engagements and non-verbal dialogue: What is evoked in me, the observer, watching someone's movement? What motifs awaken in me? These questions from psychoanalytics have shown to be productive in the understanding of movement.

The experience gained is then analysed on different levels. Levels include the movement abilities, themes of interaction, attachment behaviour, family situation and so on, to find dominant themes and make sense of movement behaviour. It has shown that movement phenomena have to be viewed in the light of cultural context and their norms. Often problems in child development can detach themselves from their actual cause and become systems of problems following their own logic and nature. This systemic dimension of movement was explicitly depicted by Balgo (1998).

Following this short introduction to the discipline, I intend to unfold a 'motological' line of argument to document some meta-theoretical findings on the matter of mind and movement. This will challenge the Descartian divide of body and mind and serve as a theoretical basis for our proposed new views on training.

THEORETICAL BACKGROUND

One fundamental reference for the theory of Motologie is *Die Gestaltkreis-Lehre* by Victor von Weizsäcker (1947).

> Wir können nichts tun ohne auch irgend etwas zu empfinden, wir können nichts empfinden, ohne uns auch irgendwie motorisch zu verhalten [We cannot do anything without feeling something; we cannot feel anything without some kind of motor behaviour]. (Weizsäcker 1932: 2, my translation)

The '*Gestaltkreis*' Model postulates the unity of movement and perception. It's concept, explained in an example of 'sensory-motor perception', suggests that when we touch an object the pattern of touch determines the pattern of sensory perception, and this sensory perception in turn enables us to touch. Here cause and effect merge as one. This could be depicted as a circular model with perception and movement together constituting 'Gestaltsein' or the shape of an action. There have been strong arguments about how this model should be interpreted, either as an open or as a closed loop (Stehn and Eggert 1997).

The 'Gestaltkreis' Model

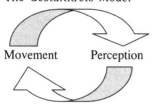

Movement   Perception

Helmuth Stolze (in Scharze and Purschke-Hein 2005) has extended Weizsäcker's notion and added a second circle to create a double circle model of human understanding that encompasses thinking and speech.

The diagram below serves to illustrate the refined model.

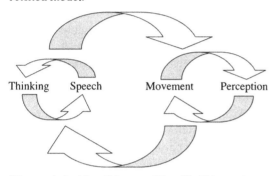

Thinking   Speech   Movement   Perception

(Diagram derived form Scharze and Purschke-Hein 2005)

COGNITION, ABSTRACTION AND MOVEMENT EXPERIENCE

According to Stolze's model, movement can be seen as a pathway cognitive development. To explain this we have to turn to cognitive theorist Jean Piaget (Piaget and Inhelder 1972). Piaget developed a cognitive-adaptation model comprised of 'accommodation' (the alteration of existing cognitive structures to fit new experiences) and 'assimilation' (the integration of experiences into existing structures). Both processes occur simultaneously in various proportions so that perception of the world changes as the cognitive structures refine and develop schemata. With regards to training, it is interesting to look into the source of Piaget's notions. He based his cognitive model on observations of his children. From the way they moved and acted he deduced inner states and formulated phases, which start with the so called senso-motor phase, the first phase of world-encounter, where infants experience most directly via their senses and motor actions. The idea that cognitive abstraction is based on movement experience is an important clue to our issue of training.[1]

EMOTION AND MOTION ARE TWO SIDES OF ONE COIN

As a range of studies demonstrates, movement plays an essential role in the communication of early childhood. The complete inter-subjective dialogue is based on expressive movement like body tension, posture, movements and gestures, vocals and so on. The mere disturbance of facial motor abilities can lead to problems in empathy. Research into the 'Facial Feedback Hypothesis' has shown this phenomenon (Hennenlotter et al. 2008). The mostly unconscious ability to engage with one´s own facial movements, copy, mirror the expressions of someone else is a pre-requirement of empathy. If facial muscles are paralysed (as in the experiment by Hennenlotter et al. with botulinum toxin) empathy is disturbed and diminished.

To go deeper into the understanding of emotional self-development, and to find more clues into the role that movement plays in outer and inner perception, we have to turn to attachment theory.

The British psychoanalyst and infant-researcher Peter Fonagy and his team have published a detailed depiction of early infant processes of affect regulation and mentalization. Mentalization, according to Fonagy, is 'the process by which we realize that having a mind mediates our experience of the world' (Fonagy et al. 2002: 3). As already pointed out, infants show their inner states via a wide range of body language, such as breath, body tension and vocalizations. The mirroring of these actions by the caregiver is crucial for the infant to realize and regulate these inner states. The baby sees itself in the eyes of the caregiver, and here lies a

[1] Today developmental science (Oerter and Montada 2002) has re-worded Piaget's phase model and pre-dated the beginnings of the sensory-motor phase into the pre-natal phase. However, Piaget's adaptation model of accommodation and assimilation is still utilized in current neuroscience (Hüther 2006).

key point: the caregiver mirrors his or her perception of the inner states of the infant and hence an interpretation of them. Inevitably a mingling will take place between the perceived emotions and the caregiver's own feelings. This mixing is there for a reason: it serves to translate the uncontrolled emotions of the child into bearable inner states of being. A too authentic mirroring, or a too dominant influx of emotion, emanating from the caregivers, is suggested by Fonagy to increase psycho-pathological proneness to borderline or narcissistic syndromes. This is all based on the perception and execution of movement. The inner regulation of feelings and emotions, as well as the perception and processing of emotions of others, are based on early inter-subjective experiences of movement and can indeed be seen as a trait of our being.

MIRROR NEURONS AND MOVEMENT

The discovery neuro-physiology of mirror neurons has given strong empirical evidence to the existing mirror theories but moreover points out the movement and bodily basis of mirroring phenomenon (Rizzolatti and Craighero 2004). The visual perception of movement evokes a similar activation pattern in the pre-motor-cortex of humans, as if we were to execute the movement ourselves. That is why visual perception of a movement arouses a feeling somewhat linked to the actual executing of it. Empathy is based on one's own body perception. The same brain regions that are responsible for the interpretation of one's own feelings are active when we interpret other people's feelings (Singer 2008).

The quality of the encounter with others determines the success of skill learning, a fact that pedagogy has known for a long time. When we start training with other people, self-perception and the perception of others are two basic parameters that determine the outcome of this endeavour. This parameter based on perception, movement and inner interpretation has to be taken into account when we engage in training in order to learn and develop skills.

EMOTIONS, DECISIONS AND MOTIVATION

The concept of the 'somatic marker' put forward by Damasio (1992) highlights the emotional basis of decision-making. Somatic markers are the physiological correlate of bodily emotions that serve to filter our decisions. In common language the 'gut feeling'. Somatic markers grow and refine together with secondary emotion (as opposed to the innate primary emotions like pain, disgust, surprise, grief, joy, fear) and remain largely unconscious. This is why they are faster than rational reasoning and function as a pre-selection. Of course this makes evolutionary sense, but if we link up further brain models to this notion we find evidence of the role emotion plays in the rational behaviour of adults. Julius Kuhl (2001) has put forward a large body of work about motivation and personality structure, which has already found practical application in various forms of training. One of his main insights is that affect-regulation is the key to successful action. Affect regulation enables the transition from one brain region to another. For instance: to switch from the planning region of the brain (left fontal cortex) to actual execution (right rear regions), we need a change of affect from a matter-of-fact state to positive emotions. Or to switch from action to analysis (left rear regions) we need a shift form positive to negative feeling. Kuhl's question was: 'What make people's actions successful?' One answer is that rational steps are propelled or hindered by affect regulation. A cross-link to the aforementioned affect regulation in early-infant development seems to come automatically to mind and demands further investigation.

MOVEMENT AS THE KEY

We have found clearly recognizable and coherent patterns relating to the interdependent development of perception of the world, movement, emotion and cognition. Infant experiences of the self and others are grounded in bodily sensation and in the understanding of others in empathy. Motivation and reasoning are based on affect regulation that is based on our social experience in childhood. If such a close relationship between these forms of development are observable in childhood, then it can be suggested that processes of bodily skill training in adult life have a greater connection to the ongoing development of emotional experience, perception of the world and sense of self than purely functional accounts of training allow for. We can furthermore develop pedagogical models for training that take greater notice of these links.

In training, adults can transform rational, mental matters into movement experiences. This can activate and regulate more of our inner self than it is possible by pure thought, a point acknowledged by participants in martial arts, sport and dance and the rationale for many movement-based therapeutic practices. On a bodily base, our experiences are intensely coloured and grounded in emotion. The acquisition of skills in training has therefore far more to do with the involvement and emotional investment of the whole self than at first sight.

What do we make out of this encounter with the inner self in training? Perhaps this should be our very starting point, and we should use bodily training as much as a path to theses experience as to the technical perfection of skill. I suggest that it is in fact imperative to start here, the premises and pre-requisites of training are the engagement of the inner cognitive and emotional structures discussed above. These structures define largely what kind of training has as an effect, what we do with it, how we engage with it and what it might do to us. If training utilizes movement to target those inner structures and activates emotions on purpose, it would enable us to work on core issues that determine the very accomplishment of any skills. Training can then be effectively tailored to an individual. It can show us how to use our resources and deal with emotions. This enables us to even work with very strong feelings, such as fear.

Functional scientific views have mostly focused the on a reciprocity between skills and training:

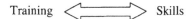
Training ⇔ Skills

The model I propose below reflects the argument that a further dimension has to be added to deepen the understanding of the role of training in the accomplishment of skills:

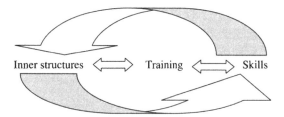
Inner structures ⇔ Training ⇔ Skills

This essay supports the argument that training mediates between inner structures of the self and skills. As such bodily training can develop physical skills and emotional sensibility when reflective methods are applied. Moreover training allows for inner structures of all types as contingent entities that are able to be reinforced, altered and established by the way we train.

Participants of martial arts, sport, dance and movement therapies have long recognized the emotional well-being, social reward and self-development tied to bodily training of various kinds. The cross-disciplinary insights of Motologie not only provide a scientific insight into the reasons for these experiences but can aid the development of holistic pedagogical models that provide a sophistication that goes beyond the dichotomous mantra of Mens sans in corpore sana.

Current cognitive neuroscience has coined the term 'embodiment' from this phenomena. This theory takes the opposite view of the 'brain in a jar' approach. The embodiment approach sees the shape and structure of our body and senses as determining the structure of our brain (Galagher 2008). This is not a new thought outside the field of neuroscience. Unfortunately the theories explaining Motologie have been published only in German so far, and its wide and fertile meta-theoretical views have not yet been recognized by an international readership.

In summary this article has connected the depiction of the central role of movement in human development with the introduction of the academic discipline of 'Motologie' and hinted at implications this might have for the issue of training. A line of argument was made to show a meta-theoretical view of the phenomena of movement and mind. Out of this argument we find many fertile lines of enquiry worthy of further investigation. These notions of movement in training provide a far more layered view than other - more function-oriented discourses - have given it in the past.

REFERENCES

Balgo, R. (1998) *Bewegung und Wahrnehmung als System: systemisch-konstruktivistische Positionen in der Psychomotorik*, Schorndorf: Hofmann.

Damasio, A. R. (1992) *Descarte's Irrtum: Fühlen, Denken und das menschliche Gehirn*, Berlin: List.

Dornes, M. (2006) *Die Seele des Kindes*, Frankfurt am Main: Fischer Verlag.

Eggert, D. and Kiphard, E. J. (1971) *Die Bedeutung der Motorik für die Entwicklung normaler und behinderter Kinder*, International Motorik Symposium, Frankfurt.

Fonagy, P., Gergely, G., Jurist, E.L., Target, M. (2002): *Affect regulation, mentalization, and the development of the self*, New York: Other Press.

Galagher, S. (2008) in M. Hubert *Körper im Kopf*, <http://www.dradio.de/dlf/sendungen/wib/722397/> (Accessed 10 Jun2008).

Hennenlotter, A., Dresel, C., Castrop F., Ceballos Baumann, A. O., Wohlschläger, A. M. and Haslinger, B. (2008) 'The Link between Facial Feedback and Neural Activity Within Central Circuitries of Emotion: New insights from botulinum toxin-induced denervation of frown muscles', *Cerebral Cortex* 19(3): 537-42.

Hüther, Gerald (2006) 'Wie lernen Kinder? Vorraussetzungen für gelingende Bildungsprozesse aus neurobiologischer Sicht', in Ralf Caspary (Hg) *Lernen und Gehirn: Der Weg zu einer neuen Pädagogik*, Freiburg: Herder Spektrum.

Kerstenberg-Amighi, J., Loman, S., Lewis, P. and Sossin, M. (1999) *The Meaning of Movement: Developmental and clinical perspectives of the Kestenberg Movement Profile*, New York: Brunner-Routledge.

Kiphard, E. J. and Schilling, F. (1974) *Körperkoordinationstest für Kinder (KTK)*, Weinheim: Beltz Test GmbH.

Kuhl, J. (2001) *Motivation und Persönlichkeit*, Göttingen: Hogrefe.

Oerter, R. and Montada, L. (2002) *Entwicklungspsychologie*, 5th edn, Berlin: Beltz Verlag.

Piaget, J. and Inhelder, B. (1972) *Die Psychologie des Kindes*, München: dtv.

Rizzolatti, G. and Craighero, L. (2004) 'The mirror-neuron system', *Annual Review in Neuroscience* 27: 169-92.

Schilling, F. (1973) *Motodiagnostik des Kindesalter: empir. Untersuchungen an hirngeschädigten u. normalen Kindern*, Berlin-Charlottenburg: Marhold.

Schilling, F. (1985) 'Probleme der Händigkeit', 13th Internationaler und Ingterdisziplinärer Herst-Seminar-Kongreß für Sozialpädiatrie, Essen: ELVIKOM Film Verlag.

Seewald, J. (2001) 'Die verstehen-erklären kontroverse in der Motologie', in K. Fischer and H. Holland-Moritz (Ret.) *Mosaiksteine der Motologie*, Schorndorf: Hofman Verlag, pp. 147-61.

Seewald, J. (1992) *Leib und Symbol*, München: Finke Verlag.

Seewald, J. and Prohl, R. (1998) 'Offene Bewegungserziehung im Kindergarten', *Motorik* 21.

Singer, T. (2008) <http://www.literaturkritik.de/public/rezension.php?rez_id=10237&ausgabe=200612> (accessed 27 Dec 2008).

Schwarze, R. and Purschke-Heinz, B. (Hrsg) (2005) *KBT auf dem Weg: Gedenkschrift für Helmuth Stolze, dem Begründer der Konzentrativen Bewegungstherapie*, Telgte: Selbstverlag.

Stehn, M. and Eggert, D. (1997) 'Ganzheitlichkeit: Zur Verwengung Gestalt- und Ganzheits-psychologischer Konzepte in der Psychomotorik', *Motorik* 10: pp. 4-18.

Weizsäcker, V. von (1932) 'Der Gestaltkreis: dargestellt als psychophysiologische Analyse des optischen Drehversuches', Pflügers Archiv, *European Journal of Physiology* 231(1) (December 1933).

Weizsäcker, V. von (1947) *Der Gestaltkreis: Theorie der Einheit von Wahrnehmung und Bewegung*, Stuttgart and New York: Thieme.

Zimmer, R. and Volkamer, M. (1987) *Manual zum standardisierten motorischen Test für vier- bis sechsjährige Kinder*, 2nd edn, Weinheim: Belz.

Wood and Waterfall
Puppetry training and its anthropology

CARIAD ASTLES

PREMISES AND PARADOXES

Little has been written in English about training for the puppeteer, and what has been written focuses predominantly on understanding the nature of the puppet, not that of the puppeteer, or concentrates on exercises and techniques. During the twentieth century, the pioneering Russian director Sergei Obraztsov suggested experimenting with the qualities of 'puppet-ness' (in contrast to the puppet as imitator of the human) (Obraztsov 1938: 78). The Swedish puppeteer and director Michael Meschke later elaborated a 'grammar' for puppetry action, through dividing and classifying types of training techniques. These included exercises such as the dead point, which he referred to as the state of concentration necessary in order to initiate clearly defined action, achieved through four clear steps: emptying the mind, abstracting the thought, focusing on the immediate task and initiating the task with passion (Meschke 1988: 54); he also analysed different categories of looks and leans, extensions, counterbalance, rhythmic and balance exercises and patterns of speed and focus engineered to develop the dynamic potential of the puppet (Meschke 1988: 48-68). Puppetry training, however, clearly goes beyond technical exercises (although these are very useful) and can be considered as a deep approach that seeks to understand the basic essence of the art of the puppeteer and their approach towards the animated object.

It is apparent that the practice of puppetry is inherently the practice of paradoxes. These paradoxes differentiate puppetry from live theatre since, generally speaking, actors wish to be seen and to have the audiences identify them as performing presences within a dramatic context. Puppet theatre presents us with a wholly different set of stylistic intentions: the puppeteer's intention is generally not to be seen, or if seen, as is usually now the case in contemporary puppetry, then not perceived as the primary focus of attention. Despite the puppeteers' so-called scenic 'invisibility', signified semiotically in contemporary theatre through devices such as the wearing of 'blacks', covering the head with caps, not making eye contact with the audience, and so on, they are required by the dramatic purposes of the performance, to generate and transmit huge amounts of energy towards the inanimate figure, material or thing, to create a sense of presence beyond their own bodies. This is the first paradox, and consequently the main question for consideration here: what is the training of a sensibility that requires the performer to locate their focus of expression outside the body while keeping the source of energy *within* the body?

A further paradox concerns the presence, absence or projection of ego on stage: how can the puppeteer successfully work with a sense of self while serving something else? Lastly, for the purposes of this article (in the Western context, notwithstanding the claims of animism, shamanism and so on), how can the puppeteer work with opposing concepts of inanimate

• *War Horse* the National's sell-out production of Nick Stafford's adaptation of Michael Morpurgo's book, directed by Marianne Elliott and Tom Morris which transferred to the New London Theatre in the West End in March 2009, currently taking bookings until 12 February 2010. *Photographer Simon Annand. Topthorn puppet, Joey puppet*

matter (for example, wood) and the abundant flow of energy (as in, say, a waterfall) required to animate that matter within view of an audience? Hence the title of this article: wood and waterfall. By 'energy' in relation to the processes of animation of a puppet, object or material, I mean the dynamic combination of force, movement and physical intention, organized differently through varying speeds, tensions, rhythms and stillnesses to give the impression of life in an otherwise inanimate object; by 'energy' in relation to the puppeteer about to animate something, I refer to the acquired and developed sense of *potential* force about to be used directionally and intentionally to indicate presence of the performing object. I seek, therefore, to analyse an approach that is a necessary process towards developing the pre-expressivity of the puppeteer: the development of this 'potential force', which is a pre-requisite for indicating presence and life in the animated object. I use the term pre-expressivity in reference to Barba's definition:

> The level which deals with how to render the actor's energy scenically alive, that is, with how the actor can become a presence which immediately attracts the spectator's attention, is the pre-expressive level ... the aim ... is to strengthen the performer's scenic bios. (Barba and Savarese 2007: 256)

FLUIDITY AND INTER-DEPENDENCE

The context for puppetry training in Western Europe (I exclude Eastern Europe here because of the development of the large-scale puppet schools under Communism) has altered hugely over the last twenty years or so, through an increase in awareness and support for the skills of the professionally trained puppeteer. This has led to a greater consciousness and hence to a rise in puppetry as part of live theatre, in particular in visual and physical performance, devised theatre, circus and so on. There are several trends within contemporary puppetry, but two still predominate in Western Europe: firstly, where the puppeteer is symbolically invisible (as in the horse manipulators in the National Theatre / Handspring collaboration of *War Horse*); and, second, where the puppeteer is clearly a stage performer (as in The Little Angel's 2008 production of *The Giraffe, the Pelly and I*), contributing to the articulation and animation of the whole dramatic event through combining skills in storytelling, manipulation and acting. In *War Horse*, giant puppet horses are manipulated by several puppeteers: all are visible to the audience, but none play a role; they are symbolically invisible. In contrast, in *The Giraffe, the Pelly and I*, the puppeteers play various roles throughout the performance, alternating between being storytellers, manipulators of different puppet characters, scene changers, singers and live performers.

These trends are not mutually exclusive, and the paradoxes expressed above apply to both, since in the first the 'invisible' puppeteers express energy through the puppets they are manipulating, and in the second the multifunctional puppeteers 'throw' their energy where it is needed. The New York-based director Roman Paska suggests that contemporary puppet theatre needs to adopt a 'primitivist' approach where both puppeteer and puppet are constantly present: 'Primitivism differs from illusionism in consciously directing audience focus back and forth between the outward sign and the inner process of simulation' (Paska 1990: 41). It is clear that contemporary puppetry needs to combine skills of neutrality and invisibility with skills of transferring, channelling or projecting energy through focus and attention. Within puppet theatre in global contexts, the symbolic invisibility of the puppeteer is addressed in a multitude of codified ways, such as having the puppets' speech distorted, using stylized movement or allowing puppets not being operated to hang in full view of the audience (Tillis 1992: 42). In Western puppet theatre, however, it is necessary for the puppeteer to move fluidly between the modes of performance and invisibility. Meschke maintains that this is best achieved by each element within performance remaining faithful to its principles (Meschke 1988: 35). Schechner, however, comments that: 'Masks and puppets actually constitute second beings who interact with the human actors' (Schechner 2002: 171). This contradicts a traditional view of puppet theatre where the puppets are protagonists, and emphasizes a relational view, where the puppet is an iconic figure uniting the performance elements. I would suggest that contemporary training of the puppeteer requires them to see themselves as part of an ecological system of scenic interdependence where they need to work generously at all times. The term 'generous' here refers to a

• *The Giraffe, The Pelly and Me*: puppet show produced November 2008 by the Little Angel Theatre, Islington. Directed by Peter O'Rourke. *Photographer Peter O'Rourke.*

process of training where the performer is consistently required to focus their attention away from themselves, towards the performing object. This concept, therefore, is associated less with the development of a puppet character expressed through the skill of the puppeteer and more with the development of the entire performance as animation through the movement of attention towards the object(s) of focus.

NEUTRALITY

In training the puppeteer to remain neutral and unobserved during performance, great attention must be given to the development of muscles of stillness and silence. There are many parallels with training in mask theatre, where actors are required to attempt to empty themselves in order to be inhabited by the neutral mask. When training with the neutral mask or puppet, for example, performers are asked to free their minds of thoughts, intentions and ego, in order to find a still place from which to respond to the impulses of the moment itself. The focus in neutral-mask work on breath-awareness is useful for puppetry; to be stilled but alert and waiting for action: 'This object, when placed on the face, should enable one to experience the state of neutrality prior to action, a state of receptiveness to everything around us, with no inner conflict' (Lecoq 2002: 36). Lecoq refers to the neutral mask as a 'stable position' where the performers are able to 'breathe freely' (39). By this he means that it is a space where performers are freed from the necessity of ego intervention or action; the use of the neutral mask is to find a calm, quiet space where performers can develop openness and naivety towards performance. In Lecoq's work, however, the neutral mask and its attendant qualities are used as preparation for performance; in puppetry training, the focus on neutrality is maintained within the performance. The puppeteer must therefore develop a dual mentality and purpose through training; neutrality within the body and expression through the manipulation of puppets or objects on stage. Exercises derived from T'ai Chi Chuan and other martial art forms have proved useful to the development of neutrality in their focus on rootedness and flexibility. A strong sense of the centre of gravity is essential for the puppeteer to enable them to move fluidly and smoothly, while not attracting attention. T'ai Chi is also concerned, like puppetry, with receiving and deflecting or directing energy; the practitioner receives energy into their body and moves it on in another direction while remaining in contact with the energy flow. Jurkowski comments on the process of energy deflection as the act of dispersion: 'I would add ... that this essential dispersion of focus by the puppeteer towards several simultaneous actions marks clearly the difference between the play of the puppeteer and that of the actor' (Jurkowski 2000: 44-5).

PRE-EXPRESSIVITY

Puppetry training shares much vocabulary with physical theatre training where the performer seeks to be open, dynamic and energetic towards the development of stage presence. Barba's concept of pre-expressivity as a prerequisite for the performer offers much to puppetry: his three essential elements of alterations in balance, the law of opposition, and coherent incoherence have clear parallels with Meschke's (and others') 'grammar' of puppetry technique; the puppet operates largely through tension in balance, gravity and counterbalance. I would like to add here, however, two further fundamental elements of pre-expressivity for the puppeteer: the law of distraction and the law of continuum.

The law of distraction is that of focusing elsewhere: a concentrated and profound act of attention derived from a sense of giving to something else. It suggests that while the performer is active and present, the act requiring attention is away from the site of the puppeteer's body. This requires, in puppetry training, the performers to work intensively through exercises concentrating their focus towards different and changing points beyond their own bodies. It also indicates not only that the audience's attention should be elsewhere but that the thing requiring attention is alive. Anna Furse comments that puppetry is the art of 'indicative attention-seeking' (2008: 21). The puppeteer is not a passive, invisible presence but a sign of directionality. Furse suggests that the puppeteer is a 'profound collaborator' in the scenic enterprise of creating *explicit illusion* (21).

The law of continuum is that which understands that all movement between puppets, puppeteers and other elements on stage is intrinsically linked, in constant motion and relationality. This law links the opposing designs of the modernists who were fascinated by puppetry's links to fine art and those of later puppet theatre directors who insisted on puppetry as a branch of dramatic art. Within a continuum, puppets can be seen as figures of geometry, symmetry, balance, or as dabs of colour interacting as in an animated painting, with misty shadows of the operators surrounding them; as the flicker of life at the end of the puppeteer's arm, a symbolic presence or distillation of the drama.

Within puppetry, there is always a physical and visual dialectic between the performers. The relationship between the puppeteer and puppet/object therefore needs to be active and in constant reaffirmation. The paradoxical co-existence of life and inanimate bodies on stage is therefore of multiple presences creating a collaboration of physical poetry. In order to prepare puppeteers for this kind of performance, they must understand the state of fluidity, where focus and presence is a moving concept, and generosity, where they give life and breath to inanimate matter. The concept of generosity here has a dual purpose: it can be seen firstly as a physical process, where the performers simply direct their attention and energy elsewhere; on another level, it can be seen as a more profound process of giving life, not only through physical action but through the belief in the intrinsic life qualities held in matter and the transmission of this belief.

DUALITY OF NEUTRALITY AND EXPRESSION

These concepts of continuum and distraction are those that enable the puppeteer to develop a duality of neutrality and expression. There are techniques to develop the practice of distraction, such as exercises focusing on the puppet's breath, eye contact, retaining a sense of gravity, maintaining a consistency of body position and shape through counterbalance and so on. These techniques, when repeated like music practice, become second nature, and the puppet is seen to be animated. What is perhaps more interesting, however, is the connection between the puppeteer and the puppet/object; this sense of the puppet as *part* of the puppeteer and not as a separate element. The process of energy-transfer is at the heart of puppet theatre. The union of breath and movement is the factor linking the source and expression of the energy. Training the puppeteer is thus to train a bodily awareness of the breath as impulse to the movement, which in turn suggests life. This is an approach to the alchemical equation associated with animation: not to pretend not to breathe, as the ventriloquist intends not to be seen speaking, but to make the audience believe that as the puppeteer breathes, so does the puppet.

The contemporary puppeteer's body seeks to distract the audience, not through trickery as in old-style puppetry but through frankness of intention. This body is in a constant process of de-egoing, decentring, of grounding, in which concepts such as flow, energy, rhythm, projection, transformation, transference and direction, which ultimately lead to animation, are more important than any sense of attraction towards it. This both frees and demands much of the puppeteer: it frees since the puppeteer is freed of self-consciousness; it demands since the puppeteer-performer common in contemporary theatre must move through performance modes expertly. Contemporary puppetry is therefore defined through a continuum of energy transference. This is achieved through intense concentration on the thing that is animated and on those relationships which emphasize this continuum.

WOOD AND WATERFALL

According to Derrida, every experienced event is defined by its relationship to that which it is not; within puppetry there is a focus on the puppet in contrast to the live human beings who operate it. Whether the material animated is solid, unresisting matter such as wood, plastic, metal or *papier mâché*, or soft, pliable matter such as fabric, clay, paper and so on, the puppeteer needs to demonstrate an awareness of the energy held in the thing, respecting the qualities of the matter itself. It holds energy through the attributes of its construction and its materiality, but the energy of breath/movement/life comes from the human source (excluding here all forms of animatronics or mechanical animation). The Western division between body/materiality and spirit/thought is less helpful here than a concept of organic unity between all elements of the performance environment, an idea that is growing in popularity as ecological and environmental philosophies demonstrate the interdependency of human and matter within the affective world. Within puppetry, this would include, for example, shows where the puppeteer is some distance from the things operated, as in the virtuoso solo shows by Ronnie Burkett where numerous string marionettes are manipulated at breakneck speed from a marionette bridge. In considering the paradoxes suggested at the beginning of this essay, training puppeteers to develop the 'potential force' mentioned earlier is essential to the development of pre-expressivity. For contemporary puppetry, this is not the art of separation of performance elements but of continuum; thus performance is created where the puppeteer does not dominate, but the process of creation is seen 'as a constant flow of interactions, processes and reactions between organic and inorganic matter' (Astles 2008: 64). Through physical practice, handling matter collaboratively between performers, puppeteers can develop a sense of themselves not as separate performing bodies but as linked essentially to each other and matter within the performance, whether that is one puppet or many different elements animated collaboratively.

All translations by Cariad Astles.

REFERENCES

Astles, Cariad (2008) 'Alternative Puppet Bodies', in Níni Valmor Beltrame and Gilmar Moretti (eds) *Móin-Móin*, Santa Catarina: Sociedade Cultura Artística de Jaraguá do Sul and Universidade do Estado de Santa Catarina, pp. 51-68.

Furse, Anna (2008) 'Committed to the Other: The ethical nature of work with puppets', *Puppet Notebook* 13: 20-21.

Jurkowski, Henryk (1988) *Aspects of Puppet Theatre*, London: Puppet Centre Trust.

Jurkowski, Henryk (2000) *Métamorphoses: La Marionnette au XXe Siècle*, Charleville-Mézières: Institut de la Marionnette.

Barba, Eugenio and Savarese, Nicola (2007) 'Pre-expressivity', in John Keefe and Simon Murray (eds) *Physical Theatres: A Critical Reader*, London: Routledge.

Lecoq, Jacques (2002) *The Moving Body*, London: Methuen.

Meschke, Michael (1988) *¡Una estética para el teatro de títeres!*, Bizkaia: Instituto Iberoamericano, Gobierno Vasco and UNIMA Federación España.

Obraztsov, Sergei (1938) *Akter s Kukloi*, Moscow-Leningrad: Gosudarstvennoe Izdatelstvo Iskusstvo.

Paska, Roman (1990) 'Notes on Puppet Primitives and the Future of an Illusion', in Laurence Kominz and Mark Levenson (eds) *The Language of the Puppet*, Vancouver: Pacific Puppetry Center Press.

Schechner, Richard (2002) *Performance Studies: An introduction*, 2nd edn, London: Routledge.

Tillis, Steve (1992) *Towards an Aesthetics of the Puppet*, Westport: Greenwood Press.

Psychophysical Training for the Actor
A question of plumbing or wiring?

DICK MCCAW

INTRODUCTION

Towards the end of the training to become a practitioner of the Feldenkrais Method, students watch a video of one of his final lessons from a training that he led in Amherst, Massachusetts, in the summers of 1980 and 1981. Moshe Feldenkrais is lying on a table, his eyes closed as he explores a movement with his fingers which he calls 'belling'; their soft opening and closing is reminiscent of a squid swimming as it bells out and flattens. The quality of the movement creates a softness in the fingers - a subtle relay between the motor and sensory nerves. He holds his belling fingers over his knee chest to see whether their softness can be imparted to the musculature of the leg. Feldenkrais' lessons in Awareness Through Movement take the form of very carefully-worded instructions to make movements which are then interpreted by the student - this interpretation constitutes the first stage of the learning process. Rather than seeing the movement and copying it, the student has to imagine what the instruction means and then try it out: from the very start of these lessons one is thinking movement. The frequent rests in between the movements are used to notice the effect they are having. Feldenkrais actively works on the relay between the spoken word, motor response and reflection upon sensory feedback: the exercise of one's experience is the means by which one can learn about oneself.

This essay will explore whether psychophysical training is about the circulation and concentration of vital energy or about the fantastically complicated operations of the brain and its nervous systems that link up the body. Plumbing or Wiring? Is it about promoting the circulation of energy or the growth of neural connections and networks? I shall argue that while these two conceptions of training are not mutually exclusive, they are fundamentally different.

TRAINING OR CONTINUOUS LEARNING?

Stanislavsky and Feldenkrais offer two remarkably similar accounts of training.

> Remember: every exacting actor, however great, at certain intervals, say every four or five years, must go back and study anew. It is also necessary for him periodically to place his voice - it changes with time. He must also rid himself of those habits which have adhered to him like dirt, as for example, coquetry, self-admiration, etc ... I repeat once more: Do not think of performance - think only of training, training, training. (Torpokov 1999: 155)

Feldenkrais insists that we engage in 'training, training and yet more training' arguing that only through training is it 'possible to cut out most of the futile labour' when we perform tasks (1985: 162), indeed, even when we are engaged in training itself. In these two quotations lie the main themes in this essay. Firstly, that training isn't about the accumulation of new skills but is often a process of questioning skills already acquired, which in turn describes the dynamic and *raison d'être* of continuing training. Training is a critically reflexive rather than an accumulative process. Both writers challenge the idea that education is a once-and-for-all process that precedes one's professional career – it is a constant process of renegotiation throughout your career. In this light, Feldenkrais's method would much better be described as re-education (and, in this context, one cannot ignore Phillip Zarrilli's use of the prefix re-). Both Feldenkrais and Stanislavsky argue that we have to learn how to recognize and then shed habits that we acquire in our professional life. These might be shortcuts, tricks of the trade passed on by 'old hands' or changes in our physical structure that result from aging and wear-and-tear. In a word, training is qualitative rather than quantitative – it is about how rather than how much. It is about achieving a constant quality of performance not amassing an increasing quantity of skills.

Before dealing with Feldenkrais's account of learning, I want to make two points. There are three types of memory; procedural, where skills like driving or riding a bike are learned and then recalled without the need for conscious reflection; semantic, where facts are learned and then recalled in a conscious act of memory; autobiographical, where events from one's life are recalled. In this essay we are dealing with a process of learning that relies on procedural memory, where the skills become 'second nature' and thus seemingly lost to scrutiny or revision. Concerning education, we have seen above that Feldenkrais places the accent on an individual's autonomous act of learning (through the *experience* of doing), rather than on being taught by someone else. The trainer creates a situation in which the student can learn, rather than teaching them.

Feldenkrais defines 'learning in the most general sense' as 'acquiring new responses to stimuli' (2005: 38), which almost brings us back to Susan Greenfield's simple moving organism. On one level this is a very functional account of learning, but on another it is the foundation for the creative development of the individual. Someone who makes the same response to a stimulus throughout their life is the best definition of a person who has a pathologically – i.e., unhealthily – arrested development. Feldenkrais defines living as a continuing process of discovering new responses to the world. In order to survive we have to learn because unlike any other mammal we are born in a highly undeveloped state with our brain weighing about 300g, 20 per cent of its ultimate weight. Animals are born with a brain nearly 70 per cent of its adult weight, which means that 'the nearer the animal brain is to maturity when born, the more stereotyped its behaviour will be' (2005: 38). In contrast to this hard-wired and stereotyped behaviour is the *plasticity* of the human brain, for which 'learning, or acquisition of new responses, [is] a normal and suitable activity' and which is 'capable of functioning with any possible combination of nervous interconnections until individual experience forms the one that will be preferred and active' (2005: 40).

Studies like Norman Doidge's book *The Brain that Changes Itself* prove Feldenkrais's claim that neural connections are formed of 'individual *experience*', which indicates that there is no distinction between hardware and software: the brain structure changes and develops through use. Feldenkrais challenges the notion that training is something that has to happen at an early age when the brain is still plastic and receptive to change: recent research indicates that the brain retains its plasticity well into maturity and thus is capable of a constant state of transformation, resulting in our lives being a process of renegotiation between self and environment. Just as a healthy organism depends on efficient circulation of vital liquids, so an intelligent organism depends on continuing plasticity in order to be able to respond to environmental changes. Both images are predicated on a dynamic rather than a static system. But how to sustain that dynamism? Proponents of plasticity and circulation both agree that it is as much about taking away as it is about adding, but how and what does one take away?

NOT LEARNING BUT TAKING AWAY #1: 'PARASITIC MOVEMENTS'

Feldenkrais examined how people perform everyday actions such as getting up from a chair and identified 'parasitic movements' that would make the action more effortful than necessary. A parasitic movement leaches strength out of the main movement. He asked the student to consider how to achieve a task not through brute force - the exertion of Will - but how they perform that task (self-awareness), then how it could be done (an act of creative imagination). The student is encouraged to read the sensory feedback and allow this information to guide subsequent motor responses.

> Learning, as I see it, is not the training of willpower but the acquisition of the skill to inhibit parasitic action and the ability to direct clear motivations as a result of self-knowledge. (Feldenkrais 1985: xiv)

Feldenkrais warns that 'men of great will power tend to apply too much force instead of using moderate forces more effectively' (1980: 58); The action fails at two levels. Firstly, at the level of execution. Like Rudolf Laban he realized that an effortful attitude that ignores the shape or space aspect of a movement will result in the needless waste of mechanical energy, and the person will tire more quickly. Intelligence is the ability to distinguish essential from futile movements and thus to perform with ease and economy. The second level is learning. Pure willing impedes learning, because the image or pattern of the action of coming to standing, say, is obscured by these unnecessary 'parasitic movements'. Quite literally, one cannot 'see' how to do it. The two levels come together when a person does it with awareness, because then she is constantly learning how she can act by examining how the given task can be achieved and how she has been going about achieving that task. One's progress through the training in the Feldenkrais Method can be gauged in terms of how much better one gets at 'awareness-ing', about becoming sensitive to the sensory feedback one gets from a movement, and how intelligent in how one makes use of the information. One's first attempts at learning a new skill are clumsy, precisely because we can't differentiate the useful from the parasitic.

> This is particularly true in learning new skills. One tenses and enacts a considerable number of unnecessary and contradicting elements of action; only later on does one appreciate how much more one did than what was actually wanted. One could swim straight away if one could eliminate all the parasitic acts and perform only those movements that propel one in the direction wished.
> (Feldenkrais 1985: 21)

The process requires that one does not do too much, and that one listens attentively. Then a person can

> make the impossible possible, then easy, comfortable, and finally pleasing. I believe it is more important to learn the way to learn new skills than the feat of the skills themselves; the new skill is only a reward for your attention. (1981: 92)

Once again, the accent is on the process of learning, learning how we can learn, rather than the skills.

NOT LEARNING BUT TAKING AWAY #2: BAD HABITS

I mentioned above that action-based training makes use of procedural memory. When we are learning a movement, we repeat it until we get it right and consider we have mastered it when it feels right, a sense of rightness that inhibits any desire for change. We can then perform it without thought; it becomes second nature. There is also a necessary economy to this kind of learning, because it allows us to address other tasks and interests. But it is also a trap, because it means that we forget how these actions are performed, and thus lose the possibility of being able to change our behaviour. This explains why early on in *An Actor Prepares* Stanislavsky insists that his students will have to relearn 'how to move about, sit or lie down' precisely because when we perform these everyday acts in front of a public they look strained and artificial.

'That is why it is necessary to correct ourselves and learn again how to walk. It is essential to re-educate ourselves' (1988: 77). Once again, that prefix 're-'.

Feldenkrais argues that we become locked into behavioural habits and use only 5 per cent of our potential because 'we tend to stop learning when we have mastered sufficient skills to attain our immediate objective', and we do this 'without realizing that [our] development has been stunted' as a result (1980: 15). But it's not just our potential that can rest unrealized, it can also be our image of ourselves. We are aware of those parts of our body that we use in our everyday lives, but this leaves parts that are 'dull or mute' in our awareness and are almost missing from our self-image when we are 'in action' (21). In order to be able to move with ease and freedom Feldenkrais argues that one needs a comprehensive, constantly updated, picture of oneself. This ability to move as an integrated and organized whole owes much to his early training in Judo where one has an 'inclusive image of one's action, so that one [doesn't] have to think cognitively about the next step (2005: xii).

A habit can also be a socially-acquired (parasitic) behaviour. Feldenkrais referred to these social habits as masks. For, by contrast with his theory of person-based learning, he regarded most institutional learning as a form of coercion and stereotyping: conditions that 'cause the majority of adults today to live behind a mask, a mask of personality that the individual tries to present to others and to himself'.

> Every aspiration and spontaneous desire is subjected to stringent internal criticism lest they reveal the individual's organic nature. Such aspirations and desires arouse anxiety and remorse and the individual seeks to suppress the urge to realise them. (1980: 6)

As did Grotowski, Feldenkrais identified the social as something that blocks the individual from spontaneous and authentic expression and realization.

Habit becomes a constraint preventing one from realizing that she has a choice of different ways of behaving. But this choice comes at a cost. It isn't easy to admit that one's habitual way of doing is inefficient, and even more difficult to return to zero and relearn these basic building aspects of living. Some will recognize that they are in a creative rut, which has deepened through repeated use and from which they want to escape. Others prefer the devil they know. Even if technique is poor, at least it enables them to do something; retraining is fraught with the embarrassment of not being able to do, of appearing ridiculous and clumsy, and with the risk that the process of relearning might not succeed. The fear of learning is what prevents many from straying too far from the comfort zone.

NOT LEARNING BUT TAKING AWAY #3: CHAT OR CEREBRATION

Both Grotowski and Feldenkrais agree on another block to spontaneous and whole-bodied movement – talking about rather than doing.

> If I observe a cat, I notice that all of its movements are in their place, its body thinks for itself. In the cat there is no discursive mind to block immediate organic reaction, to get in the way. Organicity can also be in a man, but it is almost always blocked by a mind that is not doing its job, a mind that tries to conduct the body, thinking quickly and telling the body what to do and how. (Richards 1995: 66)

Feldenkrais makes a similar point:

> One of the great disadvantages of the spoken language is the fact that it permits us to become estranged from our real selves to such an extent that we often have the mistaken belief that we have imagined something, or thought of something, where in reality we have only recalled the appropriate word. (1980: 135)

Although both agree that language, the socially-imposed, blocks access to the 'organic', the 'real self', the difference lies in that Grotowski is talking about the 'body' thinking, while Feldenkrais refers to the 'self'. A key concept in Clive Barker's Theatre Games (a book hugely influenced by Feldenkrais) is 'body think', which he glosses as the kinaesthetic sense, 'the process by which we subconsciously direct and adjust the movements of our bodies in space' (Barker 1989: 29).

> Somehow if you let the back part of the brain work, without conscious interference, the body works more efficiently. If you concentrate on making the body work, you interfere with its working ... Army instructors, taking recruits round obstacle courses, will always tell the recruit not to think about what he has to do but just do it. Those who think, fail most often to gain the objective. (18)

Like Grotowski, Barker argues that the 'body' works best 'without conscious interference', that is, when the direction to move is subconscious. While Feldenkrais is arguing against an abuse of language, both Grotowski and Barker are demonstrating a distrust of language. For Grotowski the body is a value in itself, a source of personal truth.

> Because of my physical weakness I needed the body, I was craving organicity. It was rather the need to arrive to [sic] something that would give me the ground, the support - the confirmation from my 'source'. I am sure that inside me was some hidden fear of life, of my own weakness, some need for a powerful weapon, a need for some strong basis for my ego.
> (Grotowski in Schechner and Wolford 1997: 254-5)

Feldenkrais has already stated that, like any other animal, the cat moves with speed and ease because its movement patterns are hard-wired into its brain at birth. The human's 'problem' is that we have a choice of *how* to move. We can either act automatically (and, to an extent predictably) or consciously (exercizing choice and discernment). Grotowski overlooks the obvious and fundamental point that although a human cannot be a cat, precisely because of the faculty of consciousness, a human can move with *some of the qualities* of a cat. It's a question of training.

LEARNING HOW TO TAKE AWAY

Barker's defines kinaesthesis as a 'process' by which we guide movement; *The Oxford English Dictionary* uses the word 'sense'. In a talk at the National Theatre Peter Brook (who was also close to Feldenkrais) stated quite simply 'When one does exercises, it isn't to make people more powerfully skilful, it's to make everybody from the start quite simply more sensitive' (1994: 7). Feldenkrais's lessons help students develop an ever more acute kinaesthetic sense - and this state of awareness is through conscious and not subconscious direction. But there is no conflict between keeping one's energy channels open and the need to sustain the performer's intelligence, their ability to continue learning, to continue responding creatively to their environment. Feldenkrais advocates taking away through a process of kinaesthesis, of doing with awareness, Grotowski through a process of spiritual ascesis.

CONCLUSION

I wonder if Feldenkrais (who spoke five languages fluently) realized that the words 'experience' and 'experiment' shared the same Latin root that forms the verb experior 'try, prove, or to put to the test; to find out or know by experience'. One of the OED's joyful definitions of 'experiment' is 'the action of trying anything'. Feldenkrais was always 'thinking movement', and his 'belling' lesson is just such an example. In fact, he was working in a way passionately advocated by Merleau-Ponty who argued that the scientist must not lose 'contact with himself', otherwise he will see 'his body as others saw it, and conversely, see the bodies of others as mechanical things with no inner life' (1982: 95). I imagine him describing Feldenkrais when he writes

> This representation of the body, this magical experience, which he approached in a detached frame of mind, was himself; he lived it while he thought about it. (96)

Feldenkrais was reputed to lie down in the middle of dinner parties and 'try out' a movement experiment he had just thought of. His body was his laboratory; he was a scientist who was both subject and object of his studies. How else could he have come up with such a beautiful and unexpected movement as belling? In his exploration of softness I find echoes of Tai Chi, the art of finding softness and the potent plasticity of the brain, ready to shape itself to and with every new thought. We aren't machines with hydraulic pumps and electrical wiring, we are exquisitely intricate, self-organizing organisms poised for learning, moved by a fearless curiosity to try anything.

REFERENCES

Barker, Clive (1977) *Theatre Games*, London: Methuen.

Bradby, David and Williams, David (1988) *Director's Theatre*, London: Macmillan.

Brook, Peter (1994) *Peter Brook (Platform Papers Number 6)*, London: Royal National Theatre.

Feldenkrais, Moshe (1980) *Awareness Through Movement*, London: Penguin.

Feldenkrais, Moshe (1981) *The Elusive Obvious*, Capitola, California: Meta Publications.

Feldenkrais, Moshe (1985) *The Potent Self*, San Francisco: Harper and Row.

Feldenkrais, Moshe (2005) *Body and Mature Behavior*, Berkeley: Frog Books.

Grotowski, Jerzy (1979) 'Exercises', *Dialog* 12 (December)

Grotowski, Jerzy (1991) *Towards a Poor Theatre*, London: Methuen.

Johnstone, Keith (1991) *Impro*, London: Methuen.

Merleau-Ponty, Maurice (1962) *Phenomenology of Perception*, trans. Colin Smith, London: Routledge, Kegan and Paul.

Richards, Thomas (1995) *At Work with Grotowski on Physical Actions*, New York and London: Routledge.

Schechner, Richard and Wolford, Lisa, eds (1997) *The Grotowski Source Book*, London and New York: Routledge.

Stanislavsky, Constantine (1988) *An Actor Prepares*, trans. E. R. Hapgood, London: Methuen.

Rosch, Eleanor, Thompson, Evan and Varela, Francisco (1993) *The Embodied Mind*, Cambridge, Massachusetts: MIT Press.

Zinder, David (2002) *Body Voice Imagination*, London and New York: Routledge.

Trained Performances of Love and Cruelty Between Species

PETA TAIT

EMBODYING HUMAN EMOTIONS

Big cats became popular circus performers in the first half of the twentieth century, trained to perform both ferocity and docility. Leading trainers such as Frenchman Alfred Court presented large groups of the same species (genus) or smaller groups of mixed species (genera) executing complex feats. While acts of noisy ferocity became associated with American trainers, acts of obedient cleverness became identified with European trainers even though, as outlined here, there was no clear-cut geographical distinction in practice even with Court's work. Commonly, animals were trained to do feats that reflected the chosen emotional tone within an act. While demonstrating cognition and communication between species, these acts suggested some degree of agency and co-operation from big cats or at least minimal resistance to undertaking feats. The act that delivered ferocity, however, misled spectators about this co-operation. More specifically it generated a performance in which nonhuman animals delivered theatrical emotions.

Court's memoirs and those of other trainers contain professions of affection, even love, for the wild animals that they trained and worked with in performance (Stark 1940; Roth 1941; Court 1954; Proske 1956; Bourne 1956; Kerr 1957).[1] At the same time behind the scenes, big cat performers were described by these trainers as easily excitable and volatile while their human trainers were expected to be calmly controlled.

For animal performers, an aura of wildness intersects with beliefs about emotions. An analysis of discourse about training big cats often, by the twentieth century, born in captivity reveals that for all their obedience and clever execution of tricks over years, animal wildness is collapsed into an idea of emotional wildness.

Acts that deliver ferocity suggest that big cat performers are not exempt from Diderot's proposition (1957) that performers do not feel the emotions that they perform. As Una Chaudhuri argues (2007), performance can contribute to interspecies understanding. Within training memoirs are passing acknowledgements of a telling gulf between humans and animals created by divergent sensory responses to the physical spaces for the acts. It is suggested here that what potentially contributed to the cruelty of the animal act was not found in the performed expression of ferocity in the act but in the suppression of sensory difference between human bodies and animal bodies.[2] This argument presupposes that embodied emotional experience is closely linked to the senses and can be expressed and received.[3] Trainers might well be aware of the effect of these differing sensory capacities of animal bodies, but their attention to this process remains behind the scenes in circus.

The history of trained big cat acts in twentieth-century circus performance does entail the interspecies co-operation of animal and human bodies, although it additionally involves a shift from being acceptable to unacceptable in a number of countries. The crux of defensive

[1] See Hearne (1986) for a discussion of animal training and philosophy, and see Stokes (2004) for a recent critique of the lion act in circus.

[2] Derrida (2004) posits that humans should see animals as they present themselves to be seen rather than framed as cultural metaphors. See Acampora (2006) for a discussion of cross-species somaticity, and Tait (2005) for a discussion of visceral and sensory responses to circus.

[3] See, for example, Tait (2002) for a discussion of performed embodied emotions in theatre and of distinctions between felt and performed emotions; Baines and Lepecki (2007) for discussion about the senses in performance; Damasio (2003) for ideas of the physiology of emotions influenced by culture; and Bekoff (2007) for summaries of studies of emotions in animals.

arguments for and against arising within each set of national circumstances hinges on expectations that the emotions of suffering are absent from animal lives, meaning animal bodies. Yet it can be argued that when trainers like Court profess their affection and love, they offset perceptions of emotional suffering in training and performance. Human emotions often stand in for the emotional experiences of nonhuman animals.

COURT'S ANIMAL PERFORMERS

Court is attributed a quieter style of act demonstrating compliance, but even he started out with a noisy group and presenter/trainers in Europe continued to create acts of confrontation and overt shows of physical power. Dressed in a cowboy costume with black and silver spangles, circus-owner Court took over the lion act in Mexico when his regular trainer had become too drunk to perform (Court 1954: 35). Rehearsing the act for the first time, Court watched as three lions entered the ring slowly, stretched and yawned and played peacefully and Caesar rolled over and started the act (36-7). Court cracked his whip and gave his imitation of the trainer's verbal command to take their seats, and they immediately obeyed, apparently answering to their names. As their eyes followed his every move, he wondered if they could tell he was a novice. To Court's surprise even the fourth lion, the roaring, troublesome Nero, simply leapt into position on his pedestal at the top of the pyramid. 'So, without a word from me, he had begun the act on his own!' (38). Trying to find out the cue to get Nero down and stop his roaring routine caused some anxiety, and, while avoiding Caesar's speciality of letting the trainer put his head in his jaw, Court allowed the animal performers to continue with their practised routines. Nero refused to leave until he had done his speciality, and Court recounts, 'I was, quite literally, in a cold sweat. I had not anticipated that he would stick so closely to the script' (1955: 18). When his name was shouted, Nero leapt at the chair Court was holding, striking it with force as Court recoiled, and then leapt again before turning away and going back to his seat, as he had been taught. Court realized that the cowboy costume and his imitation of the previous trainer's gestures meant that the lions were sufficiently comfortable with their environment to undertake the practised routine. He discovered that the lions were doing the performance themselves and showing him what they did, and he was simply following them.

Born in 1883 to a wealthy aristocratic French family, Court rebelled and started in circus at 16 as an acrobat on horizontal bars and became an animal trainer at 35. He became well known for a milder style of animal act than the one he had inherited and in the 1930s for mixing a number of species. Returning to Europe from Mexico after World War I, Court bought some bears from (Carl) Hagenbeck's for a zoo-circus and subsequently in 1921 acquired fourteen adult lions (1955: 53-4). Next he acquired four tigers. Court's largely untutored approach to training led him to experiment and to develop a mixed act with bears and big cats. He became a leading animal trainer in Europe in the 1920s and 1930s,

• 1922/23 Alfred Court and Maouzi, Zoo Circus

managing multiple troupes by hiring presenters to work with the animals that he trained. This was a process first developed by both of the leading nineteenth-century trainers Carl Hagenbeck (1909) and Frank Bostock (1903). Court left Europe for the United States in 1939 with the animals in his act, including sixty-five big cats, and worked there until he retired from Ringling Bros, Barnum and Bailey Circus®, The Greatest Show on Earth® (RBBBC) in 1947 (Court 1954: 82, 192; Joys 1983: 159-67; Johnson 1993: 55).

Court is credited with exemplifying the European tradition of a 'quieter' act by training an animal to execute feats of agility and balance through what Antony Hippisley Coxe specifies was parallel to Pavlov's behavioural techniques requiring the study of animal behaviour (1980: 129). While Court adopted the wearing of a white shirt with white jodhpurs and long riding boots common in more acceptable equestrian acts, his account of his work reveals a continuity with past practices and even aspects of menagerie displays rather than the complete rejection of them. He describes the retention of older sensationalist feats in his act in his early years as a trainer. For a time he put his head between a big cat's jaws; only Court managed this with a tiger, Maouzi, which was the first time a tiger was used (1954: 78). He also rode on Maouzi's back. Having observed a trained act by the world's dominant circus animal training business, Hagenbeck's, Court had all the performing big cats as well as the bears sitting up on their hindquarters (81). Working with Maouzi, Court was able to copy Hagenbeck's leading turn-of-the-twentieth-century trainer Julius Seeth's feat of carrying a lion across his shoulders although again substituting a three hundred-pound tiger.[4] This capacity to outdo predecessors typifies circus performance and makes a trainer distinctive. Court writes that the two routines most favoured by spectators involve a lion or tiger rolling a ball across the arena floor or walking a steel cable. These feats are achieved in phases. Ball-walkers are first introduced to standing on the ball for meat rewards and then grow accustomed to the moving ball under their feet without jumping off (Court 1954: 136). Only one big cat performer in ten will even venture onto thick wooden bars above ground and the width is decreased as the height is increased over time (134-5).

Court's comments about presenting animal performers in action intended to appear 'wild' confirm that he trained in the styles of both docility and ferocity (1954: 86, 134, 112). 'My cats, working 'wild' or 'tame' had the details of their work so exactly that they could have carried it to a conclusion themselves, like a piece of machinery' (134). For example, his 'wild' act in the 1920s involved using fire to drive the lions roaring into a confined space (75). In another example, based on an incident in training, he allowed Radja to get annoyed and then got him to allow Court to kiss him on the nose (86). Initially Radja's attack was a direct response to punishment, and Radja had become calmer when Court spoke to him with endearments (82). This also reveals how Radja's emotional reactions were attuned to those of Court.

Observing the behaviour of each individual animal is crucial but so too is learning the 'keys' to the disposition of each species that can be used in the act (Court 1955: 32). Court writes: 'Rewards and punishments are the basis of all training, and both must be administered swiftly; but though a blow from a stick can be understood by any animal, it is harder to teach him about rewards' (29). Animals are trained to do feats, initially through inducements like food and then through step-by-step processes without rewards. The trainer must be patient and gentle. While Court loves animals, grieving over some deaths, he must survive any fight and '[a]nimals are like human beings; love and spite, jealousy and anger exist for them too' (31). Nonetheless Court calls animal performers 'good' only if they respect or fear their trainer (1954: 61).

By the 1930s Court had discarded sensationalist tricks for an emphasis on clever feats. He created a sensation at the Blackpool

[4] A photograph of Captain Bonavita carrying a lion may mean that Bonavita developed this feat in association with Frank Bostock (Bostock 1903).

• 1941/44 Alfred Court and Nero, Ringling Bros and Barnum Bailey Circus

5 Court's act was also performed at London's Agricultural Hall prior to this and then at Manchester's Belle Vue, and Glasgow's Kelvin Hall (Court: 1954: 137; Jamieson 1998: 48).

Tower Circus in the UK and earned a big fee for a twenty-two-week season with an act of eighteen performers: eight lions, three polar bears, two black bears, two leopards, two tigers and a jaguar (Court 1954: 93; Coxe 1980: 138).[5] This signature act would evolve to include twenty-four performers. To achieve these combinations, Court used a lasso around the neck of an animal performer in early training, which is held from outside the cage by attendants as he works inside (1954: 74). As well as a diverse range of species, Court also managed his males in the act if a female was on heat. Acts with more than one species came to be praised more highly in the hierarchy of trained animal performance, and this status increased with the variety of species.

The development of trained acts from the 1890s with mixed species has a larger significance. While there is cohabitation of species in natural environments, circus animal performers mix in far closer proximity than would happen in a natural habitat and with species not found together. Wild animal acts changed from a confrontation between human and animal into spectacles in which animal species and genders were mixed together, increasing the potential for conflict between animals. Mixed acts diverted the focus from human impositions on animals to one in which animals were perceived to instigate confrontations with each other. In this manipulation of physical space, inclinations to attack another species, should the opportunity arise, in turn, could become mistaken for behaviour in natural habitats.

FEROCITY

Ferocity remained part of circus until the 1960s, exemplified by the 'hurrah' act, and such acts dominated perceptions of big cat acts in circus in the United States. A lion's roar or a tiger's snarl was part of the routine required to indicate ferocious and terrifying threat and the trainer/presenter reacted accordingly as if frightened. Given the development of acts with a quieter tone, how did hurrah acts remain viable until the mid-1960s and evade social censure? It is possible that the contrast between acts presenting docility and those presenting ferociousness confirmed that these were performances after all. Trainers asserted that big cats were humanely treated through training with rewards and methods of coaxing, and the trainers of hurrah acts strenuously and repeatedly defend their training methods in off-stage publicity. These explanations are accompanied by claims about affection for animals. The point here is that rhetoric about emotions also became significant in offsetting expressions of disquiet.

The arrival of Court's acts at RBBBC challenged the predominant and controversial confrontational mode evident in other large American circuses with admissions that treatment involved a 'blunt-pointed fork with tin cans' for noise and that all training involves some force (Anthony in Ballantine 1958: 77). The performance style of Court's later acts conveyed an opposite impression, which additionally belied standard elements in the training. Nonetheless confrontational performances persisted. For example, after World War 2 Captain Harvey in the UK and Bert Nelson in the US each wrestled with a lion. Sensationalist feats attracted attention and appealed to younger spectators (Clark 1954: 13).

Training and performing with big cats in confined spaces did contain a risk of attack for all performers. At RBBBC, Court observed his three acts there, mostly presented by other performers, and at least once had run into a ring to take over when a young presenter was attacked (Henderson 1951: 139-40). Court writes how the 'unconquerable' 'savage spirit' of animals has provided him with 'both my greatest joys and my greatest dangers' (1955: 1). Court explains that a lion understands who is master but has no conscience and does not 'sit up nights, worrying, if he's killed or crippled someone who's fond of him' (Bourne 1956: 24). A lion will remember someone who is cruel and develop what is deemed 'hate' for that person, looking for a chance to kill him or her. While conceiving that he is applying 'psychology' to training, Court outlines their emotions but notes that the behaviour of big cats was not to be understood with reason (1955: 32). Yet he specifies that reflected light or a human smell or voice tone might upset a lion and cause a behavioural change. Differences between an animal's sensory perception and that of a trainer mean that what potentially disturbs an animal performer in the physical space might be missed.

Trained acts illustrate that while the performance persona created by a trainer/presenter reflects the tone of the act, the determining effect was the way in which the animal performers presented feats. There were a number of male and female presenters for Court acts in Europe, and some, including Johny de Kok, became trainers in their own right. In 1936 Bertram Mills Circus (BMC) bought the lions from an act presented first by Violette d'Argens for Court and then by Patricia Bourne (1956), and therefore BMC hired Priscilla Kayes as the presenter (Jamieson 1998: 48).

The tigers trained by Court were less easily transferable to other presenters. First Votjeck Trubka and then his brother Franz Trubka were attacked, with Court rushing into the arena cage to assist each one (Court 1954: 130-3), and two further attacks proved fatal. While twentieth-century big cat trainers/presenters were frequently clawed and bitten, it was not common for these injuries to prove fatal.[6] Nevertheless several trainer/presenters were killed in unpredicted accidents. Although Roman Proske describes three fatalities and a serious mauling that included experienced presenters (1956: 13-17), it would seem that the inexperience of a trainer could be a factor in fatalities in Court's acts. Two novice presenters with Court, Vaniek and Mollier, were killed by the tiger Bengali (Court 1954: 113-18, 129; Bourne 1956: 15, 46).

Apparently a claim to love animals does not preclude training. Carl Hagenbeck explains that his type of business - the commercial trading of trained animals - succeeded because of 'a genuine love for animals' (1909: 7). While acknowledging that habitual routines building on reflex conditioning are the basis of animal performances, as indicated, there are repeated claims even from the earliest menagerie acts that big cats (and elephants) obey their trainers out of love (and fear). Such comments shape a belief that emotional exchanges underlie interactions between a trainer and an animal performer. If the trainer appears to work with animal performers patiently rather than by becoming frustrated and

[6] Dick Clemens was twice attacked by a lion he had bottle-fed, but this occurred during a mating season (Henderson 1951: 43).

angry or forceful and domineering, then no cruelty - or so it would seem - is involved with the animals (Al Barnes 1937: 162). The perception that there was no cruel treatment was suggested by a show of kindness or at least neutrality by a trainer/presenter. The emotional demeanour of the trainer in rehearsal and performance determines perceptions of treatment.

Trainers probably benefitted from a cultural memory of cruder nineteenth-century menagerie acts, but it does seem that performance effects overshadowed some of the actualities of twentieth-century training. The standard of animal husbandry was improved, but a trainer still imposed some physical control while proclaiming his or her affection for the animal performers (e.g., Proske 1956: 18; Kerr 1957: 26). Trainers fret when away from the animals. Barnes includes repeated declarations of love and affection, although he says that big cats do not express affection (1937: 168). He claims he had to 'train' himself to overcome grief and to have a matter-of-fact response to numerous incidents and to the dangers that cut short their lives (159-60). Court wept out of grief (1954: 60). Such confessions of love and grief by influential trainers might well have influenced perceptions of the treatment of trained animals. It might be argued that statements about emotions allayed suspicion that training inflicted physical pain, lending support to a trainer's right to control in ways that allowed trained performances to remain largely unquestioned until the 1970s.

In these transactions with other species, big cat trainers are accorded qualities of patience, perseverance and understanding for their animals. Regardless of a big cat's compliance and obedience for long periods of his or her life, all are additionally generalized about and assumed to be emotionally volatile, unpredictable and untrustworthy. This discrepancy implies that while a trainer sets out to make an animal trust him or her, the trainer cannot trust the wild animal, who might betray a trainer's affections at any moment.

In 1934 John Clarke writes that while there is 'fear and distrust of animate Nature', a trainer's 'power over animals' is a 'gift' (in Manning-Sanders 1952: 213). Alternatively, says Clarke, animals in their innocence 'know' or sense the emanations of human emotions and can become like mind-readers but should be approached as 'equals' in friendship (214). Contradictorily, since animals are outside culture, they have a sensory purity that is wild and innocent, and this allows them to see through a trainer's social guardedness.

Although twentieth-century big cat and elephant acts developed into a sequence of physical feats that were no longer referential to cultural stories external to the act as with menagerie acts, an implicit narrative of conquest and human mastery remained, and the act was no less emotionally charged. While acts were displays of control and mastery, they contained a possibility that the cats might rebel against the routine and the presenter. Consequently, trainers took advantage of this expectation and rehearsed and staged disobedience. As outlined, during the twentieth century the big cat performance often included a sequence in which the trainer seemed likely to become a potential victim of his or her big cats, only to escape at the last minute. A trainer/presenter in lightweight clothing might appear particularly physically vulnerable, and thereby a presenter under siege in a hurrah act was not necessarily deemed cruel. A cornered presenter sidestepped notions of treatment by confusing the issue with the need to constrain aggressive animals, and the staging conveyed an implicit message that an intelligent big cat was only just outwitted in a fair contest.

As trainers controlled animal movement, they shaped the emotions delivered by an act and, as outlined, the show relied on theatrical effects for impact and to spark the imagination of spectators and their emotional responses. Nonetheless animal acts do still offer insight about animal and human interactions and communication and the intelligent capacity of animals. Trainer claims of affection that circulate through animal training rhetoric as well as through act promotion reflect discrepancies in the wider society between the declared emotion and a range of behaviour that seems to be at variance with the declaration.

With a passing concession to his or her own performance anxiety about large audiences, a trainer might mention that an animal can suffer from performance anxiety with crowds. A trainer admits to having anxiety about whether the animal performers will comply with instruction during the performance, especially when he or she is starting out. The emotional drama of animal acts was multi-layered and, as in theatrical performances, constructed and expressed emotions for audiences. Certainly, claims can be made for the emotional design of an act, even when emotions experienced or expressed by a performer, including an animal performer, remained oblique.

REFERENCES

Acampora, Ralph R. (2006) *Corporal Compassion: Animal ethics and philosophy of body*, Pittsburgh: University of Pittsburgh Press.

Baines, Sally and Lepecki, André (eds) (2007) *The Senses in Performance*, New York: Routledge.

Ballantine, Bill (1958) *Wild Tigers and Tame Fleas*, New York: Rinehart and Company.

Barnes, Al G. (1935) *Al G. Barnes: Master showman*, by Dave Robeson, as told by Al G. Barnes, Caldwell, Idaho: Caxton Printers.

Barnes, Al G. (1937) *Master Showman*, edited version of *Al G. Barnes: Master Showman* (1935), London: Jonathan Cape.

Bekoff, Marc (2007) *The Emotional Lives of Animals*, Novato, California: New World Library.

Bostock, Frank (1903) *The Training of Wild Animals*, New York: Century.

Bourne, Patricia (1956) *Thank You, I Prefer Lions*, London: William Kimber.

Chaudhuri, Una (2007) '(De)Facing the Animals', *The Drama Review* 51(1) (T193): 8-20.

Clark, Ronald W. (1954) *Lion Boy: The story of Cedric Crossfield*, London: Phoenix House.

Court, Alfred (1954) *Wild Circus Animals*, London: Burke.

Court, Alfred (1955) *My Life With the Big Cats*, edited version of *Wild Circus Animals*, New York: Simon and Schuster.

Coxe, Antony Hippisley (1980) *A Seat At the Circus*, Hamden, Connecticut: Archon Books.

Damasio, Antonio (2003) *Looking for Spinoza: Joy, sorrow and the feeling brain*, Orlando, Florida: Harcourt.

Derrida, Jacques (2004) 'The Animal That Therefore I Am', trans. David Wills, in Matthew Calarco and Peter Atterton *Animal Philosophy*, London: Continuum: 113-28.

Diderot, Denis (1957) *The Paradox of Acting*, New York: Hill and Wang.

Foucault, Michel (1971) *Madness and Civilization*, trans. Richard Howard, London: Random House.

Hagenbeck, Carl (1909) *Beasts and Men*, trans. and abridged Hugh S. R. Elliot, and A. G. Thacker, New York: Longman Green.

Hearne, Vicki (1986) *Adam's Task*, New York: Alfred A. Knopf.

Henderson, J. (1951) *Circus Doctor*, Boston: Little, Brown.

Jamieson, David (1998) *Bertram Mills: The circus that travelled by train*, Buntingford, Hertfordshire: Aardvark.

Johnson, Alva (1993) 'RBB&B Big Cat and Elephant Trainers?' *The White Tops*, November/December 55.

Joys, Joanne Carol (1983) *The Wild Animal Trainer in America*, Boulder: Pruett Publishing.

Kerr, Alex (1957) *No Bars Between*, London: Cassell.

Manning-Sanders, Ruth (1952) *The English Circus*, London: Werner Laurie.

Proske, Roman (1956) *Lions, Tigers and Me*, New York: Henry Holt.

Roth, Louis (1941) *Forty Years with Jungle Killers*, by Dave Robeson, Caldwell, Idaho: Caxton Printers.

Stark, Mabel (1940) *Hold That Tiger*, told to Gertrude Orr, Caldwell, Idaho: Caxton Printers.

Stokes, John (2004) 'Lion Griefs: The wild animal act as theatre', *New Theatre Quarterly* 20(2): 138-54.

Tait, Peta (2002) *Performing Emotions*, Aldershot: Ashgate.

Tait, Peta (2005) *Circus Bodies: Cultural identity in aerial performance*, London: Routledge.

When Train(ing) Derails

BOJANA BAUER

> Careful with what you put inside your body, because what you put there once will never leave it.
>
> Steve Paxton (2001:5).

This warning from Steve Paxton is something that probably any dancer comes to realize. It would resonate with all those who have experienced the immediacy with which a given dance springs back into place once one starts moving. Yet, once we question the status of that which never leaves the body, Paxton's warning leads us into the issue of bodily knowledge and its relation to aesthetics in dance. The persistent separation of dance training as craft, skill and technical ability from the aesthetic ideal of dance-art located in theatre's representational framework has kept in dominance, through much of dance history, an instrumentalist model of the body.

Traditionally, dance training is associated with transmission of a specific body technique. The technique is acquired by practising repetition, mainly within a mimetic relation between student and master. This ensures the continuity of the movement's codification and thus inscribes it in the tradition. Paradigmatic to this model is classical ballet training, where knowledge is passed on through sustained repetition. This well-trained technique later becomes a basis for higher artistic expression in the choreographed work. Training is thus a procedure for acquiring a skill later put into service. While that straightforwardly instrumental view of the human body might appear harsh, we must not forget that until very recently dance rested on the idea of bodily control, simply putting the body to use in realizing its aesthetic goal. Furthermore, this concept of training literally gives substance to the general Western paradigm of the body as aesthetically mouldable matter. That which is mouldable is also meant to be devoid of cultural, aesthetic or subjective specificity. This in turn allowed the supremacy of a classical ballet technique based on its presumed universality.

By contrast, the development of modern dance rested on the idea that any aesthetic project in dance is deeply rooted in the specificity of the body itself and that therefore an aesthetic innovation can only be achieved through a new approach to dance technique and preparation - the training of dancers. Most of the milestone figures of modern dance history constructed their aesthetic discourse and forms on the basis of a specific body training. Creating a body for oneself meant creating a dance and choreography. According to Ginot and Launay, throughout the first half of the twentieth century the work of transmission was viewed as both creation and research (Ginot and Launay 2002: 107), playing a crucial role in the various subsequent approaches to the definition of the (dancing) body. But training itself, even if no longer as strictly disciplinary as it was in ballet, continued being instrumental in the formation of a stylistic, aesthetic and behavioural identity.

In the 1990s, authors such as Xavier Le Roy criticized both professionals and the dance education system for remaining stubbornly unaware of the underlying ideology around the production of bodies. Brought in its own right to the discursive level of performance strategies, body work comes to be seen as that which is part of the body's memory, never to leave it. It has become fairly common to see choreographic works in which dance appears as quotation, thus entering the linguistic play or exemplification of dance within dance. The question is: did the 1990s critique unsettle the concept of body as living archive that can display on demand the results of its training?

The practice of dance itself, the daily work of dancers, offers a heterogeneous picture that in fact resists homogenizing historic and stylistic categories. For when looking more closely at the training of a dancer, one can see that it always puts into tension a relationship in which the past of the body tries to meet with requirements to achieve in the future. In the moment between past and future the movement emerges. As an approach to this moment, training can become something more open than the instructed development of habits. In this sense, the work of American choreographer Deborah Hay is remarkable for its capacity to allow the body to produce new ways of looking at repetition, memory and history: 'History choreographs all of us, including dancers. The choreographed body dominates most dancing, for better or for worse. The questions that guide me through a dance are like the tools one would use for renovating an already existing house' (Hay, 2007). How do these tools work, and what do they do to the constant desire to identify a given body's historic affiliation? Answering this might help us in understanding what dance practice does to produce a shift from the concept of body as inert matter inscribed with a learned knowledge to a concept of living flesh with its own history and genealogy (Van Imschoot 2005).

Since 1998 Deborah Hay has been developing an ongoing project named *Solo Performance Commissioning Project* (SPCP) in which dancers commission a solo from Hay, who then guides and coaches them in the performance of the solo over eleven days. After this period the dancer practises the performance daily for a minimum of three months before their first public appearance. This procedure led in 2004 to *Match*, a piece which Hay worked with four dancers. In 2006, she was invited by CNDC Angers where she worked with a group of choreographers based in France.[1] They learned her solo *Room* and created the group piece *O'O* based on individual adaptations of that solo. It is the solos that preceded the *O'O* piece that will be my focus here. They were presented as autonomous performances in the Centre National de la Danse in 2006 and toured independently from the group piece. But all these works share in common questions of transmission, learning and adaptation which stem from Hay's overall artistic practice, performances and writings. She is one of the choreographers who has most meticulously, thoroughly and idiosyncratically explored, challenged and questioned the notions of training, technique, bodily behaviour and memory.

Hay's material is deceptively simple. Walking around, patting the floor, looking in a specific direction, raising the arms, talking gibberish, singing. On it goes, and none of the actions and movements require what would generally be defined as technical dance skills, athletic abilities or even more subtle, but specific, bodily coding. In Jennifer Lacey's Scoot, for example, these basic gestures are driven by the contained explosiveness gathered around the dancer's spine, spiralling outwards through her muscle mass. Her centre of gravity is solidly rooted in a pelvis that seems inexhaustibly to resource her movement. This ground level of motion is accompanied by the pulsating adjustments that persistently disturb the vertical alignment of the body. Small dances happen in the upper spine and neck, resonating with the curving in the pelvis. Those oscillations become a sort of resting point in the dance, where the body appears to be following the flux of its own postural movement in search of stability. At

[1] Nunno Bizarro, Corinne Garcia, Emmanuelle Huynh, Jennifer Lacey, Catherine Legrand, Laurent Pichaud and Sylvain Prunenec.

moments it all clicks in, propelling the dancer into series of silky yet powerful swirls, apparently skimming the space, producing weightless forms that go beyond the visible limits of physical body.

One can't not see here a trained dancer, an educated body that has been through courses of training ... Cunningham, Trisha Brown, contact improvisation. In a gesture as simple as lifting the two arms to the side, the spatial and perceptual organization exposes the traces of the body's training history. Hay's choreography - her entire process of dance-making - operates as a fine sieve that reveals the sediments of what makes the specific body move and how. More importantly, this trained body is not offering its specific skills for servicing the execution of a given choreography. The body's knowledge is not articulated as something fixed and stable, not put to use and delimited as a merely functional 'skill'. Hence the dancer's body is asked neither to fit into a choreographer's writing nor to demonstrate or quote its bodily identity. Stripped of the choreographic grid that conventionally would be giving structure and meaning to the dancer's movement, in these dances the perceptive and sensory work of the moving body is laid bare, offered to the sight as a dance in its own right.

According to Hay, learning and adapting a solo dance are about a 'singularly coherent choreographed body', where 'the dancer is not choosing to exercise the re-measuring tools needed to counter-choreograph the predominance of learned behaviour' (Hay, 2007). Hay stresses:

> I use the words 'choosing to exercise' because most of us know exactly what is required when we choose to train the physical body to adapt to a choreographer's aesthetics. Training oneself in a questioning process that counter-choreographs the learned body requires similar devotion and constancy. (Hay, 2007)

It is clear that Hay is not dismissive of training, understood in her case as an action of devotion and continuity in work. Such training is necessary if one is to engage in 'counter-choreographing', which is to be understood not as overpowering or unlearning existing knowledge but rather as triggering an ongoing transformative process. This is critical if we are to understand the role of the body's history in training and how memory can be something other than an identifying mechanism of the body (re)producing known gestures and images.. While describing Hay's dancing, Susan Foster suggests that the choreographer has cultivated her body, discovering it and re-discovering it over many years of practice (Foster 2000: ix). The notion of cultivation hints that there is a continuity of bodily practice constituting Hay's project, be it off or on stage. Hay's primary focus is on what she calls 'the training in questioning', which is nothing other than *an unwrapping of the history, an articulation of its immediacy*, where history is not a matter of chronological sequence but an object of the present. This somewhat Benjaminian perspective on the past should, however, be contextualized, as dance today faces an even more complex task of dealing with fragmented and heterogeneous knowledge. Dancers are inclined to pick from a diversified body-training supermarket. There is almost a question: which one of the body's histories do I call into the present to service a given situation? Such an artist, who has become paradigmatic of the freelance mode of life, in many ways epitomizes the subjectivity of the worker in late capitalist society, where, as Paulo Virno states, both the practice of not having a routine and training in precariousness and variability are put to good use (Virno 2004: 85). According to Virno most of the skills, and importantly most of what comes to be one's identity, are formed in the space in between: in between jobs, school, employments etc. 'To be accustomed to mobility, to be able to keep up with the most sudden conversions, to be able to adapt to various enterprises, to be flexible in switching from one set of rules to another' (85). Isn't this the image of a 'nomad' dancer, not only going from project to project but also going from class to class in between projects? What set of tools is needed for the work on and with a body trained in versatility?

This variability itself attains a status of constancy and regularity. Ballet was once considered a universal technique and no longer is, but this universalism in discourse about the body is not yet entirely extinct - even though it is well disguised in the contemporary imperative of adaptability. Training of a dancer now rests on a broad variety of techniques and practices that the dancer permanently upgrades. This may create an impression that conditions are created for the training to coincide with aesthetic projects, for the body's time and memory to be always ready to embody choreography's own temporality. But this would be a superficial conclusion. To elucidate this, let us look more closely at what it is that allows the body to question what it recognizes as its foundations. Movement analyst Hubert Godard reminds us that the dancer's training method or preparation for choreography is already a project of both a subjective and an aesthetic nature. '*It is not the repetition of movement but the experience of gesture and as such the "creation of sensory meaning" (fabrique du sens) that gives a sense, a direction, to the senses*' (Godard 1994: 30). Consequently, according to Godard, the body is a fluctuating structure that is organized and reorganized by the plasticity of respiratory, postural and perceptive phenomena.

Characterizing the perceptive organization of the body as a 'project about the world' (Godard) is to suggest that the world of a subject is created through the process of active projection rather than passive reception. It is not rare to hear descriptions of experiences from dancers that go along those lines, but all too often they are imbued by a discourse that fetishizes or mystifies 'Experience'. Indeed the experience of gesture, its perception and associated imagery, as reported by some dancers, amounts to the practice of what philosopher Miguel Benasayag calls the 'end of perception', in reference to the classic Western concept of perception as reception of stimuli by a rational subject. Perception is not a relationship between an objective exterior that leaves its imprint on a passive interior. It is a matter of creation and of decision, taking responsibility for the world the subject lives in and not the contrary. So we can talk about perceptive action inasmuch as the imaging of the world, or 'project about the world' depends on the properties of our perceptive system (neuronal, kinaesthetic etc.). The qualities of this system, in other words our capacity for action, are drawn from the history of the body. This history is not, therefore, data buried in mechanical reflexes but a living memory active in the creation of the present.

When a dancer encounters Hay's material, what happens to the history of the body? The presentation text of the project SPCP states that the artists should be prepared for and proceed by 'non-attachment' to learned or familiar techniques. Non-attachment doesn't mean negation or complete counter-education; more importantly, it doesn't presuppose any other attachment. The dancer is expected to relinquish what she knows while at the same time no other specific bodily programme is laid out. Hay leaves the dancer in the void. It is a void that is not to be filled but should rather act as a generative threshold towards the unknown. This is not a model that the dancer could try to fit with through the process of repetition. By creating a framework for learning, rather than concentrating on the object-to-be-learned, she breaks the paradigm of learning as reproduction of a model in 'the most similar possible' way. Learning the figure of Hay's dance is only the first and least important stage of the process. The French choreographers spent a mere three days memorizing spatial configurations and movements. Then they were left for three months 'really' to learn the solo through rigorous daily repetition. To understand how Hay's repetition differs from disciplinary repetition characteristic of conventional training, the process and the result of repetition have to be taken out of the representational framework. It seems inevitable, here, to invoke Deleuze's writing, since he offers some of the most insightful critiques of representation through the concept of repetition.

> Learning to swim, or learning a foreign language means composing the singular points of one's language with those of another shape or element, which tears us apart but also propels us into a hitherto unknown and unheard of world of problems.
> (Deleuze 1994: 192)

Through this example Deleuze tells us that learning does not consist of assimilating something through a set number of steps but rather that the 'one to learn' and the 'one to be learned' are two singular fields, whose mutual penetration is to form another singular field. Importantly, in Deleuze's swimming lesson, the instructor does not exist: it is an affair between the body and the sea. The body needs to allow the emergence of the movement that will create a common field with the sea. The swimmer is not there to reproduce the figure of swimming conveyed by the instructor or an image representing the movement of swimming. As José Gil comments, the sea is a system of problems whose movements and waves simultaneously offer a solution. That's to say, the creation of the solution is immanent to the problematic field and need not be mediated by a representational image. It also means that the movement emerges from the repetition of that exact movement and not through the reproduction of its image. We do, of course, form a body image while moving, but an image that is completely conscious amounts to a representation of the movement's affective quality. One could say that the learning goes in advance of the body's capacity to represent an image of itself to itself, taking place as a channelling of the imperceptible. As Gil explains, 'the problem presented to the body by the sea is one of microscopic differences that escape the consciousness, so the solution found by the body equally follows imperceptible ways' (Gil 2000: 19).

There is no metaphysics here, no implication that there are some 'more true' levels of our being that would elude rational consciousness. The body's intimate capacities, along with its cultural, geographic and aesthetic history, simply have thresholds of which it would be a mistake to expect coherence into one unifying representative image. Gil's emphasis is correct: learning is approaching a problem not as a formulation of the conditions of an empirical problem but as a creation of an always open problematic field. It comes as no surprise to hear testimonies of artists who work with Hay evoking affliction: it's comparable with drowning at first, or standing on an empty (temporal) intersection with no directions. The instability to be explored is precisely this incessant fluctuation of the body that, repeated over and over, creates ever new figures. This is quite the opposite of the effects of the imperative of variability described earlier. The hopping from one dance training to the next doesn't change the nature of learning and does little for the profound connection between the mind/body and nature (as projected world) that is sought after in Deleuzian repetition. It is more an expression of opportunism, where faster production of ready-to-use skills is going to be useful in finding a receptive niche in the market. But while it might bring one closer to the market, it will result in an even deeper disconnection from the creative process that a learning subject is capable of engendering.

What it takes to create an intersection between the past of the body and its future is a never-ending discussion among dance practitioners and theoreticians. A practice could explore, however, the opening of new fields of problems for each singular action. This then might define training as learning inseparable from creation.

REFERENCES

Benasayag, Miguel (2004) *La Fragilité*, Paris: Éditions La Découverte.

Benjamin, Walter (2000) *Oeuvres III*, Paris: Gallimard, Folio Essais.

Deleuze, Gilles (1994) *Difference and Repetition*, trans. Paul Patton, New York: Columbia University Press.

Foster, Susan Leigh (2000) Foreword in Deborah Hay, *My Body, the Buddhist*, Middleton, Connecticut: Wesleyan University Press.

Gil, José (2000) 'Prefácio: O Alfabeto do Pensamento' in Gilles Deleuze, *Diferença e Repetição*, Lisboa: Relógio D'Água.

Ginot, Isabelle and Launay, Isabelle (2002) 'L'école, une fabrique d'anticorps?' *Médium Danse* 23.

Godard, Hubert (1994) 'Le souffle, le lien' in *Marsays* 32 : 27-31.

Hay, Deborah (2000) *My Body, the Buddhist*, Middleton, Connecticut: Wesleyan University Press.

Hay, Deborah (1994) *Lamb at the Altar, The story of a dance*, Durham: Duke University Press.

Hay Deborah (2007) 'How do I recognize my choreography?' <http://www.deborahhay.com/How%20do%20I%20recognize.html>

Imschoot, Myriam Van (2005) 'Rests in Pieces', in *Multitudes*

<http://multitudes.samizdat.net/spip.php?article1984>.

Paxton, Steve, (2001) quoted by Patricia Kuypers, Introduction, *Nouvelles de Danse* 46/47.

Virno, Paolo (2004) *A Grammar of the Multitude*, Los Angeles: Semiotext(e).

Repetition and the Birth of Language

PIOTR WOYCICKI

> Repeating ... is in every one, in every one their being and their feeling and their way of realizing everything and every one comes out of them in repeating. More and more then every one comes to be clear to some one.   Gertrude Stein (1990: 245)

Endlessly repetitive sequences of movements, gestures, steps may comprise a typical training session of a classical ballet dancer. Similarly hours of practising scales and *études* can make up the daily routine of many professional musicians. In conservatoire training these abstract and compulsory exercises - often removed from context and artistic form[1] - are designed to achieve a certain standard of quality in artistic expression or gesture. The repetitive nature of these methodologies can become a compulsion, an obsession to reach perfection in an almost sport-like manner. The emphasis on craft honed through repetitiveness, together with the heavily institutionalized character of the way it is implemented and evaluated, have inspired much criticism from more 'intellectualized' approaches to methodology in arts practice. Such approaches often see this disciplining of the production of the sign through training as something limiting and anti-innovative - greatly compromising the agency of the performer/artist, merely recapitulating dominant conventions and standards in art. A famous example would be the conceptualist movements of the 1970s, which attempted to liberate art from craft. I would like to take a different stance, however. I would like to look at the creative value of repetition in craft training and assess the compulsion to repeat in terms of how it broadens one's understanding of gesture. In short, I want to explore the possibility that repetition might become a form of meditation upon 'performance excess', a self-monitoring that could become a generative force behind gesture and eventually language.

There is a dimension to gesture that is very problematic and often overlooked in the academy. It is the so called pre-linguistic, 'instinctual', immediate dimension, which is not entirely consciously or voluntarily stimulated or perceived by the subject. But how can gesture be thought of as pre-linguistic? Robert Hatten defines the categorical status of pre-linguistic gesture as an 'integrative process that animals and humans draw upon in their interactions with the world and each other, interpreting and enacting coherent movements with distinctive profiles' (2004: 97). The 'integrated sensorimotor system' (98) is capable of processing a huge amount of data to produce dynamic representations of the surrounding environment. Hatten further exemplifies these 'topographic representations' (Damasio in Hatten 2004: 98) as consisting of movement signatures of predators that become apparent by 'projecting distinctive temporal/energetic patterns as they interact with a variety of environmental resistances (a loud rustle of leaves implying a large animal)' (Hatten 2004: 98) or signs such as a peacock's display that 'enable members of a community to "read" each others' emotional states' (98). Other examples of instinctual behaviour could be quoted here, but what is key is that these

[1] Not all *études* and exercises can be considered independent artistic pieces.

processes, entrained from early on, allow for a near-immediate recognition and appropriate response to environmental circumstances. In short they are mechanisms for survival.

A lot of early training in classical music, for example violin performance, consists of training of reflexes, hand-positioning techniques and the ear's capacity in order to perform musical structures with adequate affinity for rhythmic and dynamic requirements. These technicalities have to become almost 'automatic', instinctual, unconsciously reproducible and repeatable in order that the performer can concentrate on broader issues of interpretation that adhere to high cognitive processing, cultural associations, consideration of style etc. – all in all, language. These two polarities are often referred to in cognitive psychology as bottom-up and top-down processes. Bottom-up is a form of mental processing that deals with sensory data in immediate, involuntary and schematized ways, while top-down is the opposite complementary process that analyses stimuli critically in terms of a knowledge basis that an individual possesses. This kind of take on it would presuppose that the sensory or nervous system not only has a processing mechanism capable of independent reaction to stimuli but also has some sort of independent memory and basis of knowledge. This is a crucial concept for performance and philosophy because it could negotiate performance as a unique mode of thinking in itself.

Recent findings in neuroscience shed an interesting light on this. In their efforts to discover what lies at the basis of dance and the process of learning dance, scientists contend that they have discovered a neurological 'metronome' located in the brainstem. They argue that it ensures and stimulates synchronicity and the mapping out (inscription) of the body's movements. This arguably compulsive, unconscious drive to repeat a certain scheme or pattern can potentially be an important component of learning and the organization of bodily responses in relation to 'higher order' concepts such as cultural habits. I would like to propose that the potential of this compulsiveness to 'repeat' could be a source of creativity, performance excess and the unexpected event. By 'performance excess' I mean an unexpected movement or gesture, an offset against the initial structure.

My argument begins by describing recent findings concerning the role of the cerebellum, the 'lesser brain', in the perception of dance practice and training. The cerebellum is a part of the brain located at the back of the head, behind the brain stem that links the brain with the spinal cord and the rest of the nervous system. The cerebellum is known to be responsible for the automatization of certain functions such as heartbeat, breathing and sleep cycle. It also processes feedback signals from muscles about their position and orientation and helps to maintain balance and coherence of physical movements, functioning rather like a gyroscope. Generally speaking the cerebellum function is to 'update motor commands based on sensory feedback and to refine our actual motions' (Brown and Parsons 2008: 79). Of course many of these apparently simple and rudimentary processes can be consciously overruled and 'tweaked'. There are apparently cases of people who are even capable of consciously interrupting their heartbeat.

The knowledge gained from these insights about the motor nervous system does not in itself explain the wide diversity and complexity of artistic gestures and movements seen across many cultures. Artistic expressions that come from highly organized physical movements are often seen as originating from the knowledge and influence of culture. This involves the whole of the brain and other areas where both memories and cultural knowledge are stored and processed. However Steve Brown and Lawrence M. Parsons in 'The Neuroscience of Dance' set off to explore whether this automatized processing of movement through the cerebellum's neural mechanisms has a role in scaling up of 'manoeuvres as graceful as, say, a pirouette' (Brown and Parsons 2008: 79). Their research into the activity of the cerebellum in response to stimuli that dancers experience as auditory, visual and kinaesthetic led them to postulate that it can have three important roles in dance practice. One is that its anterior vermis area acts like a metronome:

> The cerebellum as a whole meets criteria for a good neural metronome: it receives a broad array of sensory inputs from the auditory, visual and somatosensory cortical systems (a capability that is necessary to entrain movements to diverse stimuli, from sounds to sights to touches), and it contains sensorimotor representations for the entire body.
> (Brown and Parsons 2008: 81)

The second one is that the medial geniculate nucleus, an area linking the cerebellum to the lower auditory pathway, acts as a stop and helps to 'set the brain's metronome and underlie[s] our tendency to unconsciously tap our toes or sway to music' (82). They argue that the result of this is that '[w]e react unconsciously because the region connects to the cerebellum, communicating information about rhythm without "speaking" to higher auditory areas in the cortex' (82). This property can relate both to compulsions to repeat sequences of gestures during training and to notions of discipline. This idea of 'unconscious entrainment' (81) leads to the third property which is an immediate access to a 'motor image', a 'sensory-based map of one's own body, [that] helps to plot a dancer's path from a body-centred, or egocentric, perspective' (82). Brown and Parsons locate this memory, which they call a 'motor-planning system' (82), in the precuneus region of the brain. The key aspect of it is that it can only fully develop a memory basis for movements and motor-images as a result of actual training. This is because a full complex sensory package comprising visual, auditory and, most importantly in the case of dance, kinaesthetic senses is required to form a detailed mapping of movement. Finally they claim that the cerebellum also has a capacity to pre-organize gestures by placing 'units of movement into seamless sequences' (83).

This research is an attempt to map out and locate in anatomical terms the mechanisms responsible for the sub-conscious dimension of physical gestures. It is interesting that the generic mechanism that structures and organizes this 'instinctual' knowledge is likened to a metronome, a compulsion to repeat. It is almost as if the compulsion to repeat a structure through a performance that generates some sort of 'performance excess' is the generic force behind the creative development of gestural language. This rather bold assumption is interesting for performance and particularly for training because it poses a question of whether gestural language can arise out of repetition.

Thus repetition of specific sequences in training can be seen as a mode of entraining and developing 'unconscious' habits, a sensorial knowledge and ways of responding to a variety of stimuli that comprise a performance. If part of how we come to express ourselves through gestural language is indeed unconscious and ingrained in the way that these scientists have described, can training not also be an attempt to access and rationalize these habits and thus offer a creative potential for going beyond them? This might consist not merely of repeating what superficially comprises a sequence but coming to understand and perceive the logic of gesture, and doing so not only in linguistic and objectifiable terms but also through the logic of the very sensation that underlines them.

Creativity itself can be seen as a twofold process. On one side it is a conscious intentional synthesis of ideas into a construct and, on the other, an unconscious latent process that surfaces or becomes accessible to the subject independently of their 'conscious' will. This latter is often described in popular terms as the 'light bulb' moment. It is an unpredictable moment when a set of disparate ideas come together to form a more coherent whole, an 'appropriate' synthesis. One cognitive theory claims that this latent process is parallel to a conscious effortful one but that it cannot be accessed by choice or articulated through language until the 'idea' fortuitously synthesises. Perhaps repetition in training can be seen in this light as a form of meditation upon the pre-linguistic, a way of stimulating unconscious processes and the wealth of information in them, in order to bring it out and make it accessible to conscious faculties.

Theatre has a history of researching methodologies that not only tap into these unconscious areas of the mind but also, more importantly, enable the artist consciously and deliberately to access the apparent wealth of information that can affect the complexity of artistic craft and thus performance language. Interestingly these methodologies became, in essence, an exploration of a subject's agency. One of the more notable of such approaches is the Stanislavskian system.

Stanislavsky's system emerged at the turn of the nineteenth century and historically coincided with some leading scientific breakthroughs. For example, Charles Darwin's theories outlined in works such as *The Origin of Species* (1859) not only provided a new way to define human beings and their 'origins' but also inspired a scientific inclination to search for generic causal chains. In particular, Stanislavsky was interested in developing a training methodology for actors that could uncover the generic building blocks behind action. His initial attempts led him to develop a psychological method through which an actor could stimulate action. The ability to produce action on stage would be dependent on 'three inner forces' (Leach 2004: 29): feeling, mind and will. That feelings were difficult to arouse and control posed a challenge for the performer. Using the 'mind' consisted mainly of using memory mentally to induce a notion of specific circumstance. Great attention was to be paid to the particularity of the situation recreated so as to avoid generalizations. The will to carry out action would arise out of the latter two and become 'the key motivating force' (29).

Thus the question of the will to act was always conditioned upon the interdependence of feeling and mind. These two 'forces' whose interdependence resulted in gesture had to be orchestrated. Initially a psychological approach was taken which included emotion memory, the *magic if* and a breakdown of the performance text into blocks of objectives, super objectives and given circumstance. All in all these were methods of montage, since the emotion essentially required a verb, a temporal approach, and a change from one state to another. One was not supposed to act *being* in love but *becoming* in love. The rationalization and the conscious use of memories as analogies served as ways to source the will to carry out action. In later practice this highly intellectualized and somewhat autocratic approach to training shifted to an investigation of physicality and a possible change of emphasis to training physicality as a basis for sourcing the will to carry out action.

This latter approach became known as the 'Method of Physical Actions' and was oriented around a more free improvisational style and an emphasis on rhythm. The old workshops were substituted by repetitious improvisations comprising a sequence of actions that would enable the actor to further their understanding of what makes them act as opposed to how they would react in a given circumstance. This separation of the mind and the body led to the development of the 'silent *étude*' where actors were 'asked to perform the actions without the benefit of words to examine its coherence, logical progression and ability to communicate' (Leach 2004: 39). The methodology based on rhythms and repetitions was directed towards the latent memory and the possibility of unconscious spontaneous gestures surfacing during the rehearsal process. It would enable actors to generate material and refine gesture by a form of meditation upon their craft, to find and articulate subtleties in seemingly trivial and banal actions. The whole concept of developing 'sensitivity' through craft may very well be connected with entraining and stimulating the unconscious, involuntary dimension of mental processes that underpin gesture. A further development of this methodology was made by Lee Strasberg and called 'sense memory'.

Stanislavsky's ultimate goal was to bring out

these nuances like the involuntary muscular tensions of a liar's facial expression and integrate them into a piece that had a specific meaning. These nuances of an actor's physicality would be made to resonate with the meaning 'intended' by the dramaturg/director. Thus the gesture would be turned into a clearly readable theatrical sign. But there are other practitioners who explored the gestural abyss opened through repetitions of laboriously trained craft and used it for ways of complicating the perception of social gesture and thereby creating a new theatrical language.

The aesthetic strategies of Pina Bausch's theatre explore the relationship between repetition in training, rehearsal process and notions of individual agency. In a famous scene in her production of *Bluebeard's Castle*, a female performer repetitively re-enacts sexually charged poses in front of a male only to be constantly rejected by him throwing lipstick in her face. This is synchronized with repetitions of musical sequences from Béla Bartók's opera. These 'torturous games' may initially appear as a representation of victimization of the female. The repetitive sequences can be initially read as entrapment, where the body of the performer is powerless and incapable of going beyond the imposed rhythm. But the repetitive compulsive actions also draw attention to the physicality and craft of performance. The duration of this scene turns it into a rehearsal, a form of bizarre training and tuning of the body's movements. The prolonged extent of these repetitions begins to trouble, to complicate, the initially easily readable stage, making it difficult, unreadable. The ever more and more tired body of the performer becomes apparent within the hitherto clearly organized structure; the performance produces that which is in excess of itself. This is an example of how the rehearsal process and craft become not only a way of sourcing material but also a subject matter for the performance.

There is something unsettling about trying to articulate the unconscious, involuntary dimensions of gesture through performance by paring down what could be initially apprehended as language. Emphasis on craft in arts training can provide opportunities to reflect on and monitor one's body to gain a better understanding of the notion of agency. However, the subjectivity of such experiences often poses problems for a rigorous theorization of these issues. On the other side, the neuroscientific approaches that seek to provide objective discourses to develop our understanding of performance result in an ethical problematic. To what extent can science objectively theorize gesture by monitoring human bodies and their performance while still being able to allow space for an individual's agency? And if we are to accept the often generalized findings that invite trans-historical readings, then what value do they have in furthering the understanding of the complex social evolution of gestural language? These uneasy relationships between discrete discourses that seek to define performance and human subjectivity from generic bases have begun to be interrogated and explored by contemporary artists such as Stelarc - most notably his work on prosthetics and cyborgs that modify gesture by means of technology. Perhaps in this light the role of training can be re-thought so as to define it as a methodology that develops a specifically performative discourse - or in fact a way of thinking through performance. In a world where we are becoming more and more removed from the physicalities of our existence, where high-powered, mediated modes of perception substitute direct sensations and engagement, training as a form of meditation upon gesture might help us to re-articulate what is at stake in the contemporary social being.

REFERENCES

Brown, S. And Parsons, L. M. (2008) 'The Neuroscience of Dance', *Scientific American* (July): 78–83.

Hatten, R. S. (2004) *Interpreting Musical Gestures, Topics and Tropes: Mozart, Beethoven, Schubert*, Bloomington: Indiana University Press.

Leach, R. (2004) *The Makers of Modern Drama*, New York: Routledge.

Stein, G. (1990) *Selected Writings of Gertrude Stein*, New York: Vintage Books.

Spinal Snaps
Tracing a back-story of European actor training

JONATHAN PITCHES

PRELIMINARIES

Cervix (C1-C7), thorax (T1-T12), lumbar (L1-L5), sacrum (S1-S5) and coccyx (Co1-4): the spine is the 'power centre of the body', one 'long limb' connecting head to pelvis (Tufnell and Crickmay 1993: 9-10). As you descend the vertebral column the spine becomes thicker and weightier, before it (literally) tails off and loses flexibility; the final two sections comprise fused vertebrae located deep in the centre of the body. Each of these five spinal segments has a character and function of its own, evoked in no small way by their Greek and Latin names and on whose etymology I will draw freely to justify my range of perspectives here.

The aim in this essay is to use varying understandings of the spine to help examine specific examples of European and Russian performer training. But to do this it is necessary to place these understandings in associative collision with other sources: ones that draw on the domestic, the documentary and the dramaturgical. What follows is a set of contrasting registers and responses to the spine in performance: snapshots, drawing structurally on the physiology of the spine itself. Given that one of the many connotations of the spine that needs questioning from a training perspective is its neat linearity, this is not a strictly predictable journey. Instead the questions of training raised here are arranged rather as an archeologist might come across a set of bones in the dirt - in fragments, which may or may not be assembled into a meaningful whole. It is a speculative attempt to 'give voice' to the spine.

INTRODUCTION: C1–7: THE CERVICAL SPINE

The topmost vertebra (C1) is called the Atlas and joins the head to the spine

Atlas: from Greek Mythology: a Titan whose name probably means 'he who carries' or 'he who endures'. Charged with holding the sky up in perpetuity.

In their second co-authored book on performance, improvisation and imagination, *A Widening Field*, Chris Crickmay and Miranda Tufnell set their readers a challenge:

Let the pelvis listen to the head through the spine ... let the head hear the pelvis. In your mind's eye, travel the pathway of the spine

Let the legs and arms ... open as branches ... from its length
Open the soles of the feet ... sense the ground
Open the crown of the head ... let in air ... light

Let the whole body open and move from the length of the spine
Write and make to give the spine a voice.

(2004: 209, my emphasis)

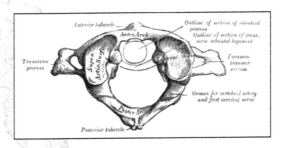

This *written* article can only address half of Tufnell's and Crickmay's tantalizing final invitation, although it is worth noting that their constant coupling of the terms 'making' and 'writing', their almost seamless manoeuvring between the page and the studio, is part of a strategy to collapse these traditionally separate activities into one fluid continuum of performance practices – a provocation to find enduring and tangible meeting points between earthbound modes of making and the limitless horizon of the imagination, a kind of Atlantan project in microcosm.

Their purpose in *The Widening Field* is clear: to provoke the reader's imagination and to encourage its use as a defamiliarizing tool when working with the body. In their writings the mind's eye is constantly invoked to open up the body and scan it from impossible perspectives; it is used mentally to 'unfuse' the fused vertebra of the sacrum, to spread outwards the wings of the ilium or, even more radically, to 'imagine you have no bones' at all (2004: 195). Yet these invitations to engage imaginatively in a deconstruction of the body are rooted in a deep and enduring interest in anatomy, osteology and the spine; Tufnell is a cranio-sacral therapist as well as a dancer, for instance, and this duality is reflected in a constant interplay in their work between the entropic forces of creativity and imagination and the more measured and objective descriptions drawn from science.

To capture a flavour of this interplay and to evoke the complexities associated with the word, here is a selective overview of the currency of the spine in performer training, organized into four types of understanding: i) psycho-physical, ii) genealogical, iii) dramaturgical and iv) osteological.

THE PSYCHO-PHYSICAL

Given its centrality in the daily functioning of the body and its connectedness to the entire gestural resource-pack of the performer (neck, back, shoulders, abdomen, hips), the spine is understandably a key discussion point for performer trainers. These articulations have taken many different forms: for Eugenio Barba, artistic director and founder of Denmark's Odin Teatret, the spine is 'energy's helm', offering a benchmark for the anthropological analysis of 'all extra-daily body techniques' (Barba and Savarese 1991: 232). Since the company's founding in 1964, Barba's intercultural theatre ensemble has viewed training as a fundamental voyage of personal discovery; training regimes are devised by each performer and maintained daily so that the meaning of the work, in his words, 'belongs to them alone' (244). The common reference point is the actor's spinal column, which Barba describes as a 'yardstick' with which to measure the actor's work, one which can then be applied to 'all other physical, psychological and social oppositions' (244). The spine is not simply the centre of energy, then, but an auto-didactic tool of analysis.

The Polish ensemble Gardzienice, whose director Włodzimierz Staniewski shares with Barba a common inspiration in the figure of Grotowski, also emphasizes the spine in its training. Known colloquially in Polish as 'the cross', the spine in Staniewski's book is the psycho-physical source of a performer's energy and serves as a fundamental meeting point between actors, developing what he sees as a prerequisite for performance training, mutuality:

> We know that the work of the spine releases physical and mental energy ... The attitude (posture) of the cross when the solar plexus is exposed, is an attitude of questioning, inviting, it's a challenge, readiness, and the beginning and end of action. The importance of the cross for dialogue in partnership, for cooperation of one actor with another is unquestionable. (in Hodge 2000: 234)

Grotowski, too, spoke of *la croix* in his 1989 essay 'Tu es le fils de Quelqu'un'. Like Staniewski after him, Grotowski thought of the spine, or the 'sacrum-pelvis complex' as he defined it (Schechner and Wolford 1997: 297), as the source of the performer's creative energy. 'That's where the impulses begin [*la croix*]' (Slowiak and Cuesta 2007: 124), Grotowski argued and justified this by paralleling the work of actors and the movements of African, Mexican and Bengali hunters in the bush. All, he maintained, adopt a 'primal position' (Schechner and Wolford 1997: 297), where the spine is inclined and the knees slightly bent, a position of ultimate efficiency and responsiveness that is held in place by the sacrum-pelvis complex. Developing a physical understanding of this primal position thus became a key part of Grotowski's later training methods, and specifically through the exercise of the Motions.[1]

THE DRAMATURGICAL

Beyond these body-based understandings, there are dramaturgical interpretations of the spine, related to the actor's treatment of text and character. Taking their cue from Stanislavsky, Richard Boleslavsky and, later, Lee Strasberg and other Group Theatre members, developed the notion of the 'spine of the role' in their work with actors in America from the mid 1930s. Boleslavsky had worked with Stanislavsky at a pivotal moment in the development of the latter's psycho-technique from 1906-1920 and had then exported this early version of the System to the United States, colouring it with his own imagination but not departing from the script in the way Michael Chekhov or Vsevolod Meyerhold did. Tracing the usage of the term 'spine' to indicate the through-line a character takes in the play, or alternatively the 'overall meaning' of the play itself, reveals a fascinating transmission of ideas crossing over a number of Russian and American schools. Boleslavsky used the term in his laboratory in New York in the mid-1930s Michael Chekhov was still using it at Dartington in Devon in 1937, as I will detail later, although it is not a word that features prominently in his published books. Harold Clurman from the Group Theatre in the US, also a trainee of Boleslavsky's, refers to the spine of the character or play in his book *On Directing* (1972: 78-9), Elia Kazan in his explication of *Streetcar* (Jones 1986: 140-1) and Strasberg in his unpublished lecture series on Stanislavsky delivered to students in 1958.[2] Indeed, while Strasberg and Stella Adler famously fell out over their interpretations of Stanislavsky's system after their respective visits to Moscow in 1934, terminologically, at least, the spine represented a point of connection for the two: it is placed significantly as the point of 'transaction' between 'complete internal' and 'complete external' work in her sketch of the System made that same year.[3]

Four years later, with the publication in Russia of *An Actor's Work on Himself* in 1938, the Stanislavskian root of all of these spinal metaphors was revealed in glaring pictorial terms for in the preface to his *magnum opus* Stanislavsky pictured his whole system as two creative 'lungs', bisected by a spine complete with individual vertebrae. His point was at once literal and symbolic: a play, like a spine, is made up of individual actions or vertebrae, which through the industry of the performer are linked seamlessly together in the backbone of the part. Or, more symbolically, the creative energy of the artwork is fed by the balanced *inspiration* of those oxygenating lungs: *voploscenie* (scenic embodiment) and *perezhivanie* (internal experience).[4]

THE GENEALOGICAL

At a further level of abstraction, it is possible to read the backbone as a metaphor for the process of transmission itself - the spine as a model of a training lineage - as the Moscow-based director Kama Ginkas does: 'I wasted enormous amounts of energy battling with the schooling I received', he stated in 1998, 'but your schooling sits deeply in you. It's genetics. It's your backbone' (Ginkas 1998: 10).

Ginkas's sentiments expose a particular Russian (and continental European) view of training as 'family inheritance' and the training ground as a family 'home'. Eugenio Barba refers to his family tree in many publications - with his

[1] 'There are three cycles of stretches ... Each cycle is one specific stretch/position executed four times, once toward each of the cardinal directions ... Separating each cycle is a stretch called nadir/zenith, a quick stretch down followed by a quick one up' (Thomas Richards in Slowiak and Cuesta [2007: 126]).

[2] I am indebted to Bobbie Ellermann for giving me sight of these fascinating records of Strasberg in action.

[3] For a reprint of the diagram, see Pitches (2006: 119).

[4] Stanislavsky's diagram is reprinted in Carnicke (1998: 99).

[5] See Barba's 2003 essay 'Grandfathers, Orphans and the Family Saga of European Theatre', for one salient example.

grandfathers identified as Konstantin Stanislavsky and Vsevolod Meyerhold.[5] Anatoly Vasiliev, formerly of the Moscow School of Dramatic Art, now working in Lyon, describes himself as 'the student of the student of Stanislavsky', and his contemporary and director of the Maly Drama Theatre, Lev Dodin, locates his place in the same lineage via Stanislavsky's student Boris Zon and his training at GITIS. In the parallel French tradition of training, Etienne Decroux and Jacques Lecoq have recently been described by Leabhart and Chamberlain as, 'starting from the same artistic parent, Jacques Copeau and uncle, Gordon Craig' (2008: 11).

It is Grotowski, however, who perhaps best embodies questions of lineage, going to calculated lengths to ensure his own family line remained 'pure':

> It is a terrible business, because there is, on the one hand, the danger of freezing the thing, of putting it in a refrigerator in order to keep it impeccable, and on the other hand, if one does not freeze it, there is the danger of dilution caused by facility ... The burning question is: Who today, is going to assure the continuity of the research? Very subtle, very delicate and very difficult.
> (Schechner and Wolford 1997: 471)

As is well known, he answered this question by placing Thomas Richards as the legal executor of all of his papers and effective inheritor of the Grotowski tradition. The neat linearity of this (Schechner calls it Grotowski's need for 'control') is part and parcel of the mode of transmission, a function of orature, as opposed to literature, or, more specifically of direct, physical delivery, to return to the Latin root of the word tradition.[6]

[6] Tradition: from *tradere*: to give up, transmit (Collins).

THE OSTEOLOGICAL

An osteological view of the spine in performance brings together the longview of a tradition with the instant snapshot afforded us by new technologies - in this case the MRI. The advent of Magnetic Resonance Imaging has allowed remarkably detailed readings of the spine to be made based on multi-perspectival recreations of the vertebral column. MRI scans let you observe the spine from any angle, in two dimensions or three, anterior or posterior, paralleling in digital form the *imaginary* surveys of Tufnell and Crickmay - 'see the view from the tip of your spine [down]' (1993: 7), they advise in *Body Space Image*. The images produced by MRIs offer a monochrome window onto an often colourful past, a past which, from an osteologist's point of view, is inscribed on one's bone structure as clearly as the rings of a tree trunk or the sediment patterns in an Alaskan ice core reveal their individual histories:

> Bone holds our deepest and oldest memories, it reacts to joy or shock, breathes and fails to breathe ... Bone carries the imprint of all that we do, and of where we have been. Throughout our lives our bones subtly change and record the directions we have taken.
> (Tufnell and Crickmay 2004: 199)

But this statement of osteological certainty begs questions: what use might be made of the relatively new archeological resource of the MRI in the distant future? How might these hitherto unseen markings be drawn on in the examination of recent histories, now that mortification and exhumation are no longer precursors to becoming intimate with the insides of humankind?

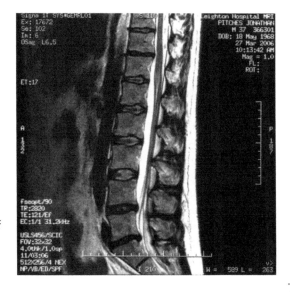

And what of the traces even bone forensics can't uncover? Where does the corporeal archive of the body's past fail us? At what point are other forms of mediation necessary, those that recognize that all lineages, even those of a vertebral nature, are subject to hidden and unmarked forces, reproducible only through the performative capacity of the imagination?

S1–5: SACRUM

[from Latin sacred, or holy bone, because it was used in sacrifices].

> The sacrum is the root bone, that spreads our weight downwards to the earth and also, as the keel of a boat, supporting the rise of the head and spine ... The sacrum, more than any other bone, is shaped by the weight and movement that passes through it.
> (Tufnell and Crickmay 2004: 218)

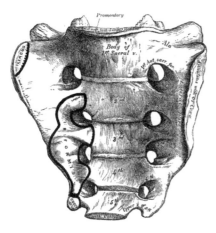

A report from Consultant Orthopaedic and Spinal Surgeon, Mr Krishnan, South Cheshire, Dated 10th April 2006:

> The gentleman reports that he has had back problems with niggling aches from a young age. He recalls having physiotherapy when he was about 14 years old after which his acute symptoms settled down and he has only had the odd twinge since then. In August 2005 he loaded heavy kit in his car when he felt a 'tearing sensation' in his back. He had severe back pain for about a week and then had non-steroidal medication and his back pain settled down. Unfortunately it recurred in September 2005 and worsened steadily ... He managed to carry on and his symptoms settled down to the point that he was able to do quite a lot of walking in the Lake District and mountain climbing in December. He had a further recurrence in January 2006 with back pain and right leg pain from the buttock with severe cramps in the right calf and a numb right foot ... He went off work in February 2006 ... He continues to have severe right leg pain, paraesthesiae in the right leg with a numb right foot which is pretty much constant. There is no bladder or bowel dysfunction ... The MRI of his lumbar spine from the 27th March 2006 was available for scrutiny. The scan shows focal pathology from Lumbar 4 to Sacrum1 ... At Lumbar 5/Sacrum 1 there is loss of signal with advanced disc resorption and marked loss of height. There is also retrolisthesis which is quite noticeable and not mild as reported by the radiologist ... In addition there is a large disc prolapse which is postero-lateral to the right ... with impingement of the right S1 and S2 roots and the disc protrusion is extruded behind the sacral body. The spinal canal is wide and capacious which obviously explains the absence of major neurological physical signs.

It's tempting to ask what else Mr Krishnan can tell from this scan that he is keeping quiet. Vestiges of the many trips and falls occasioned by beach shingle? Traces of the days and months spent in the distorted shapes of biomechanics? Markings of the many times one's children have been tossed onto ill-prepared shoulders? What are the joys and shocks of the last forty years, and how are they recorded?

L1–5: THE LUMBAR REGION

Of, near, or relating to the part of the body between the lowest ribs and the hipbones

From Latin *lumbus*: loin.

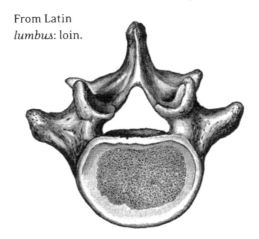

1997.jpg

1998.jpg

1999.jpg

2000.jpg

2001.jpg

2002.jpg

2003.jpg

BORTH BENCH

I've never been one for religious ceremonies – my brief flirtation with Catholicism in the early 1970s made sure of that. Yet for over a decade I have been making a pilgrimage of sorts – to the holiday resort of Borth, near Aberystwyth in West Wales, or, more specifically, to the bench-outside-the-Family-Shopper-supermarket-on-the-front-at-Borth, although there remains some dispute about which bench it is, exactly.

We are, in truth, a small sect. We began with just four pilgrims, but in recent years our numbers have swollen to six and may rise still further in the future. But the modesty of our congregation does not limit the zealotry with which we pursue our aims – year in, year out, we travel hundreds of miles to observe a simple ritual: to gather briefly in a designated, (if disputed) space, facing the sea on the prom. Here, we pose for the 'annual photograph', collectively, if momentarily, suspended in thrall to the self-timing device of a digital camera. Then we disperse.

Inevitably, there are a host of unspoken understandings which inform this ritual: the camera always rests on the breakwater wall, demanding a sprightly return to the bench from its operator; the order on the bench must religiously be observed and sub-pairings maintained (although the last five years have seen some significant promotions from lap to bench). And it must always feel that we have just one shot at getting 'that picture' in any one year, even though we might visit the same beach three or four other times in as many days and in any case will be staying in the neighbouring village of Tre-Taliesin, just 15 minutes away across the flood plain; there is an urgency and necessity to get the job done and equally a strange sense of deflation once the photo has been taken, as if, in some way, the main purpose of our annual holiday has been achieved in that fleeting moment of a shutter-click.

In recent years, as I have watched the montage created by this tradition grow steadily on the wall, I have begun to think of our ritual and the art objects that have been produced from its observance, as a new sub-genre – as a kind of *domestic* durational performance. Clearly, we are not walking from one or the other end of the Great Wall of China to meet, spiritually and personally in the middle, as Marina Abramovic and Ulay did, nor are we spending a year on the streets, or the same time physically bound to another artist like Teching Hsieh and Linda Montano; endurance is not, at least not explicitly, part of the package. But central to this modest ritual on the beach in Wales are similar overarching concerns: the need to find appropriate means to mark and map the passing of time, to establish firm and unyielding ground rules that draw attention to the 'timeliness' of time, to make known the limitations and simplifications of constructed narratives.

Here, the visual telescoping of a decade of human development, made briefly present by our yearly punctuation marks, draws explicit attention to what is so obviously missing and untraceable in the story. And yet, as a personal visual history, these photos record by inference the backbone of my life-story. In these twelve years, I have moved from newly-wed to parent, from the Midlands to West Yorkshire, from lecturer to professor. Within a few miles of this site I have met (and often re-met) academics and practitioners who shaped my thinking and determined my future trajectory: Eugenio Barba, Ted Braun, Robert Leach, Mel Gordon, Simon Murray and Richard Gough. Here, for a few precious years, the CPR Past Masters conferences were held with almost the same frequency as our more modest gatherings on the bench. A beachstone's throw away from Borth, I practiced Meyerhold's biomechanics with one of his pupils' pupils, Alexei Levinsky, enjoyed the tireless play of my children on the sand dunes of Ynyslas and (almost at the same time) witnessed the unfathomable pain of close relatives. These are some of the variegated backstories to this piece.

What distinguishes this performance from

Abramovic or Hsieh is its open-endedness. Unlike 'Night Sea Crossing' (1981) or Hsieh's various 'One Year Performances' (1978-86), I have no idea when the piece will finish and, more to the point, who might be seated on the bench when it does. In my wildest fantasies my two sons become as motivated as I am to continue the tradition, bringing with them every August to Borth, their children and their grandchildren, but the 2009 photo (no. 13 in the series) could just as easily be the last. It is this contingency that situates this work in the domain of performance, that our collective art work is subject to all the vagaries of life, that while it is still being performed, it is forever under the shadow of 'circumstance', that it both captures and at the same time illustrates the impossibility of capturing our (and my) story.

It is, perhaps, important to remember this inbuilt contingency when analysing other more elevated traditions - the performative backbones which are so often constructed by practitioners and critics (including myself) to trace the 'Grandfathers of Modern actor training'. What are the backstories, and who's missing from the bench?

T1–12: THORACIC SPINE

(Meyerhold, Decroux and Michael Chekhov)

Thorax: the part of the mammalian body between the neck and the abdomen also: its cavity in which the heart and lungs lie

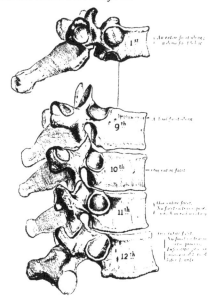

Coming from two separate but related traditions of performer training, Meyerhold's biomechanics and Decroux's Corporeal Mime define a particular approach to the performer's spine based on the compartmentalizing of action and the near-scientific analysis of the body itself. Meyerhold located the centre point of the actor in the sternum or breast-bone; it is around this point the actor literally 'groups' their actions and gestures to give them a sense of centre (located near the top of the thoracic spine) and to ensure a conscious balance between left and right. This action of 'grouping' - or *groupirovka* as master practitioner Gennady Bogdanov terms it - is explained by one his actors:

> Gennady asks actors to be aware of *groupirovka* at all times, it is perhaps best illustrated, in training, during the biomechanic run and to its most extreme level in the *étude* 'The Dagger'. During this *étude* the victim moves from a completely open position leaning back with his/her arms outstretched, they then group around the sternum before opening up again and falling to the floor. (Mann 2009)[7]

Biomechanical actors are trained to develop their spatial awareness by imagining that this centre is a constant reference point, in relation to all the other shifting parameters provided by the performance space - the walls, the floor, other performers: 'imagine lines spreading from your sternum outwards, in all directions', Bodganov preaches in his classes, 'lengthening and shortening as you move around the space, and at all times ensuring your momentary awareness of place' (Mann 2009).

Etienne Decroux, one of Jacques Copeaux's students at the Vieux Colombier in Paris, took anatomical analysis to an even more exacting level, again concentrating on the spine or 'trunk'. This he classified as: 'the head plus neck plus chest plus waist plus pelvis' (Leabhart 2007: 116). Anne Dennis describes this spinal chain as: a 'principle source of corporeal expression' in which 'emotion is reflected through breath' and where 'it is precisely the vertebrae that permit this emotion to become visible' (1995: 62).

2004.jpg

2005.jpg

2006.jpg

2007.jpg

2008.jpg

2009.jpg

7 Terence Mann, formerly an actor with Talia Theatre, from an email conversation with the author (2 April 2009).

[8] For details of these exercises, see Leabhart (2007: 116-24).

[9] For examples of *études* from the 1920s to the 1990s, see Bogdanov (1997).

[10] It is for that reason that Decroux has been likened to postdramatic understandings of the body; such an observation would never be possible with Meyerhold. (See Chamberlain and Leabhart 2008: 12).

[11] I am very grateful to Professor Thomas Leabhart for providing me with video documents of this exercise. Leabhart notes: 'Decroux also spoke of a center "like a sun shining between the shoulder blades" but the most important center for him (and fixed point or fulcrum around which the lever of his counterweights operated) was the point a few inches below the navel' (email conversation 30 March 2009).

Decroux's 'Inclinations on a Lateral Plane' evidence the level of precision and segmentation in Corporeal Mime - it is just as important to know when you are not moving part of your body as when you are - and illustrate, too, the uses of his specific spinal taxonomy: head, hammer, bust, torso, trunk.[8] These Inclinations can be developed and made more complex by adding physical contradictions or by transforming the vertical 'bar' which mentally bisects the actor into a curve or chain. In either case, the body becomes a 'keyboard', as Decroux put it, played using a detailed and sophisticated manipulation of the spine. Decroux sought to expose that keyboard and celebrate the physicality of the performer by covering the face (which he thought simply 'sweats reality') and revealing the body:

> The nude body expressing what one receives generally from words and from the gaze, transports us to another world ... Face re-presents and the body creates. (Chamberlain and Leabhart 2008: 41)

Meyerhold's biomechanical training has a similar tradition of blank-faced performers and near-nude practitioners. From the earliest snippets of training films from the 1920s to the more recent videos of Bogdanov demonstrating *études*, an exposed and well-developed muscular torso has been a focal point.[9] This, combined with a collective interest in the historic performance traditions of *commedia dell'arte* and Japanese *Noh*, suggests that Meyerhold's and Decroux's training methodologies occupy considerable common ground. But it is arguably in their devising of *études* (or actors' technical studies) where the two systems meet most significantly. With no personal experience of Decroux's system, my analysis here is inevitably read through the lens of biomechanics, but such a perspective reveals some striking spinal synergies. There are clear similarities in purpose between Decroux's exercises and the range of études devised by Meyerhold: each take workaday actions and extend them, both to estrange the activities themselves and to develop physically demanding and formally exacting tasks. There are degrees of abstraction here that might differentiate Decroux from Meyerhold - Meyerhold did not experiment with pure physical form, for example, and, unlike Decroux, the simple narrative retained a degree of importance and visibility for him.[10] But a comparison of Decroux's Extensor (interpreted by Thomas Leabhart)[11] and Meyerhold's Shooting the Bow (here performed by his collaborator Nikolai Kustov) nevertheless reveals a number of common imperatives.

Both exercises constitute short and repeatable crystallizations of an action (stretching a body-building apparatus and a bow, respectively); both defamiliarize this action through the use of an extended gestural vocabulary, rhythmic contrast and play; both have an 'inner music' informing the actor's work (Leabhart sings to himself as he performs the Extensor); and both actively and consistently put out of balance what has previously been in balance or centred by virtue of the performer's training. Both forms, then, exploit a heightened consciousness of the spine first to stabilize and then to destabilize the actor at work, recognizing that it is this creative tension that leads to visually arresting performance or to that much-debated term 'presence'.

These two examples illustrate a distinctly rationalized, even atomized, approach to the spine and more generally to creative play, an approach which reaches its apotheosis in Decroux's 1960 article 'Bodily Presence':

> The body is in fact remarkable and impossible to pulverize. It's a pity. The advantage would be clear if, without killing this body, one managed to reduce it to powder or to carve it up into tiny cubes. These parts, too small to interest the eye, too uniform as well, would be arranged as one wished; then one would reveal to the world the arrangement of these specks concealed from the world's view.
>
> (Chamberlain and Leabhart 2008: 53)

Michael Chekhov's interpretation of the spine is characteristically different, emphasizing the non-rational and intuitive, the imaginary rather than the material body. Just a year before the publication of Stanislavsky's great spinal model, Chekhov was appropriating his teacher's terminology in his classes at his new Studio in Dartington. But even then, as his Technique was coming into focus and sixteen years before it was first published, his emphasis was more synthetic than atomistic. In his unpublished lesson from January 1937, entitled 'The Spine or Main Line, The Whole', Chekhov conflated the linear, dramaturgical function of the 'spine of the role' with what he called the Fourth Brother – or the feeling of the whole. In this transcript of the class from the archive at Dartington, Chekhov is keen to distance himself from what he sees as the dry, analytical thinking associated with the former:

> The whole method I am trying to give you is directed towards escaping this bad way of intellectualizing about the play, which kills the possibility to be in the aura of the play. The intellect is not able to enter into the aura of the play. It kills it.

Betraying his anthroposophical leanings, Chekhov focuses on a play's hidden aura – a Rudolf Steiner-inspired alternative to his better-known feeling of *the Whole*. He then goes on to detail how one goes about entering into the aura of the play: imagine, before you approach the play in detail, you are sitting in the theatre after the curtain has come down on a performance of it, sitting in a mood of openness to the impressions received throughout the piece. 'Revisit' in your mind each act as it might have been performed to you and allow a refined sense of the totality of the piece to enter your thoughts. Only then, Chekhov argues, in this imaginative space of prediction, in this site of creative augury:

> There is this beautiful moment when you can catch with your whole being the result of the play.[12]

Later, in *On the Technique of Acting*, Chekhov described this process as 'the past and the future, being experienced acutely as the present' (1991: 133). Perhaps, in Chekhov's holistic re-definition of the spine there is a prefiguring of what Tufnell and Crickmay mean: the spine as 'one long limb' not as a set of separately articulated vertebrae ...

C01–4: COCCYX: TAILPIECE

The small triangular bone at the end of the spinal column in man and some apes, representing a vestigial tail.

From Greek: *Kokkux*, or Cuckoo, from the likeness of the bone to a cuckoo's beak

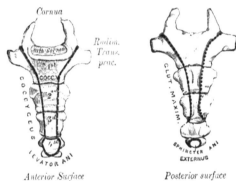

Anterior Surface   *Posterior surface*

The snapshot by definition breaks up an observable fact and detaches it from its natural home. This process of 'pulverizing' (to use Decroux's rather frightening metaphor) can be helpful as an analytical tool, but it runs counter to the function of the spine itself: as a connecting point for the whole of the body. In physical terms the spine is a living representation of this tension between atomism and holism,

[12] I am grateful to The Dartington Hall Trust Archive for giving me permission to quote from the Michael Chekhov collection. Catalogue Ref. MC/S1/21/E.

comprising thirty-three separately labeled components (or vertebrae) but linked from atlas to coccyx and suffused in spino-cerebral fluid flowing continuously between head and tail – 'a constant tide of connection' (Tufnell and Crickmay: 1993: 3).

While in medical terms the coccyx is a redundant evolutionary hangover from our primate past – a tail for which we no longer have a use – in performance terms it is an ideal place of conclusion. For it is precisely this quality of *vestigiality* (a hint, a mark, a trace?) which is so central to the phenomenon of training and its inherent contradictions.

Training undoubtedly makes its mark on the trainee, but this mark remains largely hidden until the act of performance. Indeed, in *indirect* traditions of acting,[13] the training base of the performer is often not in evidence even then – at least not explicitly. Within a given tradition, training often functions as a shared language of *unspoken* understandings: a bond between director and performer, if both have the same training roots, and between performers themselves, particularly if there is an element of risk in the work. That hidden understanding, from a spectator's perspective, provides the basis for what often looks like an uncanny 'togetherness' in a cast of performers, a quality of *mutuality* that is as tangible as it is difficult to describe. Training is, in effect, the backstory to any performance.

One antidote for this loss of visibility is for a practitioner to claim highly visible roots to their training – to delineate definable histories. While this is increasingly difficult in a Western context of multiple and simultaneous training, there are still many good reasons for protecting the spine of 'deep training': training that is longitudinal, developmental and confined to a specific set of practices. The most obvious symbol of this (justifiable) protectionism is the model of training transmission as 'family inheritance' and the training laboratory as a 'home'. This 'undiluted' (to use Grotowski's term) but potentially parochial model allows for a level of quality assurance in training processes and militates against dilettantism, though it brings with it all the fractious politics of the family power dynamic. And while the grandfather-father-son model of direct training still remains popular in some practitioners' rhetoric, in truth it is as utopian as my wish to see my grandchildren's children holidaying in Borth in the late twenty-first century.

A more enduring symbol identified in this article is the injury and its place in training. I have tried, here, to set permanent injury within a context of natural osteological developments and changes in the physical form – to the spine specifically. But injury operates at another level, too, as an enforced objectifier or defamiliarizing agent. It is no coincidence that both Moshe Feldenkrais and F. M. Alexander were inspired to develop training systems by their own limitations (from a knee injury and respiratory problems respectively), for these restrictions forced them to think outside of their own habituated behaviours and posture. Thus, in specific circumstances, it is possible to make discoveries from sometimes shocking changes to one's physical capacity, to make gains from any initial loss. Meyerhold, Chekhov and Decroux were not, of course, motivated by the same causes as Feldenkrais and Alexander, but they shared with them the belief that training is a route to new understandings of the self and of one's own functionality.

All three practitioners featured in the Thoracic section of this article view the spine as a tool for analysis, even though that tool might have been used in varying ways: from Decroux's often starkly anatomical approach to the imaginative projection of Chekhov. Advances in technology – which even now extend way beyond Magnetic Resonance Imagery to Paraspinal Thermal Imaging, for instance – have extended this idea of the spine as an index of balance, health and connectivity. And at the same time they intensify the image of the spine as our personal archive, steadily accumulating and recording the shocks of life as we progress towards our end.

[13] Ian Watson (2000: 1-2) draws a distinction between 'direct training' where the trainee learns a specific repertory from a master and 'indirect training', which focuses on generic skills to be applied to a range of contexts.

If there is an overarching discovery to be made from this layered survey of spinal understandings, it is to respect the interstices between verterbrae, the resonances, half-truths, metaphors and etymologies that define the spine itself, while retaining a healthy suspicion of any claims to undisputed verticality.

AFTERWORDS (OR 33 SPINAL SNAPS)

Spine as tradition
Spine as archive
Spine as keystone
Spine as lineage
Spine as pain site
Spine as benchmark
Spine as fragment
Spine as limb
Spine as complex
Spine as witness
Spine as window
Spine in 2D
Spine in 3D
Spine as ice core
Spine as trunk
Spine as backbone
Spine as absence
Spine in curves
Spine as chain
Spine as trap
Spine as role
Spine as pathway
Spine as connector
Spine as divider
Spine as bone
Spine as fluid
Spine as support
Spine as deluder
Spine as communicator
Spine as axis
Spine as cross
Spine as long-view
Spine as snap

REFERENCES

Barba, Eugenio (2003) 'Grandfathers, Orphans and the Family Saga of European Theatre', *New Theatre Quarterly* 19(2 (May): 108-117.

Barba, Eugenio and Savarese, Nicola (1991) *A Dictionary of Theatre Anthropology: the Secret Art of the Performer*, London: Routledge.

Bogdanov, Gennady (1997) 'Meyerhold's Theater and Biomechanics' (video), Berlin: Mime Centrum.

Carnicke, Sharon (1998) *Stanislavsky in Focus*, London: Harwood Academic.

Chamberlain, Franc and Leabhart, Thomas (eds) (2008) *The Decroux Soucebook*, Oxon: Routledge.

Chekhov, Michael (1991) *On the Technique of Acting*, New York: HarperCollins.

Clurman, Harold (1972) *On Directing*, New York: Macmillan.

Dennis, Anne (1995) *The Articulate Body: The physical training of the actor*, New York: Drama Books.

Ginkas, Kama (1998) 'Russian Theatre is not a Time Killer: John Freedman Interviews Kama Ginkas', *Theatre Forum* 12 (Winter/Spring): 4-13.

Hodge, Alison, ed. (2000) *Twentieth-Century Actor Training*, London: Routledge.

Jones, David Richard (1986) *Great Directors at Work: Stanislavsky, Brecht, Kazan, Brook*, Berkeley: University of California Press.

Leabhart, Thomas (2007) *Étienne Decroux*, Oxon: Routledge.

Mann, Terence (2009) email exchange with the author.

Pitches, Jonathan (2006) *Science and the Stanislavsky Tradition of Acting*, Oxon: Routledge.

Schechner, Richard and Wolford, Lisa (eds) (1997) *The Grotowski Source Book*, London: Routledge.

Slowiak James and Cuesta, Jairo (2007) *Jerzy Grotowski*, Oxon: Routledge.

Tufnell, Miranda and Crickmay, Chris (2004) *A Widening Field: Journeys in body and imagination*, Hampshire: Dance Books.

Tufnell, Miranda and Crickmay, Chris (1993) *Body Space Image*, Hampshire: Dance Books.

Watson, Ian (2000) *Performer Training: Developments across cultures*, Amsterdam: Harwood Academic.

On the Production of the Body Ideal

VÉRONIQUE CHANCE

• Prop No.1
©Véronique Chance
2005–6

> The lithe and energetic body, tight and slim, with its toned up boundaries is a powerful image of contemporary culture, especially as articulated in advertising and consumer culture. Not only has the toned body become a commercial icon, but also the gym has become highly visible as the site where this body is produced.
>
> Roberta Sassatelli (1999: 227)

1.

The past decade has seen a proliferation in the building of fitness centres, as highly visible urban sites, which sell fitness regimes that refer to the cultural image of an ideal body. In recent art work I have used photography and video footage taken inside the contemporary site of the fitness centre 'gym' to look at the body's relationship to training and its relationship to the equipment and machinery involved in the physical process and performance of transforming and perfecting the human body.

This has resulted in two series of works: a set of large photographs that focus on the individual fitness machinery and equipment used to 'train' the body and a series of looped video performance sequences that focus on the particular movements made by the body when using these machines. In the former, the machine stands alone, a powerful, desirable sculptural object and a prop in waiting that also becomes a replacement for the human body. In the latter, the human body has been isolated from its environment in order to express the forward thrust of a singular action that is continuously and mechanically repeated without end.

In a gym the body 'performs' actions on machinery and equipment that 'work' certain parts of the body, separating it out into its constituent parts. The body thus becomes fragmented and rearticulated in terms of its various parts, in terms of specific 'gestures' or movements that relate to those parts and in terms of the particular machinery or 'props' on which these gestures or movements are 'performed'. The body and its parts become re-considered in terms of how they function or perform these movements on the machinery, which is itself considered in terms of how it functions, how it performs and how it is used.

> The usefulness of a thing, Marx writes, makes of this thing a use-value. This usefulness or use-value of the thing is therefore inseparable from its material support. It has no autonomous, independent existence. But [this use-value] is at the same time a property of the thing that is only realized in [its] consumption ... Use-Value, according to Marx, always refers in the final analysis to the needs and organs of a living body.
> (Hollier 1995: 136-7)

The 'use-value' of something describes its purpose, what it is for. With regard to this I wish to start with a consideration of the body in terms of its functionalism, thinking about the 'use' and 'value' of exercise in this context (about the usefulness, purpose and intention of exercise) and of exercise training as a 'practice' used as a means of transforming and putting the body to 'work' towards the making and production of an 'ideal' (or idealized) body. Central to this idea are the 'mechanics' of the body: not only in the articulation and performance of its various 'parts', but mechanics in relation to the machinery and equipment used to exercise or to train the body and in the relationship these machines have to the body: in their anthropomorphism, in their aesthetic and in their relationship to use-value as objects that have the specific function and purpose of 'putting to work' a particular part of the body towards a desired or intended output or end.

In using exercise as a process and methodology in my art work, I consider gestures and movements in terms of sequences and actions in their own right: how they perform (or are performed), how they 'operate' in relation to the carrying out of certain actions or tasks and how they might be re-articulated in relation to the body and its representation as art. Temporal associations become particularly important in the relationship between the still and moving image, as what is reflected in an exercise or an aspect of exercise becomes repeated in its visual and aural representation.

2.

In a way, one could say that in a gym, the machine 'controls' the body and its movements (the body is forced to move in a particular way by the machine), but these movements are, in turn, also shaped by the body's operation of the machine, which the body controls through the selection of different levels and programmes of training, different levels of speed or different levels of weight or resistance. The machine acts as a material framework for the body, with and against which the body moves. Its operation is performed through the intentional and (en)forced movement of a specific part of the body and the practice of a particular technique assigned to it. This technique has to be learned and perfected in order for the machine to operate safely and effectively and for it to 'do its job' (that is, of [re]building and [re]forming the body).

The idea of 'making' or 'producing' a body is not a new one and has historical associations with military and social 'discipline'. Discipline here refers not only to a 'practice' but to an idea of control, in terms of enforcing either self-control or control on others (or both) and of

• Prop No.4
© Véronique Chance 2005–6

obeying set (or sets of) rules, instructions and regulations. The idea of being 'disciplined' invokes obedience and complicity together with enforced punishment if one does not obey the rules. (One also talks about exercise as a 'punishing' regime in relation to a kind of self-punishment or masochism, something not so much imposed by others as by oneself). Thus in the production of the ideal body, there is a suggestion of the body being subjugated, tamed, *made* 'docile' in order to maximize its efficacy and its utility.

In his book *Discipline and Punish*, Michel Foucault opens his chapter on 'Docile Bodies' by referring to the 'ideal figure of the soldier' in terms of the deportment, movements and anatomy of would-be soldiers of the seventeenth century, as instantly recognizable 'signs' of soldiers in the making, which belonged to a 'bodily rhetoric of honour'. By the late eighteenth century, however, he continues,

> the soldier has become something that can be made; out of formless clay, an inapt body, the machine required can be constructed; posture is gradually corrected; a calculated constraint runs slowly through each part of the body, mastering it, making it pliable, ready at all times, turning silently into the automatism of habit. (Foucault 1991 [1975]: 135)

The body has become something that can be controlled, manipulated, shaped, trained, re-arranged, 're-made' to make it work 'automatically' and to perform (tasks) more 'efficiently', more powerfully, like a machine. Movements, exercises and gestures are repeated, learned, remembered, practised, so that an individual does not even have to think to be able to perform them to perfection, it becomes an 'aptitude'. These 'machine bodies' keep mind and body separate: the focus is entirely on the body and its 'production', its being 'made' or transformed and its unquestioning complicity in this. Production also refers to the body's usefulness or utility in economic terms: in other words, to its labour power or 'use-value'.

Foucault modelled his theory of the 'docile' body on theories of '*dressage*' found in the book *L'Homme Machine* written by Julien Offray de La Mettrie in 1747, and in particular on methods and regulations adopted by institutions such as the army, prisons, schools and hospitals, for 'controlling or correcting the operations of the body' as a body which can be 'subjected, used, transformed and improved.' (Foucault 1991 [1975]: 136) For Foucault, discipline was a 'machinery' and a 'mechanics of [institutional] power', a mechanism for controlling individuals, which he called 'political anatomy': 'How one may have a hold over others' bodies, not only so that they may do as one wishes, but so that they may operate as one wishes, with the technique, speed and efficiency that one determines' (138). In this way Foucault also recognized the paradoxical counter-productiveness of (enforced) training and discipline: that while on the one hand discipline 'increases the forces of the body (in economic terms of utility)', that is, in the body's usefulness or productivity), on the other hand discipline decreases 'these same forces (in political terms of obedience [in its complicity and in its being made "docile"])'. In other words 'it dissociates power from the body ... [O]n the one hand it seeks to increase capacity, on the other hand it reverses the course of energy'. Thus Foucault established in the disciplinary coercion of the body a direct link between 'an increased aptitude and an increased domination'. (138)

• Prop No.7
© *Véronique Chance*
2005–6

3.

Consider the site of the contemporary fitness centre as a replacement for the military institution, as a social site where the body can be shaped, trained, re-arranged, re-made (for there are analogies that can be made in the disciplining, transformation, 'production' and making of the modern body [ideal]). The fitness centre has become a contemporary cultural phenomenon and 'a highly visible site where the body is "produced"'. (Sassatelli 1999: 227). It is a site where a range of disciplinary body techniques and activities are practised and performed. These conform to established standards and patterns of bodily control in the form of 'training' that purports to 'improve' the body. Users comply with and follow time-tabled 'controlled activities' or obey sets of instructions as part of a group or as individuals, which take place over set periods of time or at particular times of the day. In the case of the 'gym', individuals are assessed and given 'programmes' of activity to follow, which are monitored, measured, quantified and periodically reassessed to 'suit' individual body requirements set by the institution. It is a site for making the body 'docile'.

Like Foucault's military institution, it is a site of 'enclosure', where one can be observed, not only by instructors and other users but also by passers-by. The site is also one of exposure and display: the large panels of glass which are often incorporated into the features of the architecture are a means by which one can see not only from the inside out but from the outside in. What is on 'view' becomes a spectacle for those passing by, and for users there is an increased notion or awareness of 'being on view' or 'being seen'. This is further emphasized by the banks of mirrors that line the interior walls of 'training' rooms and fitness studios, which transform the disciplinary site from one of 'increased domination' to one of desire and pleasure in an increased physical and cultural narcissism and fetishization [of the body], 'which permits the unashamed display of the human body' (Featherstone 1991: 177) both inside and outside its walls.

However, while Foucault acknowledges a certain level of visibility, he does not acknowledge any presence of desire or pleasure in his text, either in terms of the (individual's) desire of a body ideal or of any pleasure on the part of those being dominated or dominating others. Foucault's *Discipline* is discipline at the level of repression and coercion. While one could talk about this as the body being on display to those observing it, this actually is a level of subjugation and domination in which the individual is enclosed and cannot see those observing him or her, or is unaware of being observed. He or she is driven to the body ideal only by force, as a perfection of the discipline in relation to labour power and to avoid being punished – not at the level of desire. Therefore he or she is unable to take any pleasure from it. This is where the two sites differ.

As 'fitness' increasingly becomes a part of consumer culture, it becomes a commercial (body) production venture, an 'exchange-value', selling 'customers' and 'clients' exercise through glamorized images of the (young) 'fit', 'healthy' body as the desirable cultural ideal and standard to which to conform and aspire. 'Images of the body beautiful, openly sexual and associated with hedonism, leisure and display, emphasize the importance of appearance and "the look"' (Featherstone 1991: 170). Control and power are still in the hands of the institution but rather more subversively, as emphasis is placed on individual consumer 'choice' and an increased responsibility for one's own body in terms of 'maintenance' and 'self-preservation' within a regime of fitness, sold as a 'life-style' choice in itself. The body is 'proclaimed as a vehicle of pleasure' and

> discipline and hedonism are no longer seen as incompatible, indeed the subjugation of the body through body maintenance routines is presented within consumer culture as a precondition for the achievement of an acceptable appearance and the release of the body's expressive capacity.
> (Featherstone 1991: 171)

• Prop No.9
©Véronique Chance
2005–6

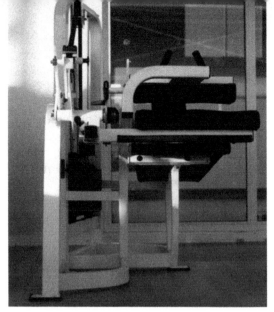

4.

In his later writings, Foucault was to take further his earlier theories of discipline that focused on institutional power and on the domination and control of the body by others in order to consider practices of self-discipline in the pursuit of self-knowledge through 'technologies of individual domination [and the control of one's own body by one's own 'self'], 'in the mode of action that an individual exercises upon himself [or herself]' (Foucault 2000: 225). Shortly before his death in 1984, he was developing a theory that he called 'Technologies of the Self.' In it, he outlined a practice of self-empowerment that emerges out of his system of domination and bodily control. Based on the idea of taking pride or pleasure in one's own body, it operates on a physical level and outlines a way in which one might 'attain a certain state of happiness, purity, wisdom, perfection or immortality' (225) through an understanding of one's 'self' through the body, through a knowledge, practice and training of its limits, capabilities and capacities (and of its desires and pleasures), that are self-imposed rather than imposed by others. Foucault referred to this as the 'revolt of the body' and as 'technologies of individual domination', in a kind of self-mastery and ascetic practice that concerns the mode of activity on practises upon oneself. He claimed:

> Mastery and awareness of one's own body can be acquired only through the effect of an investment of the power of the body: gymnastics, exercises, muscle-building, nudism, glorification of the body beautiful ... leading to the desire of one's own body.
> (Foucault 1980: 56)

In a shift from the earlier text on coercion, he moves to a statement of self-control as an autonomous practice, in 'an exercise of the self on the self, by which one attempts to develop and transform one's self and attain a certain mode of being' and a development, through training, that *exercises* and disciplines both mind and body (2000: 282). Foucault refers to the etymology of the word gymnasium, in this context, from the Greek term *gymnasia*, (meaning 'to train oneself'), which applies to 'training in a real situation, even if it has been artificially induced'. Coming from a tradition of 'sexual abstinence, physical deprivation and other rituals of purification' (240), it has analogies with the rigorous training and exercise undertaken in the realm and contexts of bodybuilding, which has its roots in the fitness gym.

Such self-control also has analogies, I suggest, within the traditions of performance and body art-practices, in rigorous performance acts and feats of physical endurance that test the limits and thresholds of the human body through the desires and discipline of excessive bodily expenditure. It is no accident that artists such as Chris Burden, Carolee Schneeman and more recently Matthew Barney have turned to the contexts of body-building and athletic training, using their own bodies as props and/or props 'tailor-made to interact with [their] own [bodies], in order to investigate specific sensual experiences' (Nemser 1971: 41) and to effect different processes of transformation.

5.

Contemporary fitness gyms, although disciplinary institutions, (appear to) appeal to notions of individuality and individualism in the adoption of practices of self-discipline and care of the 'self' that are tailored to the needs of the individual 'client' or 'consumer' through emphasis on the individual and individual choice. This implies a certain autonomy and freedom set 'within the confines of responsibility and self-control', where individuals are invited to 'work diligently and with humble determination toward their own goals, in short, to discipline themselves'. Exercise thus not only exists as such but it also acquires a certain 'value' (Sassatelli 2000: 406).

In addition, exercise acquires value by appeal to the idea of 'training in a real situation' and in relation to the 'naturalness' of the (physical) act (Foucault 2000: 282; Sassatelli 2000: 405). Exercise is therefore considered to be 'natural' because it demands the actual 'action' of the body (on the subject's own body) to be involved in a process that depends on physical effort, capability and willpower. In a gym the body is made to 'act directly' on itself by means of its own strength and physical movement, even when 'it has been artificially induced' (Foucault 2000: 240) – and even when it involves the use of exercise equipment or machinery. The function of a fitness machine is to train or 'work' a specific part of the body, working with its natural movement to 'improve' its strength and physical characteristics.

In her essay 'The Commercialization of Discipline: Keep-fit culture and its values', Roberta Sassatelli suggests that this 'docile instrumentality of the body alludes to a better, stronger individual, more in control of him or her self', with the 'naturalness' of fitness 'allud[ing] to an authenticity and willingness to "act" and to endure fatigue for self-improvement' (2000: 405).

However, the strong emphasis placed on 'pleasure and satisfaction', as opposed to fatigue and physical effort, suggests that there are also values produced around the 'enjoyment' of physical exercise. This confirms the seemingly ambivalent position of the contemporary fitness gym, which through commercialization and the notion of choice has taken disciplinary techniques into the 'sphere of leisure' and into the production of a body that responds to consumer culture though the 'enhancement of the individual' and generic notions of 'well-being' rather than through the rigours and specifics of (a) particular training or through training for something in particular.

On one hand the gym seems to make reference to the aesthetics of an ideal body, defined by specific physical characteristics (such as muscle tone, strength, energy, agility and vitality), but these characteristics, on the other hand, remain relatively abstract and are governed by the body's functionality rather than just by its physical appearance (Sassatelli 2000: 399).

In his earlier essay on *Discipline*, Foucault claims that a 'disciplined body is the prerequisite of an efficient gesture', able to sustain a range of actions and movements. This suggests a body that is resourceful and proficient and that has value. It also suggests a capable body and a body in control of self as an autonomous subject (Sassatelli 2000: 402).

6
My latest artwork takes up this concept of autonomy and self-control in a disciplined activity that takes place outside the gym environment and in the environment of the outside world. Taking the act of running as one of the most basic and natural forms of human activity that requires little or no additional equipment or machinery (to take place or to be performed), I have been developing a series of moving image/performance works that use mobile camera technologies worn on the head and body to record a series of long-distance runs.

• Prop No.16
©Véronique Chance
2005–6

• Prop No.23
© Véronique Chance
2005–6

What is recorded is the run in its entirety from my eye-view and experience of running the event. I have deliberately chosen long-distance runs as a means of working with a distance that is by its nature solitary, self-governed and physically challenging and that requires rigorous self-training, self-control and self-discipline.

Less concerned with the actual physical appearance of the body in the image, the activity and the body are framed by duration, physical effort and endurance. These control the appearance and physical movement (in the image) of the natural environment surrounding the body in which the activity (of running) is performed and recorded (where the movement of the image is directly affected by the body's physical movement). The sound of the activity also becomes a dominant feature of the work, where the body's physical effort and willingness to 'endure fatigue' becomes particularly apparent in the continuous and alternating rhythms of heavy footsteps and heavy breathing combined with the rhythm of the moving image.

This work suggests the autonomy and capability of the human subject, 'in control of him or herself through the rigours of a particular training that is self-imposed (rather than imposed by others)', but it also points to the limitations and inefficiency of the human body, where in carrying out the activity there is a continuous tension that it might not succeed or go the full course. This element of possible failure does not feature in Foucault's texts on discipline and technologies of the self, nor is it an element that is made apparent in the commercialization of discipline and in the values of keep-fit culture. In the Production of the Body Ideal, the body is made to act upon its own strength and physical movement, through which it tests its capability and willpower, but in that process there are times when the body must inevitably fail. For me there is value to be placed in this notion of failure, for the body after all is only human.

REFERENCES

Featherstone, M. (1991) 'The Body in Consumer Culture', in *The Body: Social process and cultural theory*, London, Thousand Oaks and New Delhi: Sage, pp. 170-93.

Foucault, M. (1980) 'Body/ Power', in Colin Gordon (ed.) *Power/Knowledge: Selected interviews and other writings 1972-1977*, Harvester Press, p. 56.

Foucault, M. (1991 [1975]) 'Docile Bodies' and 'The Means of Correct Training', in Michel Foucault *Discipline and Punish: The birth of the prison*, Harmondsworth: Penguin, pp. 135-69 and 170-94.

Foucault, M. (2000 [1994]) 'Technologies of the Self', in Paul Rabinow (ed.) Ethics: Subjectivity and truth / Essential works of Foucault, 1954-1984, vol. 1, Harmondsworth: Penguin, pp. 223-49.

Hollier, D. (1995) 'The Use Value of the Impossible', in Carolyn Bailey Gill *Bataille: Writing and the sacred*, London: Routledge, pp. 133-53.

Mettrie, Julien Offray de La (2008) 'Machine Man', in Ann Thompson (ed. and trans.) *Machine Man and Other Writings*, Cambridge: Cambridge University Press, pp. 1-40.

Nemser, C. (1971) 'Subject-Object Body Art', *Arts Magazine* 46(1) (September-October), pp. 38-42.

Sassatelli, R. (1999) 'Interaction Order and Beyond: A field analysis of body culture within fitness gyms, *Body and Society*, vol. 5(2-3), London, Thousand Oaks and New Delhi: Sage, pp. 227-4.

Sassatelli, R. (2000) 'The Commercialization of Discipline: Keep-fit culture and its values', trans. Anne Collins, *Journal of Modern Italian Studies* 5(3): 396-411.

Acting Freely

JOHN MATTHEWS

There is a profound dichotomy in all regimes of training: while each regime seeks to increase a participant's capacity for a particular form of action, this is frequently, if not necessarily, accomplished by reducing and restricting the ways in which trainees can act. This refers to acting both in the *theatrical* sense and in the *political* sense (associated with individual liberty; an individual's 'freedom' to act in any given setting). Negotiating this dichotomy requires managing the repressive strictures of training's regimented practices alongside the emancipating effect these regimes purport to induce. In the West, this dichotomy may be a legacy of a particular theology and efforts to manage it the bequest of ascetic monastic traditions that, according to Foucault, infiltrated subsequent social institutions and that provide something of an ur-model of training for performance (Matthews 2008: 249-56). This dichotomy can be understood through an examination of the overlap between different notions of what it means to 'act freely' in theatrical and non-theatrical situations and with reference to the co-embeddedness and 'overlap' of what has been called a 'real' and a 'virtual' world (Gordon 2006).

In the interest of exposing a meta-disciplinary feature of training for performance, this article traces a single point of 'overlap' in disciplinary rhetorics and practices by drawing from my own experiences of training in three sites - in the studio, in the clinic and in the monastery.[1] This article considers the relationship between skill-acquisition and a capacity for acting via an assessment of what is entailed in *acting freely* in the different performance environments proposed by religion, rehabilitation and theatre. This entails thinking through and interpreting what Robert Gordon has called the 'myth' central to each practice of training identifiable in the language with which practitioners describe their practice:

> each of these rhetorics becomes a kind of shorthand by means of which they can indicate the particular attitudes or methods of their craft, but at the same time each rhetoric constructs an aesthetic vocabulary that aims to validate the process it ostensibly describes. These rhetorics function as myths *justifying* the principles they express.
> (Gordon 2006: 4-5, emphasis as original)

Tracing one feature of training through these three sites requires holding in suspension three brief 'trains of thought'.

FIRST TRAIN OF THOUGHT: ACTING *THEATRICALLY*

There are few opportunities in British culture to be naked in a room of fully clothed people, but theatre affords one, well, two actually. In the twentieth-century anatomy theatres and playhouses have facilitated this experience on their stages and operating tables and in their rehearsal studios and examination rooms. Perhaps surprisingly, this was what was going through my head as I was stripping to my underwear in preparation for a physical

[1] My own participatory experiences in these three sites includes practising training exercises with members of the Odin Teatret, time spent conducting research on rehabilitation wards in South Wales and the South West throughout 2007-2008 and a period of research spent living in Worth Abbey, a Benedictine Monastery in Sussex. The physical examination that provides the central point of reference for this article was conducted on 1 January 2008. In keeping with the wishes of the physiotherapist who conducted the examination, further details have been withheld.

[2] Berlin argues that such an individual liberal ideal of freedom would appear to be a very modern doctrine because discussions of individual liberty as a political ideal are scarce in the ancient world (1969 [1958]: 129). In considering the various historical versions of this doctrine in Hobbes, Mill, Locke and others, Berlin states that such doctrines are characterized by a commitment to protect a sphere of negative freedom while accepting (to varying degrees) that limitations must be placed on the complete expansion of this sphere so that individuals can function as and within a *polis*.

3. While Alan Read (2008) has preserved some currency for the term 'acting' in Performance Studies via his mobilization of Bruno Latour's Actor Network Theory (2005) and Nicholas Ridout has aligned the term 'acting' with the 'relational aesthetics' of contemporary performance, the present moment, where makers of performance 'cannot be untheatrical enough', remains one in which acting, like 'theatricality', is a key (and negative) term (Ridout 2006: 5).

examination on a rehabilitation hospital ward in the South West of England as part of my research into rehabilitative training. Given my train of thought, it is perhaps less surprising that, as I manipulated my almost naked body for the analytic gaze of the physiotherapist, the iconic textbook images in *Towards a Poor Theatre* (1991 [1965]) of y-front-wearing actors in the studios of Jerzy Grotowski sprung to mind. Indeed theatre, as Jean-Paul Sartre observed, puts us in all kinds of situations, just one of these situations being stripped to our underwear in a room full of strangers.

In his essay 'For a Theatre of Situations' Sartre retraces the divisive line conventionally located between tragic forms, observing that the subject of the forces of fate and the subject of social or psychological forces have quite different roles to play in their own tragic demise. The concerns with a sense of existential freedom that dominated Sartre's philosophical thinking emerge in his theatrical work also, where he shuns the characters of what he calls 'psychological theatre', whose actions are 'never anything but a composition of forces whose results are predictable' (Sartre 1998 [1947]: 43), in favour of human subjects with a sovereign capacity to act:

> if it is true that man is free in a given situation and that in and through that situation he chooses what he will be, then what we have to show in theatre are simple and human situations and free individuals in these situations choosing what they will be. (43)

The different cathartic possibilities proposed by a character who is free to act and one who is freely acted upon are of no small interest to 'the theatre', but, in my particular situation, something else is also at stake in the contradicting realities of what it might mean to act freely.

SECOND TRAIN OF THOUGHT: ACTING *POLITICALLY*

Another eminent philosopher of freedom – though one less prone to writing plays – Isaiah Berlin, explored this same tension between acting and being acted upon inherent in the philosophical question of freedom in his famous essay 'Two Concepts of Liberty' (1969 [1958]). In it, Berlin traces the contrasting subjects of Sartre's theatrical situations through more than two hundred senses of the word freedom and situates these characters within a social and political context. Berlin concludes that all versions of what it means to posses freedom to act are reducible to two opposing concepts, which, he calls, 'positive' and 'negative'.

In defining negative freedom, Berlin writes, 'I am normally said to be free to the degree to which no man or body of men interferes with my activity (1969 [1958]: 122). Negative freedom, in the historical traditions of philosophy that Berlin addresses, is concerned with the reduction or absence of coercion or infringement placed on one human being by another or others.[2] Partly because of this, and partly because of the range of variables or 'magnitudes' to which it is subject, negative freedom 'is something the extent of which, in a given case, it is difficult to estimate' (130). Nevertheless, Berlin argues that it is possible to estimate the scope of an individual's freedom provided that 'total patterns of life [are] compared directly as wholes' (130), accepting that the method by which a comparison is made and the reliability of the conclusions will be difficult or impossible to demonstrate. Berlin's insistence on direct comparison between specific realms of freedom acknowledges the contingency of all notions of freedom upon their operational sphere and makes explicit the 'ecological' qualities of human action.

The notion of 'positive' freedom identified by Berlin describes a sense of the term defined by 'the wish to be a subject not an object' and to be 'self directed not acted upon by external nature or by other men as if I were a thing, an animal or a slave incapable of playing a human role' (Berlin 1969 [1958]: 131). Berlin concedes that negative freedom, as a freedom from coercion or enslavement, is not at a 'great logical distance' from a concept of positive freedom as the capacity to liberate oneself from such fetters (131).

THIRD TRAIN OF THOUGHT: ACTING IN THE OVERLAP

Tracing any correspondence between these competing concepts of freedom and the different situations of theatrical characters takes on an added complexity when one considers that 'acting' can also be understood in at least two ways. Given the ambiguous meaning of the phrase 'to act', and the ambivalence with which contemporary performance regards traditional notions of acting,[3] it is probably unsurprising that Robert Gordon recently defined it as a term that denotes two primary meanings, which overlap. He writes that acting as *doing* in the sense of acting 'in the real world' is difficult if not impossible to fully separate from acting as *pretending* in the sense of acting 'symbolically' in what he refers to as 'the virtual place' of play (2006: 1-2).[4] The co-embeddedness of the real and the virtual, and the overlap of what is entailed by 'acting' in each, has been dramatically demonstrated by numerous deaths 'in play'; Molière's collapse during a performance of *The Hypochondriac* a suitably dramatic-ironic testament to the failure of virtual times and spaces of play to exempt participants from biological imperatives.

With these three trains of thought now in play and held in suspension, I resuscitate the description of me in my underwear before, as it were, I catch a cold.

FIRST SITE: IN THE CLINIC

The tasks I undertook during my examination, instructed by a physiotherapist, replicate what the rehabilitation community calls 'real world kinematics', or the simplified components of the more complex activities that make up daily life. Each of these simplified components must be repeated several times during examination so that the physiotherapist can observe the range of a patient's movement and so, for over an hour, I found myself engaged in simple repetitive activities: getting in and out of a bed, sitting down in and getting up from a chair, raising a glass to my lips and lowering it to a table and walking up and down a hallway, while the physiotherapist looking on diligently made notes. After all this I was presented with the document shown in Figure 1, and I was struck by the fact that I, an apparently fit and healthy individual, am presented with a significantly effaced diagrammatic chart representing my body. Each pencil line and scribbled note details a weakness or misalignment, the most alarming to me being an westward facing arrow drawn across my groin bordered by the words 'lateral shift' - of all places to have lateral shift! In my consultation with the physiotherapist after my examination, I was

4. This is, he maintains, because childhood role-playing informs and supports the kind of social role-playing on which society relies, but it also is the case because to act 'symbolically' is also to act 'really', since, when an actor on stage sits down or accepts a cream bun, they *really* sit down and *really* take the cake. Conversely, the kind of social role-playing in which things *really* get done in the *real world* relies on the symbolism of action as so many, following Searle (1969) and Goffman (1959), have shown.

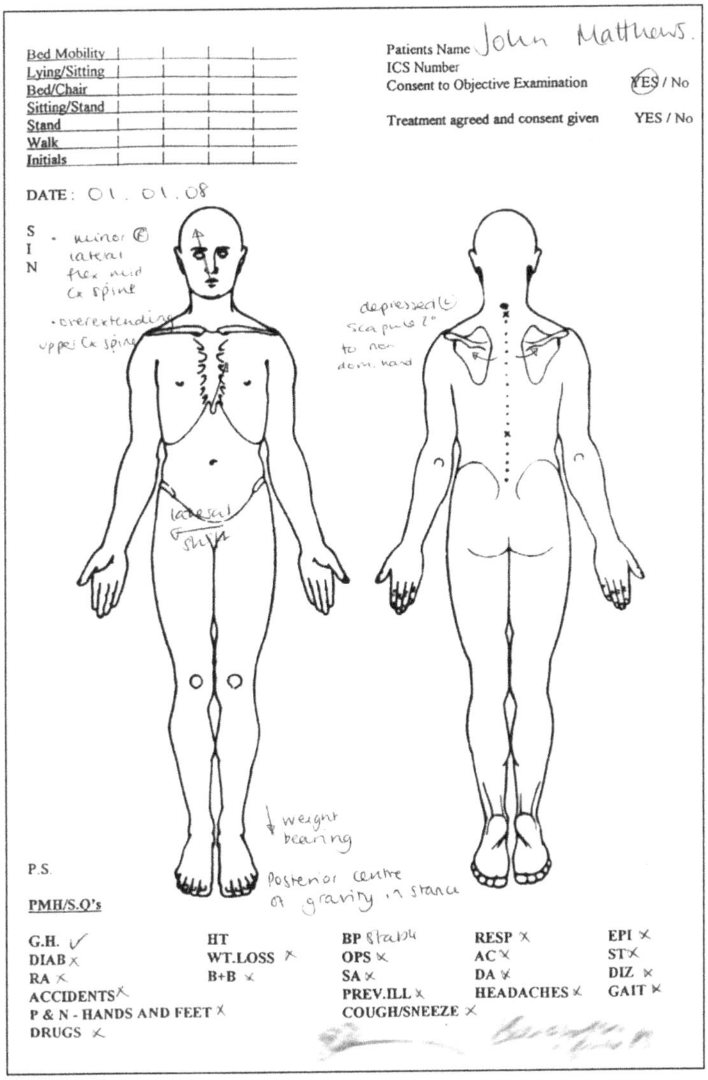

• Figure 1

relived to discover that this lateral shift gave no great cause for concern – my spine shows 'no abnormality' (see Figure 2) – but somewhat alarmed to learn that the tightness in my calf muscles and subsequent failure of my knees to fully extend (see Figure 3) may actually require a therapeutic response. The physiotherapist showed me a simple calf-stretching exercise, as one might do before playing sport, and advised me to undertake this on a daily basis to lengthen the muscles and prevent further tightening. This exercise, involving placing both feet in a straight line heel to toe with one foot about half a meter in front of the other and leaning forward, would, I was told, with repeated practice, make my walking and running more efficient and reduce the strain on my hamstrings, which were currently compensating for tightness lower down in my legs.

Having spent time leading up to this examination conducting research into rehabilitative training after stroke on residential hospital wards and in care homes in South Wales, I was well aware that my own diagrammatic was not as heavily graffitied as the charts of many others, such as Ian Wilding, a resident at Dan Yr Bryn Care Home in Cardiff who contributed towards this research. Diagrams such as those shown in this article are produced at regular intervals during the treatment of a patient undergoing rehabilitation and are compiled along with other medical records, treatment schedules and prognoses in a giant lever-arch folder usually referred to as an Individual Care Plan. Just as with mine, Ian's physiotherapeutic examination had given rise to a treatment schedule that included stretches not dissimilar, though more extensive, to those proscribed for my tight calf muscles. His daily programme of stretching exercises, which includes stretches for all his limbs, is designed to strengthen muscles and keep them strong, prevent stiffness from becoming permanent, improve coordination and blood circulation, reduce pressures, sores and, perhaps most importantly, regain functional abilities.

In the context of rehabilitation, 'functional abilities' refer to the combination of simple bodily movements associated with the necessary activities of daily living such as bathing, eating and drinking. Functional abilities are those that enable an individual to sustain their own social and biological life. Ian has recently contributed to a television advertising campaign for a group of care homes wherein he explains the obstacles to the practice of his own functional abilities through telling an anecdote about buying sweets for his children:

> I tend to only go to places that are accessible. Recently I've come across places which aren't, which are a bit difficult for me. I only wanted to buy some sweets for my children and I went down to the sweet shop and I couldn't get in. Makes me feel a bit cross,

• Figure 2

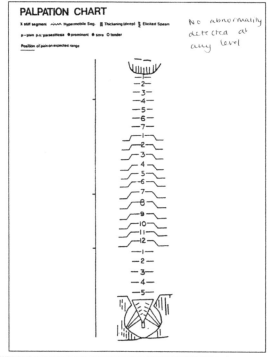

• Figure 3

really frustrated more than anything. I lose the will to get sweets then.   (Wilding 2008)

Ian's anecdote is followed by a female voice admonishing the viewer to 'look again at disability'. The story Ian tells in this commercial evinces the fact that the 'real world' is constructed to suit certain bodies, or rather to suit individuals who can *do their bodies in certain ways* (Matthews 2008: 48-56). The invitation to look again invites one to see that, apart from the social and professional disablement caused by a physical disability, which is supposedly mitigated by equal opportunities legislation, there is the rather more prosaic question of the ergonomics of the 'real world' and the kinematics these proscribe. To be free to act in the real world is a matter of acquiring the kinematics of functional abilities predetermined by the human construction of the real world. The constructed ergonomics of such a real world give rise to what Hughes and Paterson note are 'vast tracts of space [which are] no-go-areas' (2003: 146). The response of the real world to impairment has been what they call 'anthropemic' in denying disabled people access to sites, spaces and practices of power and privilege (including, of course, theatres). The construction of the real world to assist in and insist on the performance of particular kinematics is extensive, and providing disabled access to certain spaces, while going some way towards offsetting the anthropemic effects of these ergonomics, does not constitute a sufficient retooling to make this world comfortably inhabitable by the physically impaired, as Ian explains. While the advertising campaign aims to generate momentum in a drive towards such a retooling, Ian's own therapeutic treatment operates under a more limited objective in the sense that, rather than stimulating a reconstruction of the real world, it aims to train the individual so that they can perform its already designed and subsequently obligatory kinematics.

One only needs to look at the unmarked body outlined in Figure 1 - well nourished, proportional, complete - to confirm what Deborah Lupton has shown, that the idealized body of Western medicine is the obligatory body of such a real world, a virile body that is also affluent, as is implicit in the simple fact that it has access to nutrition and treatments (1995: 124). The kind of freedom to act that rehabilitative physiotherapy aims to provide for recovering patients is similar to, if not identical with, the freedom of action they enjoyed before onset of injury or disability and, as such, is always oriented by the activities of the real world. Indeed the main assumption underpinning Carr's and Shepherd's 'motor learning approach' (1987, 1989, 2003) is that 'regaining activities of daily living ... requires a relearning process that is similar to the learning process for non-impaired people' (in Barnes et al. 2005: 229). Within this process, the activities of everyday living, which are associated with the capacity to act in the real world, are said to consist of essential components, 'the invariant kinematics of an activity', which are both 'task and context specific' (229). In order to regain the ability to accomplish the tasks of daily living and to act freely in the real world, training replicates the task and context of a given real world movement to create functional tasks in functional settings. The therapist observes and analyses, noting the 'missing' or poorly controlled sections of the kinematics of a particular functional task, which are then transposed into physical exercises practised extensively in training, not only under the supervising gaze of the therapist but in a range of non-supervised environments in order to promote 'carry-over' into real world situations. The operation of what Foucault called the 'great myth of the free gaze' (2003 [1963]: 61) that 'traverses a sick body [and] attains the truth' (72) is as essential to this process as any other clinical treatment. What is particularly interesting about this treatment, however, is the emphasis placed on 'carry-over' by the focus on functional settings for training exercises that not only replicate but are the same as those of the 'real world'.

Williams, Davids and Williams, studying skill-acquisition in the attendant bio-medical field of sports science, emphasize the need to understand the relationship between an environment and the development of functional kinematics that operate within an environment, a relationship that 'implies that the performer and environment can best be understood as a system' (1999: 194). They argue that the focus of study on skill-acquisition 'should be on how animals typically produce a tight fit between the environment and their actions' (194-5). Recognizing that the constructed environment of the real world produces an ecology that specifically enables and supports the performance of non-impaired activities, Robert Fawcus points out, in his book on stroke rehabilitation, that re-learning of everyday skills must map onto the 'action schemata' of activities within this ecology;

> during motor learning and re-learning we are acquiring action schemata ... If therapy is developing the acquisition of schemata or prototypical knowledge about the skill under training, then it follows that the quality of the required schemata depends largely on the variability of practice. Taken in conjunction with the plasticity of the neuromuscular system, only the faithful repetition of normal movement patterns in all relevant situations will rehabilitate sensorimotor skills effectively. (2000: 76)

Fawcus's notion of action schemata, like the notion of the kinematics of an activity, recognizes the ecological nature of skill-acquisition and performance. Indeed Fawcus points out that, given the accord between particular ecologies and particular bodies, 'learning by means of isolated non-action-specific movement will be useless' (76). Instead, Fawcus argues that the challenge for rehabilitation is to enable a trainee to acquire action schemata that don't easily produce what Williams et al. call a 'tight fit' with impaired bodies. To mobilize Gordon's terms, the freedom to act within an everyday ecology, while undoubtedly tied into the symbolic activities of social existence (i.e., Ian Wilding's role as father and consumer) is, in the case of rehabilitation training, intimately associated with biological survival because of its focus on an individual's independent performance of 'real world' action schemata of eating (sweets?), drinking, cleansing and other activities coupled with the biological life of an organism.

It is very important to be clear at this stage about precisely how Berlin's notion of political freedom must be understood within the realms of everyday living, particularly with respect to rehabilitation patients, given that Berlin is clear that mere incapacity to attain a goal does not constitute a lack of freedom (Berlin 1969 [1958]: 122). Berlin is unequivocal that infringements on negative freedom can only be affected on a human by other humans, and it is the very fact, as testified to by Ian, that the 'real world' is as artificial as the 'virtual' reality of theatre that results in the curtailment of the negative freedom of physically impaired actors, and if anyone should doubt the seriousness of such curtailment, they need only reflect on how it stands between Ian and the satisfaction of his biological needs.

SECOND SITE: IN THE STUDIO

Entering back into the overlap between the virtual and the real, alongside skill-acquisition in rehabilitation I want to consider a different example of training – an exercise I participated in with actors from the Odin Teatret (one of a select group of contemporary theatre companies who practise training daily). In this exercise two trainees work together with a length of strong ribbon or rope, holding either end as though engaged in a tug of war. In the first phase of the exercise the two trainees explore the possibilities of movement enabled by the support of their partner's weight at the other end of the rope. Both find that they can, with the support of their partner at the other end, lean, crouch, reach and make new shapes with their bodies. In the next phase the two trainees devise a short choreography that includes three balances (in tableau) using the support of the rope. The partners practise this sequence until they can both move comfortably from one balance to the next and hold each balance in a controlled fashion for a short period of time. In the final phase of the exercise the rope is removed and the trainees have to find a way to perform their sequence without the support of their partner at the other end of the rope. The support that was coming from the partner at the other end of the rope must now be found within the body, and between the body and the floor.

This exercise would appear to focus on the acquisition of decidedly 'virtual' skills, given that it culminates in a 'symbolic' representation of a realistic dramatic fiction. In this respect the exercise has a very actorly application for performers in a modern tradition of a theatre of verisimilitude: through repeated practice participants develop and refine the ability to convincingly represent the absent rope and to maintain the representation of the presence of its absence throughout the choreography. However, unlike the functional kinematics of rehabilitation, these action schemata are seldom transposed directly into performance but rather are for 'the formation of actors' (Barba 2002:100).

Since the advent of what Eugenio Barba has called 'the age of exercises' (Barba 2002: 100) in the twentieth century, skill-acquisition has played 'a secondary role' (Watson 2000: 219) in practices of actor training in Europe. In the wake of Grotowski's 'via negativa' and the increased awareness of 'Eastern' actor and performer training routines and techniques in Europe, twentieth- and twenty-first-century training practitioners have focused on the 'eradication of blocks' (Grotowski 1991 [1965]: 17), in place of the acquisition of skills, and the channelling of 'pre-expressive' performance capabilities (Barba 1995: 104) as well as the cultivation of affective 'states' (Zarrilli 2002: 182) or 'conditions' (Watson 2000: 219) of body and mind. Towards the end of twentieth century Joseph Roach tracked the connections between the decline of actor training programmes consisting of skill-acquisition exercises and the rise of what Barba has called 'exercises for the formation of the actor' (Barba 2002: 100) alongside developments in physical therapy and psychotherapy to show that in a late-twentieth-century moment, 'we [now] believe that spontaneous feelings, if they can be located and identified, must be extracted with difficulty from beneath layers of inhibition' (1993: 218).[5] In focusing on the eradication of blocks and the return to a prelapsarian, 'pre-cultural' or 'pre-expressive' state of embodiment, these late-twentieth-century models of actor training lay claim to what Barba has called a 'transcultural physiology' (Barba and Savarese 1991: 118) that pre-exists all culturally codified modes of expression. The Odin's programmes of actor training, rather than focusing on the acquisition of performance skills – which would be allied to the delimited kinematics of codified systems for the signification of meaning associated with any given culture – have attended to 'acquiring through training ... certain bodily tensions and oppositions, certain ways of moving, vocalizing and gesturing [that] lead performers to their "extra-daily" bodies, their special non-ordinary bodies' (Watson 1993: xi). Laying claim to a transcultural physiology is problematic for a number of reasons, not only because of the apparent insensitivity it enacts towards the ownership of cultural practices but also because it lays claim to a unified and unifying notion of the human self. Here, this tradition of twentieth-century actor training comes into contact with the central paradox Berlin identified in his study of forms of freedom. He argues that any system that lays claim to an essential self must negotiate between the self-realization of the individual (his or her positive freedom) and their enslavement (or reduction of negative liberty) because the proponents of such a system can 'ignore the actual wishes of men or societies ... [and] bully, oppress, torture in the name and on behalf of their "real" selves' (Berlin 1969 [1958]: 132).

Clearly there is a difference of 'magnitude' between any such 'oppression' in voluntary

[5] It is important to note that, as Nicholas Ridout has observed, despite the declining importance of skill-acquisition to European actor training, the 'necessity' of the reconciliation of 'repetition with the equally exacting necessity of apparent spontaneity' has remained central to modern theories of acting (Ridout 2006: 20).

[6] Several academics have explored the 'eastern' spiritual and performance-based influences on Jerzy Grotowski during his studies in Moscow and his travels in central Asia (Meyer-Dinkgraefe 2006: 74-80; Lavy, 2005: 175). With respect to other religious traditions and practices Schechner refers to Grotowski's research into 'old forms of Christianity' (1997:476) and Osinski notes the 'hermit ... asceticism' (1997: 398) of his work.

[7] Dykstra's description of the wide-reaching effects of formation - 'the faith community has formative power in the lives of people. It can nurture their faith and give shape to the quality and character of their spirits' (in Astley et al. 1996: 252) - reflects what he calls a 'general consensus ... among religious educators at the present time' (252).

[8] According to Kumiega, Grotowski asserted that Stanislavski's primary legacy to the profession of acting was his emphasis on the need for daily training (1987: 110) and Wolford observes that in her experiences 'Grotowski consistently upheld this mandate, requiring the actors under his direction to engage in regular physical and vocal training' (in Hodge 2000: 198).

[9] John Dillon observes that the archetypical practices of restraint and denial can be traced back through the historical development of Western traditions of asceticism to Plato's Phaedo and two implied conceptualizations of the relationship between body and soul. One interpretation of the

participation in actor training regimes and the state-based oppression of a tyrant. If we take Berlin's advice and compare total patterns of life directly as wholes, we also couldn't fail to conclude that the voluntary participant in actor training is more free, even in a negative sense, than a physically impaired individual trying to operate in the 'real world'. Likewise, if we do compare directly these situations as patternated wholes, we cannot fail to conclude that they are of the same *order* even if not of the same *magnitude*.

Any conception of the human that is predicated upon certain essential qualities of self necessarily generates a 'myth' of self-development in the terms of positive freedom, precisely because the recognition or uncovering of these essential qualities must entail a more 'true' realization of oneself. Here, as Berlin notes, we are on dangerous ground because, with enough manipulation of the definition of a true self, 'freedom can be made to mean whatever the manipulator wishes' (Berlin 1969 [1958]: 134). It is at this point in history that, perhaps incongruously, the myths of actor training begin to resonate with the myths of asceticism, not only in the sacrificial rhetoric of 'holy' actors but in the negotiation between a curtailment of negative liberty and an increase of positive freedom.

In appropriating the term 'formation' from Christian monasticism to denote the evacuation of skill-acquisition exercises from actor training in the twentieth century, Barba is, perhaps unwittingly, achieving more than the continuation of the 'religious impulse' that Joseph Roach identified in the theatre practice of his mentor (Roach 1993 [1985]: 225).[6] What formation describes for Barba and for monastics is the deeply personally-felt cultivation of the self and the experience of making enduring changes to the self at levels that transcend the possession of new skills acquired through the practising of tasks.[7] Formation is more than a process of acquiring the capacity to perform new functional or aesthetic skills; it is also a process of undergoing significant and lasting changes that

affect aspects of a trainee's lived experience extending beyond training.

THIRD SITE: IN THE CLOISTER

The time I spent living in a Benedictine monastery in Sussex in 2006 as part of my research into performance training confirmed what Richard Marsden, following Foucault, has written about monasteries: that the monastery has spawned many transformative institutions and practices because it is 'the ideal-typical enclosure [and] source of many contemporary organizational techniques' (1999: 159). The daily training of the Odin recalls the daily timetabling and organization of activities in a monastery that deliberately and conspicuously foreclose on an individual's negative freedom. What Foucault called the monastery's 'three great methods' for controlling activity - 'establish rhythms, impose particular occupations, regulate the cycles of repetition' (1991 [1975]: 149) - which infiltrated schools, hospitals, workshops and workhouses, may have only been properly instituted in European actor training during the twentieth century.[8] The freedom that is attained through such restrictions of an individual's negative liberty in the monastery - restrictions, it is important to note, that are actively chosen by the subjects of training unlike the subjects of Discipline (Matthews 2008: 138-41, 165-73) - is tied into a belief in an essential self associated with the divine. It is precisely because the freedom achieved through monastic training is one associated with a transcendental spiritual dimension of divinity that it is mapped into a 'real world' ecology of restraint and denial.[9]

The routines of morning and evening stretches and medical examination I observed on rehabilitation wards also reflect the organization of the monastic day. In the clinic, the myth of the essential self is associated with the healthy ideal body of Western medicine - the differential between my body and the ideal made explicitly clear in the scribbled notes in Figure 1. The different situations identified by Sartre are, of course, representative of differing philosophical concepts of selfhood, and this difference maps onto the paradox Berlin observes inherent in any estimation of an individual's capacity to act freely. Just as acting theories have wrestled, and continue to wrestle, with Diderot's paradox (Roach 1993 [1985]: 116-59, 218-26), theatrical and non-theatrical trainings negotiate Berlin's paradox as they prepare and equip actors to act in specific 'real world' and 'virtual' contexts. However, it is precisely because acting in either context entails an overlap of the symbolic and the real that training involves redefining the relationship between an individual's 'real' biological self and their 'virtual' social or cultural 'self'.

Patrick Olivelle argues that there is a tension inherent within monastic asceticism whereby 'creation' rubs up against 'deconstruction' in a process of ascetical transformation as the body as biological material and latent transcendent capacity separates from the body as social construct. He argues that 'ascetic creation' is in actuality 'a deconstruction of the socially created body', and that, as such, 'the ascetic deconstruction of the body has to be located ... within the socially constructed correspondence between the two bodies - the physical and the social' (1995: 188-89). As Molière has shown, the biological continues alongside the social even as it is particularly done by it and the correlation between these two bodies corresponds to the overlap between 'symbolic acting' and 'real acting' in the co-embedded ecologies of the real and the virtual. While what it means to act freely in each particular real and virtual context of performance entails the acquisition or possession of certain specific capabilities, at a meta-disciplinary level, training to act in the cloister, the clinic and the studio entails the redefinition of the correspondence between the 'physical' and the 'social' self and the balancing of negative and positive freedom. As Ian Wilding has testified, the physical capacity for action is intimately connected with the capacity for social and political action, and both are entailed in the definition, to ourselves and to others, of who we are in every situation - naked or otherwise - wherein we act.

REFERENCES

Barba, E. (1995) *The Paper Canoe: A Guide to Theatre Anthropology*, trans. R. Fowler London and New York: Routledge.

Barba, E. (2002) 'An Amulet Made of Memory: The Significance of Exercises in the Actor's Dramatury' in Zarrilli, P.B. (ed) *Acting (re)considered: A Practical and Theoretical Guide*, London & New York: Routledge, pp. 99-106

Barba, E. and Savarese, N. (1991) *A Dictionary of Theatre Anthropology: The secret art of the performer*, London and New York: Routledge.

Barnes, M. P., Dobkin, B. H. and Bogousslavsky, J. (eds) (2005) *Recovery After Stroke*, Cambridge: Cambridge University Press.

Berlin, I. (1969 [1958]) 'Two Concepts of Liberty', in *Four Essays on Liberty*, Oxford: Oxford University Press.

Carr, J. H. and Shepherd, R. B. (1987) *A Motor Learning Model for Stroke*, Oxford: Butterworth Heinemann.

Carr, J. H. and Shepherd, R. B. (1989) 'A Motor Learning Model for Stroke Rehabilitation', *Physiotherapy* 75: 372-380.

Carr, J. H. and Shepherd, R. B. (2003) *Stroke Rehabilitation: Guidelines for exercise and training to optimize motor skill*, Oxford: Butterworth Heinemann.

Dillon, J. (1995) 'Rejecting the Body, Refining the Body: Some remarks on the development of Platonist asceticism', in V. L. Wimbrush and R. Valantasis (eds) *Asceticism*, Oxford: Oxford University Press, pp. 80-87.

Dykstra, C.R. (1996) 'The Formative Power of the Congregation' in Astley, J.F, & Crowder, C. (eds) *Theological Perspectives on Christian Formation: A Reader on Theology*, Grand Rapids: Eerdmans, pp.252-265.

Fawcus, R. (2000) *Stroke Rehabilitation: A collaborative approach*, Oxford: Blackwell.

Foucault, M. (2003 [1963]) *The Birth of the Clinic: An archaeology of medical perception*, trans. A. M. Sheridan, London: Routledge.

Foucault, M. (1991 [1975]) *Discipline and Punish: The birth of the prison*, trans. A. M. Sheridan, London: Penguin.

word *phroura*, 'prison', in Socrates statement 'we men are en tini phrourai and one ought not to release oneself from this or run away', led to the development of a 'world-negating' version of asceticism (1995: 81). This version is also associated with a Pythagorean dictum, known to Plato, that the body (*soma*) is a tomb (*sema*) for the soul. But Dillon also explains that *phroura* as well as meaning 'prison' can also mean 'guard post', and it is through this interpretation that a 'world-affirming' conception of asceticism develops that views restraint and denial as associated not with rejection of the world but with a 'refining of the body, to make it a worthy, or at least non-injurious receptacle of the soul' (81).

Goffman, E. (1959) *The Presentation of Self in Everyday Life*, New York: Doubleday.

Gordon, R. (2006) *The Purpose of Playing: Modern theories of acting in perspective*, Ann Arbor: University of Michigan Press.

Grotowski, J. (1991 [1965]) *Towards a Poor Theatre*, London: Methuen.

Hodge, A. (2000) (ed) *Twentieth Century Actor Training*, London and New York: Routledge

Hughes, B. and Paterson, K. (2003) 'The Social Model of Disability and the Disappearing Body', in A. Blaikie (ed.) *The Body: Critical concepts in sociology*, London: Routledge, pp. 146-163.

Kloczowski, J. (2000) *A History of Polish Christianity*, Cambridge: Cambridge University Press.

Kumiega, J. (1987) *The Theatre of Grotowski*, London: Methuen.

Latour, B. (2005) *Reassembling the Social: An introduction to actor network theory*, Oxford: Oxford University Press.

Lavy, J. (2005) 'Theoretical Foundations of Grotowski's Total Act, Via Negativa and Conjuctio Opposortium', *The Journal of Religion and Theatre* 4(2): 175-88.

Lupton, D. (1995) *The Imperative of Health: Public Health and the Regulated Body*, Thousand Oaks, California: Sage Publications.

Marsden, R. (1999) *The Nature of Capital: Marx after Foucault*, London and New York: Routledge.

Matthews, J. (2008) *What is Called Training? A meta-disciplinary study of training for performance*, University of Surrey, doctoral thesis.

Meyer-Dinkgraefe, D. (2006) *Approaches to Acting: Past and present*, London: Continuum.

Olivelle, Patrick (1995) 'Deconstruction of the Body in Indian Asceticism', in V. L. Wimbrush and R. Valantasis (eds) *Asceticism*, Oxford: Oxford University Press, pp. 188-210.

Osinski, Z. (1997) 'Grotowski Blazes the Trails: From Objective Drama to Art as Vehicle' in Wolford, L. & Schechner R. (eds) *The Grotowski Sourcebook*, New York: Routledge, pp. 385-403

Read, A. (2008) *Theatre, Intimacy and Engagement: The last human venue*, Basingstoke, Hampshire, and New York: Palgrave MacMillan.

Ridout, N. (2006) *Stage Fright: Animals and other theatrical problems*, Cambridge: Cambridge University Press.

Roach, Joseph (1993 [1985]) *The Player's Passion: Studies in the science of acting*, Newark: University of Delaware Press.

Sartre, J.-P. (1998 [1947]) 'For a Theatre of Situations', in Brandt (ed) *Modern Theories of Drama*, Oxford: Clarendon Press.

Schechner, R. (1997) 'Exoduction: shape-shifter, Shaman, Trickster, Artist, Adept, Director, Leader, Grotowski'; 'A Polish Catholic Hasid' in Wolford, L. & Schechner R. (eds) *The Grotowski Sourcebook*, New York: Routledge, pp. 157-160, 462-494.

Searle, J. R. (1969) *Speech Acts: An essay in the philosophy of language*, Cambridge: Cambridge University Press.

Watson, I. (1993) *Towards a Third Theatre: Eugenio Barba and the Odin Teatret*, London and New York: Routledge.

Watson, I (2000) 'Training with Eugenio Barba: Acting Principles, the Pre-expressive and personal temperature' in Hodge, A. (ed) *Twentieth Century Actor Training*, London & New York: Routledge, pp. 209-223.

Wilding, Ian (2008) in 'Creature Discomforts', <www.creaturediscomforts.org> (accessed 2 January 2009).

Williams, A. M., Davids, K. and Williams, J. G. (1999) *Visual Perception and Action in Sport*, London: E. and F. N. Spon (Routledge)

Zarrilli, P.B. (2002) "On the Edge of a Breath, Looking": Cultivating the Actor's Bodymind through Asian Martial/Meditation Arts in Zarrilli, P.B. (ed) *Acting (re)considered: A Practical and Theoretical Guide*, London & New York: Routledge, pp. 181-199.

Partisan Warfare
Training, commitment and the politics of entertainment

WOLF-DIETER ERNST

1.

One of the subjects of the performance 'We are all Marlene Dietrich FOR' by the Iceland Dance Company is the process of training. In this regard what we as the audience see during the show are trained dancers, performers and musicians. The performance leaves no doubt that the ensemble as a whole has undergone an intensive training. Unlike in classical ballet, where the routines appear to be performed with no trouble at all, in 'We are all Marlene Dietrich FOR' we witness how the performing bodies sweat, struggle and fall. As in a fitness studio or in rock 'n' roll performances, our attention is drawn to the body working hard.

Additionally, training is explicitly questioned. In one of the scenes, at which I now want to take a closer look, the dancers train the audience. A coach with a red feather boa around her neck enters the stage and starts to explain and demonstrate a simple movement and breathing exercise to the audience. Her voice has the constant cheery undertone that the entertainers at Club Med have. Her instructions are as follows:

• Fig. 1 Doing the splits. Scene from *We are all Marlene Dietrich FOR*.
© Iceland Dance Company.

Okay, we are going to start with something simple. Just clapping our hands. Everybody. Clap your hands! Everybody can do this! Really work those muscles. Okay. And every time you work those muscles, we need to stretch them. So we just stretch up. And down. Relax. And again. Stretch up and down. One more time. Stretch really high. And down. Good. Now we do some stomach exercise. For all those beer bellies. And we just are going to go. Hah! Hah! Come on! Louder. Very good, people. Now we just are going to relax. Wave our hands side to side. Everybody to the same side. Don't hit the person next to you. Okay. And on every side we say. Yeah, yeah … Yeah, very good people. Okay. Now we are going to put it all together. Make like a little routine. So we do two of each. We do two claps. Two stretches. Hah! Hah! and Yeah! Yeah! (transcribed from the DVD)

The audience follow these instructions willingly. But as the performance continues, the atmosphere obviously changes. The audience for example has to witness the dancers doing the splits and at the same time ending up in the most uncomfortable positions over and over again. Their dislocated bodies during that process even try to move forward. The dancers deliberately reduce their appearance to being both mere creatures and objects of the voyeuristic glance. For the audience it is rather irritating to realize how the seemingly agonized bodies on stage appear to become less human.

The aspect of severe discipline in physical training also becomes apparent in some visually intriguing sequences of 'We are all Marlene Dietrich'. We see the drum player bandage his own head with gaffer tape, one of the dancers starts to fill her mouth with what appears to be nails as if to silence herself, another dancer declaims a text while remaining in an extremely difficult Yoga-Asana. While she is bending her legs up behind her ears, her body rests on her palms. One might even say, this performance in some ways resembles the Body Art of the early 1970s.

Having seen the above-mentioned painful acts and the reminiscence of self-humiliation they invoke, the audience is asked to show commitment again. At the end of the show, the animation routine is repeated, and of course it fails. This time, the spectators remain seated. What the company performs, reminds me of what Judith Butler has pointed out as the logic of performative citationality: the training sequence is a citation of previous performances of training. Training can be copied – and, indeed, most of the time performers are keen to perform a copy of what has been rehearsed – but it can also be counterfeited. The latter is demarcated by the repetition of the sequence. According to the well-calculated failure of the performance, the audience becomes aware that by its very presence it always has an active role in the performance. It is up to the audience to decide whether one should show commitment or should remain passive. Through the experiment in training the audience, the performance leaves the realm of entertainment, or rather entertainment is both questioned and reinforced.

The title of the piece is telling: It refers to the German singer, actress and sex symbol Marlene Dietrich, one of the greatest entertainers of her time. It is of particular interest that Dietrich supported the Allied Forces in World War 2. Moreover the prefix 'FOR' reminds us of recent NATO peacekeeping actions (e.g., KFOR) or those led by the UN and recalls images of bombing and bloodshed in Serbia and Kosovo during the late 1990s. The title contrasts the moral integrity of Dietrich as an entertainer, who was acting politically, with the contemporary state of global warfare, which bears less clarity. Thus, the title already raises the question of whether entertainment can promote a moral standpoint at all. Or is it true that entertainment especially is always on the wrong side, as it only compensates for the wounds caused by a politically motivated use of violence. The performance of 'We are all Marlene Dietrich FOR' refers to a political dilemma concerning entertainment. In its claim not to be political, entertainment might be a powerful political tool. This, however, would question the notion of entertainment in its literal sense, which is to hold together, to prevent from collision or falling apart, to keep a group of people interested or amused. In entertainment the audience normally would participate passively, as in cinema, theatre, circus, dance and music. More active participation, as in games and sports, can rather be associated with the notion of recreation. While the title states a moral dilemma, the embodiment of entertainment poses a paradox. The more the performer's trained body would try to hide that it actually promises entertainment, the more we would be curious to learn about this secret art of entertainment! How, then, can a trained performer deny that he has undergone training?

In order to discuss this paradox of training and its political implications it is helpful to refer to Carl Schmitt's 'Theory of the Partisan'. I will borrow the concept of the partisan, which Schmitt discusses in its political setting within military history and political theory, as a metaphor to describe the twofold nature of training. As I would like to argue, training is a prerequisite for accomplishing certain objectives, but it also carries in itself an uncontrollable aesthetic effect on the beholder. Let us first recall the political theory of the partisan according to the German professor of law Carl Schmitt (1888-1985).

2.
Carl Schmitt is probably best-known as the author of 'The concept of political' (1996 [1932]), an essay in which he tries to define state autonomy upon the distinction between friend and enemy, alias the other. While this attempt to get away from party politics is widely noticed and discussed within legal and political philosophy by thinkers including Jacques Derrida, Giorgio Agamben and Heiner Müller, it is of particular interest in discussing the paradox of training to look at a later text by Schmitt, 'The theory of the Partisan' (2007 [1963]). In this essay, Schmitt observed that the demarcation of friend and enemy, which his earlier work claimed to be crucial, becomes blurred in post-war partisan conflicts. The partisan draws Schmitt's attention, because he is defined by a set of extraordinary features: a partisan is not uniformed but nonetheless acts collectively, which often takes the enemy by surprise. The partisan has undergone extensive training and drill; he is therefore highly efficient even in combat against stronger and better-equipped enemies. The partisan is more mobile and tactically more efficient than any unit operating within ordinary military structures. And finally, in spite of his weak position between conventional battle lines, he is more motivated than any other soldier. While the latter is being paid for conducting military operations, the former fights for immaterial or symbolic profit, which he also gains in the form of civil resistance by citizens of the opposing nation. It is especially this moral support, caused by partisan warfare, that corrupts Schmitt's concept of the political as being defined by a clear-cut definition of friend and enemy. The partisan, in his super-motivated action, aims at a target outside the battlefield. At least this was the case in the Vietnam War, when US peace activists called for support for the Vietcong. The success of the Vietcong partisans was in raising awareness and winning moral support for their interests by others, e.g., the media. Their military actions aimed at the enemy, and at the same time they referred to an off-scene, which is not actively taking part in the battle. In theatrical terms, this would be the audience.

This brings me back to the training routine in The Icelandic Dance Company's production of 'We are all Marlene Dietrich FOR'. If we think of the paradoxical attempt to try to hide the evidence of the trained body, the metaphor of the partisan reveals a certain double bind of the partisan's action. It is the partisan, as well as the trained body, that acts indirectly, hidden and in a moral sense obscene. Playing via the off-scene, he seems to raise extra attention, to show extra motivation, even moral support. But at the same time, in doing so, he transforms the spectacle into something else. In Schmitt's case, the partisan undermines the logic of friend and enemy. In our case, the trained body subverts the subject of the spectacle when trying to make a point against the legal and moral entanglement of entertainment and warfare. In doing the splits, screaming and crawling, the body is apparently trying to avoid producing a pleasant spectacle, but at the same time it is showing dazzling technical skills.

3.

After discussing the metaphor of the partisan to understand the paradox of the trained body, a question arises. Could any form of staged training ever compete with the logical and substantial results of training processes in the military, revolutionary or even terrorist field? At least this is a question indicated in the call for papers for this issue. Are political and aesthetic conflicts really comparable with each other? One would say, no. In contrast to the stage performance, the acts of soldiers or suicide bombers are irreversible. I remember that by the time I saw 'We are all Marlene Dietrich FOR' in 2005 in Groningen, I had just stated this very sentence in front of my students at the Theatre Department of the University in Hildesheim. They had brought up in class the idea of attending a military training. It had been their task to provide a proposal for their practice-based research project on the subject of 'Collective Bodies in Art'. They were obviously attracted to the experience of the severe discipline in the German Bundeswehr barracks, where the students intended to stay while doing their research. Of course, there was a certain aspect of provocation in it, too. They embraced the idea of becoming part-time members of the army, while usually all German art students try to avoid conscription using any excuses they can think of.

After I saw 'We are all Marlene Dietrich FOR', I changed my mind about reversibility being a strong argument against the concepts of training and drill. I was intrigued by the feelings of uncertainty and uneasiness the collective performance of the dancers and musicians caused in me. There surely was a certain kind of entertainment to it, entertainment in terms of skilfully produced visual and acoustic effects or pleasant moments. These moments, on the other hand, are carefully counter-balanced with what might be perceived as shocking and violent

• Fig. 2 Confronting the audience. Scene from *We are all Marlene Dietrich FOR*. © Iceland Dance Company.

moments, e.g., the bonding, the 'spasm routines', the screaming addressing the audience directly.

But most of all, the performers leave the audience feeling the line of thought they provoked is incomplete and open to interpretation. The issue of the dilemma of entertainment is raised in an intensive, almost tragic manner, but the problems are not being solved. There is no relief, nothing that would indicate how to take up political action or what would even give us hope or any reason to 'smile in the end'. This open end that the performance leaves behind is already indicated by the enigmatic title 'We are all Marlene Dietrich FOR'. 'We are all' is a rhetorical phrase, and it signifies that there is no position beyond political involvement with violence. The training scene, when the dancers exercise with the audience, is far from being didactic, and although it contains a certain amount of irony, it is certainly not making a mockery of military training routines. Rather, the group on stage confronts itself with one possible outcome of the training routine they had gone though. In this Brechtian sense of the dialectics of teaching and learning, the performance collective appears to be keen on learning to the same degree as the audience might learn - or, for that matter, as we all might. The subtitle of the performance reveals a reflexive turn: 'Performance for soldiers in peace keeping missions'. Since hardly any active soldiers will ever find their way into this show, the title addresses us all, the civilians as soldiers. It says: We are all always and already likely to end up in violent actions, because whether we do training, whether we watch a show or work in the entertainment business, we already act politically. Our peacekeeping missions aren't faultless.

Maybe I should have encouraged the group of students to undergo the military drill. It is not that I am now convinced of the artistic outcome of such an endeavour or that I would overlook the superficiality of the idea of comparing a short period in the barracks to long, professional training. The students would not have found the core of military violence and training, neither in theoretical reading nor on the training ground itself. After having experienced the uneasiness that the view on training presented by The Iceland Dance Company had caused in me, I am convinced that there is no such thing as a clear-cut enemy or other. But there is a latent state of violence, which I would distinguish from Johan Galtung's concept of structural violence, which rather demarcates the institutional, typical in, e.g., the governmental, military or the terrorist executive. Latent violence, rather, obtains its power from the bottom up, from physical training and imaginative journeys. If my formulation of the latent violent character of training turns out to be true, and if we all already are part of a training process as a 'social experiment', as Brecht described his *Lehrstück* concept, then it does not really matter to which outcome - be it dance, peacekeeping or terrorism - your training is supposed to lead. What matters is to start to question the training process itself.

REFERENCES:

Brecht, Bertolt (1967) 'Mißverständnisse über das Lehrstück', in Bertolt Brecht *Gesammelte Werke*, Frankfurt a. M.: Suhrkamp, pp. 1025-7.

Galtung, Johan (1969) 'Violence, peace and peace research', *Journal of Peace Research* 6(3): 167-91.

Schmitt, Carl (1996 [1932]) *The Concept of the Political*, foreword Tracy B. Strong, trans., introduction and notes George Schwab, notes on Schmitt's essay Leo Strauss, trans. J. Jarvey Lomax, Chicago and London: University of Chicago Press.

Schmitt, Carl (2007 [1963]) *The Theory of the Partisan: Intermediate commentary on the concept of the political*, trans. G. L. Ulmen, New York: Telos Press; originally published as *Theorie des Partisanen: Zwischenbemerkung zum Begriff des Politischen*, Berlin: Duncker und Humblot.

Iceland Dance Company (2003) 'We are all Marlene Dietrich FOR: Performance for soldiers in peacekeeping missions' Erna Ómarsdóttir and Emil Hrvatin, Ljubljana: Maska Productions (DVD) (special thanks to Katrin Hall and Johanna Pálsdóttir).

In Permanent Process of Reinvention

Guillermo Gómez-Peña, Roberto Sifuentes and Kimberlee Pérez pause to reflect upon La Pocha Nostra's permanently unfolding methodology and pedagogy

An extended version of this conversation will be part of Gomez-Peña's and Sifuentes's new book Radical Performance Pedagogy, forthcoming from Routledge.

January 2009: Tucson, Arizona;
February: Virtual space

Guillermo Gómez-Peña and Roberto Sifuentes discuss the currency of their performance pedagogy while they conduct their two-week intensive performance workshop involving twenty-five local and international artists.

For four years, the Pocha Nostra summer and winter schools have become amazing artistic and anthropological experiments in how artists from three generations and many countries, from every imaginable artistic, ethnic and subcultural background begin to find common ground. Performance becomes the connective tissue and lingua franca. Chicana cultural theorist Kimberlee Pérez enters the conversation via the Internet. Her interventions generate another layer of issues and demand that the dialogue expand in a non-linear manner.

PART 1 THE BEGINNING OF A NEW ERA

Guillermo Gómez-Peña: With the arrival of Obama, the US and the rest of the globe are now breathing a deep sigh of relief. It's like we just woke up from an epic nightmare. We are experiencing a radical political shift, and there is tremendous public optimism, a naïve optimism regarding the immediate future. And the question for us is – how is this major paradigm shift going to affect our art work? Will this new zeitgeist require a new methodology? I just don't know.

Crucial pedagogical questions remain. How can we develop a stronger and more inclusive sense of community, even if temporary, through art-making? How can we become better border-crossers and well-rounded citizens? How can we exercise our full citizenship through performance and not feel so marginalized? And how can we stand up and talk back to power, ¿que no?

Kimberlee Pérez: I love the way your questions move through the layers of performance and its possibilities, the political doing of it. You describe a pedagogy of radical inclusion – community generates resistance. While I find communities *can* be productive, I am also suspicious of 'community'. Do you find in workshops that some voices are silenced by those with more power or cultural capital? How do you negotiate a politic of resistance while confronting the unequal relations of power among participants?

Roberto Sifuentes: Our objectives are to create free zones, 'demilitarized zones', where volatile issues can be addressed. There is a distinction between the work of creating images and the power dynamics that might come out in the group. In those cases, the group members will often call each other on their shit. Of course, it has happened that sometimes people go too far in exerting power over another participant, and we have to take them aside and talk with them.

KP: So, overall, as groups develop their identity as a collective they begin to dialogue across difference. What do you do when self-segregating groups form and branch out on their own in the workshop?

RS: Socially, people will inevitably gravitate into groups for one reason or another. Our pedagogical approach during workdays is to shift partners around so that people don't work exclusively with their friends and they create new, unexpected bonds through performance work. But everyone is their own social being, and people have different ways to decompress after the workshop, and we have to respect that as well.

GGP: One of the challenges in this respect is to try to avoid clicas – small groups of people who tend to gravitate towards those who are similar to them as a mechanism of defense.

KP: Give me some examples.

GGP: Say the five or six theatre students who are a bit intimidated by the more adventurous performance artists or by the image-savvy art students ... or the heteros who are dealing with their fears of proximity vís-à-vís the gays and lesbians. They tend to hang out together, especially in the first three days. And when we sense it, we pair them with people they normally wouldn't collaborate with. It's a delicate matter, and it has to be done indirectly and diplomatically as to not make anyone feel self-conscious. The ultimate goal is to create a common ground.

KP: Outside of the microcosm of any particular group, can you discuss your motivation for holding workshops?

GGP: There are several objectives. To name but a few (I quote from a workshop document), 'To develop new models for relationships between artists and communities, mentor and apprentice, which are neither colonial nor condescending ... To find new modes of being and relating laterally to 'the other' in an un-mediated way, bypassing the myriad borders imposed by our professional institutions, our religious and political beliefs and pop-cultural affiliations. To experience this, even if only for the duration of the workshop, can have a profound impact in the participant's future practice'. Another important objective is to discover new ways of relating to our own bodies. Firstly, decolonizing them, then re-politicizing them as sites for activism and embodied theory, for memory and reinvention, for pleasure and penance. All these motivations overlap.

RS: Certainly one of the many objectives of the workshop is to create a network of rebel artists. Hopefully the Pocha methodology becomes a common language for these artists to jam together, to exchange ideas, to create art groups in their own cities. We see these networks sustaining themselves through blogs and social networking sites, creating projects and festivals with one another in different cities and countries. And, most importantly, these new networks happen without us. Although, it is harder to gather these artists when the globe is in the midst of total economic collapse. This will have a very direct and immediate impact in our work and our pedagogy.

GGP: You mean from now on we have to buy cheaper props? [laughter]

PART 2 OPENING UP THE METHODOLOGY

'Roberto and I are taking a break from the workshop and having a beer at the Congress Hotel. As exhaustion begins to sink in, we feel a bit insecure about the methodology. Part of our political praxis has been to open up our methodology to criticism and use this criticism as a challenge to constantly reinvent and expand the Pocha method in situ. We reflect on the shortcomings and challenges of our border methodology. Kimberlee enters the dialogue laterally, forcing Roberto and I to step out of our zones of comfort.' (Gómez-Peña)

RS: Most of the responses to our methodology have come from actual participants during a workshop. And in the days following, we respond to these challenges by shifting the nature of certain exercises and inventing new ones on the spot.

GGP: It's a living method for live art practice. For the past twelve years we have been developing this performance practice and these training methods as we tour, in between projects and with very little time to reflect.

RS: It's the same way we develop our performance work, in response to the moment, with a sense of urgency and immediacy ...

GGP: ... case by case.

RS: So, how do we translate our adaptive practice to other artists working in similar situations?

GGP: Tough question. Here's another one: How can we translate all the challenges of a live art workshop such as ours into a book format, a performance handbook for the twenty-first-century young bohemian?

RS: How can we even find the respite and support to reflect on the praxis and write about it? These questions and frustrations are at the centre of our living praxis.

[Kimberlee enters the discussion via the Internet]

KP: Ethno-techno begins some of the descriptive work of how you practice the methodology, but I am also interested in your pedagogical praxis - to theorize these kinds of reflections and experiences. Where does your pedagogy meet your methodology? How do you as facilitators/pedagogues navigate the politics of relation among participants? What do those moments look like?

GGP: Today, in our clumsy attempt to be more egalitarian, we have ceded a lot of control to some of the participants, and they are running

with it. This is good in the sense that it empowers them tremendously, but it is also affecting the normal course of the exercises. It's a delicate border we have to negotiate.

RS: Definitely, some stronger voices and personalities have taken the power. They have even somehow militantly structured how the group engages in dialogue in order that everyone is 'heard'. It's interesting to watch how they are figuring it out.

KP: An ecstatic, if messy, process for sure. Can you talk about your positionality when power-shifts, complex interactions and images and messiness take over the workshop in ways that do not move the workshop in productive directions?

RS: Our subtle performance strategy is to simply turn off their microphone and eventually they get the hint. (LOL)

GGP: Or take one of the antagonists of a conflict out for coffee or for a long walk and talk to them individually, and with compassion try to sort things out.

RS: Really, those are some of the adjustments that happen on a day to day basis. You remember in Portugal, from a very small group there emerged a strong puritanical opposition to the presence of wine in the evening sessions of the workshop. All of the sudden we were devoting a whole dialogue session to the subject of temperance, where some attempted to impose their morality on the group. This was certainly a heavy moment of imposed power. The group as a whole eventually came to an understanding that people could do whatever the hell they wanted to, rather than be driven by a moral and minority opinion.

GGP: Performance is a unique and elliptical form of democracy, a wonderfully clumsy form of democracy. You get dirty, but it works. It's a horizontal model. It involves the active participation of everyone present, the constant fleshing out of our civic, aesthetic and theoretical muscles. But the rules and dynamics change depending on the composition of every group. Some groups work better than others. And this you just can't predict.

KP: Certainly. I would also like to hear you talk about your strategy for generating democratic performance communities in the workshop setting. What are your base premises, foundations, and how do you introduce, maintain, and develop them as the workshop unfolds (or unravels)?

GGP: The strategies for inclusion require a specific knowledge that comes with experience. How to make everyone feel included and everyone's voice feel important. How to not be authoritarian, while at the same time be able to lead. How to listen to the participants' needs and complaints and incorporate them into the process. These are the challenges of a performance facilitator, an intellectual MC, and I want to believe we are getting a little better at it every year.

RS: Right. And the workshops invite and appeal to a range of participants, from multiple kinds of artists to students and theorists who are not necessarily familiar with the language of embodiment. As facilitators, it is important to allow the participants who don't necessarily come from a strictly movement background to discover and invent points of entry into the process. Though we often have requests for participants to only step back and observe, it is important for everyone to do the physical work. After some days of participating in all of the exercises, they translate their own métier into the Pocha process organically.

GGP: These are questions and challenges continually raised by theorists and other pedagogues. One theorist from NYU once asked us a very pertinent question: Can artists who aren't physically trained as performers enter our practice? I think it is useful if participants have some kind of performance, theatre, dance or martial arts training in their background, but it isn't absolutely necessary.

RS: As performance artists, the body is essential to our practice. So if an artist has an extreme phobia of being looked at or even touched, then perhaps this is not the right workshop for them. There are always artists with less physical training than others, and that's fine. Each workshop changes depending on the make-up of the group. Visual artists, sculptors and video artists have found our method useful in the sense that the exercises help them to develop unusual, original imagery that they can apply to their practice.

GGP: Curiously, theatre practitioners have a harder time, despite their training, because they are used to being directed, and we don't really 'direct'. We merely animate. We like to think of ourselves as performance DJs. We step in and out, hold the outer membrane of the workshop and share certain strategies, and by the end of the first week, we begin to encourage autonomy, and that flips them out.

RS: What about theorists who are interested in performance but rarely use their bodies? Many theorists are looking for a way to embody their theory and a Pocha workshop can be very useful.

KP: What I find generative and exciting about the workshops is the way Pocha maintains a border methodology towards the theorist/practitioner binary and emphasizes embodied theory. Can you talk more about how the teachers and theorists who aren't necessarily performers enter the workshop?

RS: We always engage and invite theorists who have never done any form of performance practice and who are interested in experiencing performance in their bodies and writing. We encourage them to integrate or adapt what they experience in the workshop into their own classroom pedagogy. They find new strategies in the workshop setting.

GGP: I welcome wholeheartedly the presence of theorists in the workshop, but they have to be willing to participate in all the exercises, not just observe. I welcome their presence because we also learn from them. It's an interesting negotiation: both sides feel a bit awkward. We feel a bit 'observed' by them, especially if we know they are writing about our practice, and at times they feel self-conscious. And to me, this unease is necessary and can be a generative place for dialogue. Uncomfortable situations are always fertile ground for developing performance material.

KP: As I recall, it was out of a passionate and awkward moment between us that we came to this conversation. How can we, as performers and theorists, develop collaborative relationships more often and thoroughly? How can we find more productive ways to communicate and embody theory, to generate one out of the other? What is the role of theory in your performance work?

GGP: I see myself as both a theorist and an artist, and to me this isn't a contradiction. I divide my time between writing and theorizing and making art, and both activities overlap. I don't even see where the border between them is located.

RS: Each workshop represents an evolution in our artistic and theoretical practice. So yes, the workshop space (and this very conversation) is part of a Pocha Laboratory that hopefully generates theoretical discourse, unique images, and ideas. Perhaps we can imagine the workshops as 'embodied think tanks'. But 'theory' does not figure overtly in the workshop context.

GGP: This is yet another challenge we have faced from theorists: How can La Pocha introduce theory and discussion during the workshop in a way that does not disrupt the hands-on work? We haven't entirely solved this one.

KP: Another messy moment – embodiment and talking about embodiment. It is difficult to ask participants to read theory, though suggestions are made that, at the minimum, participants enter with a familiarity of Pocha's methodological and performance practice, available in Ethno-techno and previous publications. But I do think it links back to our discussions of the dis/connect between aesthetics and political consciousness. They are sometimes mutually exclusive practices, and participants inevitably, without consciousness or sometimes discussion, construct images or engage in relational dynamics that are violent or damaging in colonialist and other power-laden ways. Theoretical introductions and interventions in these moments can be so productive at consciousness-raising and understanding. Not that you can't, or don't do this work, but perhaps an in-residence theorist/performer as a Pocha member in your next workshop might be a more overt catalyst to address these challenges?

RS: You're hired! We always have a number of theorist performers as part of the workshop, and they are invaluable to the process both within the workshop and at the discussions after hours. We encourage people to discuss the work outside of the workshop, at dinner time, in the bars or the cafes, but they often tell us it is not enough.

GGP: Also during our one-hour Zapatista-style discussion circles, we try to create space for participants to discuss pressing theoretical issues, but it doesn't seem to be enough. This is one of the main challenges we are currently facing.

KP: How about constructing a theoretical parallel to the 'quick and dirty' approach to image construction – don't think too much, just jump in and do it. Quick and dirty theorizing. It would be an interesting approach to integrate theory and performance without disrupting the flow and energy required for long workshop days. As we've discussed, participants need to stay on their feet and move, because once we sit down the energy goes with it. Doing both simultaneously would lend to developing a taxonomy of aesthetics and consciousness more overtly in ways that allow us to continue it outside of performance contexts and into other public realms. The question seems to be figuring out how to attend to the moment of an image or an issue without collapsing from the weight of the attending emotion or visceral responses.

RS: Those moments of instant reflexivity often occur during live performances of La Pocha's 'Performance Karaoke'. At the end of a given performance we often have an open structure where the audience is invited to join us onstage and create their own imagery. Guillermo freezes the action during the most radical moments and calls out for the audience to look at the image and make critical changes. Perhaps the critical 'discussion' does not have to be long talking sessions but also moments of physical intervention and reinvention.

GGP: Making art in situ out of the delicate issues that emerge in the process seems to be one of the solutions. Remember the Oaxacan workshop of 2007? The repression of the teachers' insurrection took place as we were conducting our summer school down there. And we had a discussion about this. Do we stop the workshop and join the teachers' strike, or do we continue doing what we went there to do? After a day's discussion, the consensus was to respond to the political moment with our work and with the kind of imagery we were developing; to use the charged political context as a way to energize and clarify our work. When we presented to the local community our final performance, we invited a lot of teachers and protestors to come into the museum, and they loved it. To them the museum became a temporary sanctuary, a place for reflection.

RS: If La Pocha wishes to be congruent with our beliefs, that we are a sanctuary of rebel artists from all métiers, national origins and conditions, we have to learn to walk the talk. And this means that the pedagogy has to address the needs of multiple communities, including those experiencing physical, theoretical and other challenges. We are not a theatre school or an academy of art. We are not interested in only 'skills training' but in the civic and ethical dimension of art-making.

KP: That's an important distinction. When you place yourself in the position of pedagogue, and articulate that kind of intention for yourself, even when it is one that is in a continual process of becoming, there are still questions of accountability. If one of your motivations is to calibrate cultural rebellion, how do you come to place yourself in the position of pedagogue? How do you navigate the hierarchy and power dynamics laden in even the most radical models? Who are you, and why do you want to teach, to hold workshops? When you extend your own methodology to others, how does it intersect or construct a radical pedagogy? What is radical pedagogy, how is it lived differently than the university, and how it is related? How do you theorize through this kind of pedagogy with its attention to multiple existing and ongoing communities? Why the workshop at all?

GGP: Ay Kimberlee, Roberto and I are writing an entire book called *Radical Performance Pedagogy* to play with these questions. In a sense, *This* conversation is part of figuring *it* out, workshopping ideas through dialogue. It's all about asking the hard questions, just like the ones you are asking right now ... but in a nutshell I can say that the purpose of a Pocha workshop, at least the conscious one, is to share some artistic strategies for people to become border-crossers and better artist-citizens. But I don't want to speak for Roberto. *¿Y tu carnal?*

RS: We are interested in an ongoing development

of the artist as border-crosser and radical intellectual. Our emphasis is not pure physical training, creating an arsenal of famous or fantastical 'super performance artists'. The mainstream public swiftly maintains discourses of dismissal and ignorance. Rather, our interest is in nurturing socially conscious artists working in experimental art forms interested in collaboration across international borders.

KP: And so the workshops participate in motivating cross-collaboration, emphasizing the intersections of aesthetics and politics? If Pocha's performance and pedagogical imperative is to reflect, engage and be a part of an ongoing cultural critique and shift, how do you structure your praxis in ways that account for the never-ending indeterminate nature of the global politic and make choices that reflect that in the workshop?

GGP: Really what we are saying is that much of the new work of our pedagogic praxis happens long before the workshop ever takes place. It is not a typical process of convocation and selection. We have to be engaged in ongoing recruitment all year long. Our performance colleagues around the globe become informants, pointing us towards younger artists in the cities where we perform and conduct workshops. Our responsibility is to make the effort to return to these cities and countries on a regular basis to sustain the network of newer 'Pocha associates' and support their work as well.

RS: Building a network of 'graduates' and associates is at the heart of the praxis. Whether we initiate it or not, participants create extending circles of collaborators and supporters. The community of performance is indeed a global community in a very immediate sense. From the UK's New Work Network to Facebook and others, we are connected in ways that were not possible years ago.

GGP: Perhaps the next step is to create a website with an embedded blog where people can exchange ideas and collaborate in upcoming projects across borders, a place where young performance artists can go to plan, exchange,

dialogue and engage in even more practical matters: I need a certain prop or costume, does anyone out there have it? I'm looking for an electronic composer to create music for one of my upcoming pieces, anyone out there interested? Or, I'll be going to Brazil, next month, can anyone put me up? It would be like a resource and exchange centre for performance artists connected to La Pocha.

RS: Part of what we are saying here is that we find that the work opened during the workshop continues beyond its close. Part of that means generating performance actions that culminate in, and extend to, public audiences in our final performance. The performative conversations among workshop participants and audience members in that public space is a productive site for what we believe performance can do – radical community-formation, public criticism, the practice of doing things differently, and being part of the emerging contemporary culture of hope. We hope that the shared 'language' of this performance methodology can provide a base for these ever-shifting communities of radical artists, in whatever ways they continue and manifest beyond the workshop context.

TO BE CONTINUED

• *Photos R J Muna*

BOOK REVIEW

Out of Now: The Lifeworks of Tehching Hsieh

Out of Now: The Lifeworks of
Tehching Hsieh
Adrian Heathfield and Tehching
Hsieh
Live Art Development Agency /
MIT Press, 2009
ISBN: 978-0-262-01255-3
383 p £29.95

Let's start by revisiting the bare bones of the performance projects by Taiwanese-American artist Tehching Hsieh, realized between 1978 and 1999. Six projects in all, beginning with a series of five year-long performances. First, one year of solitary confinement in a sealed cell with no communication. Second, a year of punching a time clock on the hour every hour and photographing this action: 24 frames a day for 365 days. Third, a year living rough outside on the streets of New York, drifting and seeking shelter, never going inside. Fourth, one year tied at the waist with a rope to the performance artist Linda Montano, with a prohibition on touch. Fifth, a year spent abstaining wholly from art, its making and its spheres of influence. Finally, a 13-year project in which Hsieh proposed to make art without ever showing it in public, a project during which he effectively disappeared. On New Year's Eve 1999, at the cusp of the new millennium, in a brief event at the Judson Memorial Church to mark the project's ending, Hsieh simply told those who had gathered that he had succeeded in keeping himself alive.

The publication of this superb monograph is timely indeed. To date very little of substance has been published about this most remarkable artist and his profoundly unsettling body of work, despite the fact that its contours and challenges are etched indelibly into the psyches of so many involved in contemporary art and performance. We know these deceptively simple shapes, the sculptural forms of the bare bones outlined above, and they are as honed as the shapes of some of Beckett's most economical work. Or rather we *think* we know them, for they linger on in unresolved reverberant forms within us. In reality, individually and collectively these works confront and resist claims to knowledge: about art and its parameters; about the passage of time, meaning, identity, freedom; and ultimately about what really happened in the seconds and minutes and hours and days and months and years of these extraordinary 'lifeworks'.

In a brilliant opening essay, 'Impress of Time', Adrian Heathfield contextualizes and unfolds the implications of Hsieh's 'life lived at limits' (58) with consummate sensitivity and thoughtfulness. He treads lightly and respectfully throughout, refusing to explain this work away in any singular and inevitably reductive 'reading', instead approaching each work in turn not as a referential or symbolic narrative structure but in terms of what it does. In this way, he seeks to articulate something of the affective 'force' of this body of work as a 'constellation of *enduring ideas*, echoing in the present' (58).

As well as providing detailed descriptions of each of the projects in turn, Heathfield explores a wide range of such ideas, including: Hsieh's conception of art and life as simultaneous processes; his embodied instantiations of radical paradox, including the ambiguity of relations between constraint, solitude, freedom and thought in his work, and his deconstructive 'binding together of activity and negation, production and redundancy', public immersion and isolation, movement and stasis (45); the differing temporalities of photography and film, and the unstable epistemological status of documentation; Hsieh's embodied stagings of an ethics of alterity, relationality and civility; his recurrent engagement with aspects and structures of 'the law' (he cites Kafka as a core stimulus), set alongside his vulnerable status as an illegal immigrant in the US; his decelerative 'wasting of time' in non-productive and uneventful works of extreme duration, and the critical frictions his 'use-less' slowness seem to propose within the accelerated temporalities of late capitalism. En route, Heathfield also traces relations with Conceptualism, Performance Art, Body Art in the West, and connections with a range of other artists including Bas Jan Ader, Harry Houdini, Hiroshi Sugimoto, Abramovic and Ulay and, perhaps most startlingly as a deterritorializing line of flight, the tightrope walker

Philippe Petit. These connective genealogies are invariably and finely attuned to differences, and Heathfield resists collapsing this relational cartography into any homogenizing empire of the selfsame.

The bulk of the book (pp. 63–315) is given over to Hsieh's exhaustive documentation of each of his 'lifeworks'. Scores, flyers, maps, punch cards stamped and signed, legal documents attesting to Hsieh's own 'rules' having been respected (cells and ropes sealed and unbroken, punch cards stamped etc.) and thousands of photographs. Hsieh also includes calendars registering minor breakings of his strictures, such as hours missed in the punching of the time clock: 133 absences in the total of 8,760, each one catalogued in relation to one of three possible 'reasons' – 'sleeping', 'late', 'early'.

Many of the beautifully reproduced images comprise lengthy series of stills cumulatively registering the passage of time, in dated punch cards, say, or gradual hair growth. It's intriguing to revisit the hourly photographs of 'Time Clock Piece' in this print context, laid out on 31 consecutive pages, each page containing 12 vertical columns / film strips of 24 images (i.e., one day per strip, 12 days per page). The lay-out produces an uncanny juddering temporality, and at the same time foregrounds the sheer enormity of the (t)ask. Its astonishing difficulty is somewhat elided in the high-speed, suppressed-hysteria energetics of the 6-minute stop-motion animated film version, within which each day – each column within the book – is condensed into a second (see Hsieh 1999). On the page one can skim and flick, or endeavour to accept it as a kind of meditation exercise: an invitation to engage with the im/possibility of paying attention to each image, to the rare blank spaces when Hsieh failed to make it and to the infinite blank spaces of the unimaginable 59 minutes or so *between* images. The labour of attempting to 'read' it as a (ruptured) continuum takes time and real effort. Cumulatively it's incapacitating, one soon struggles with a kind of 'blindness' and defaults to skimming; and in the end we come no closer to understanding what really happened. One recognizes Hsieh's absolute clarity of purpose and will-full integrity in the work, but 'he' is always elsew/here.

Ultimately, Heathfield locates Hsieh as 'a sentient witness of time' (11), engaged in practices of 'aesthetic duration', with each work *'a sense passage in which corporeal attention is drawn to (a) time reforming'* (22). Each of Hsieh's 'untimely' projects constructs a space of severe, self-imposed privation and constraint within which time passes and thinking happens. Each performance elaborates a rigorously precise architecture for the event of thought as art; but none of those thoughts is communicated. The internal life of the being in human being – Hsieh's lived experience of brutalizing bare life *in extremis* – is forever withheld in an economy of denial that serves to create empty spaces for our own projections and dealings with incomprehension. As Tim Etchells puts it in his letter to Hsieh, the extensive documentary traces of the work that survive 'show everything but tell nothing' (357). Hsieh moves implacably towards the self-erasure of ever greater illegibility, invisibility and silence to leave us confronted with 'a sculpture of nothingness', and we are pulled back endlessly to 'a face off with the void' (360). Or, as Hsieh puts it with characteristic economy and lack of sentimentality: 'Living is nothing but consuming time until you die' (335).

The book draws to a reflexive end without closure in a long and engaging interview/exchange between Hsieh and Heathfield ('I Just Go On In Life') and a series of open letters to Hsieh by Peggy Phelan, Marina Abramovic, Tim Etchells, Santiago Sierra and others from Hsieh's personal archive. The latter include a hand-written note from an irate and anonymous Chinese person – 'Artist? UGH!' (354); and a delightfully formal letter of support from a (real) estate agent in Michigan – 'I don't totally understand exactly what you are doing but I do think it is very important. Keep on with your good work ... ' (350). The letters allow different modalities of writing to open up other more intimate perspectives on and creative responses to the work, most effectively to my mind in the exquisitely performative contributions of Peggy Phelan and Tim Etchells. Finally, Carol Becker writes back into and out of the book in an elegant summative post-script, in which she applauds Heathfield's approach to the curation of these materials. His framing, she suggests perceptively, creates 'a safe holding environment where the work can rest ... The intent of the pieces appears intact, allowed to exist in its emptiness and silence, still elusive even after so much has been said' (369).

David Williams

REFERENCE

Hsieh, Tehching (1999) *One Year Performance Art Documents, 1978–1999*, DVD-ROM. See http://www.one-year-performace.com Also available through the Live Art Development Agency's online Unbound: http://www.thisisunbound.co.uk/

Performance Research: On Training
Notes on Contributors

THE EDITORS

Ric Allsopp is a founding editor of *Performance Research*. He is currently Senior Research Fellow in the Department of Contemporary Arts at Manchester Metropolitan University, UK, and Visiting Professor at the University of the Arts, Berlin.

Richard Gough is general editor of *Performance Research*, a Professor at Aberystwyth University, Wales, and Artistic Director for the Centre for Performance Research (CPR). He has curated and organized numerous conference and workshop events over the last 30 years as well as directing and lecturing internationally.

ISSUE CO-EDITOR

Simon Shepherd is Professor of Theatre and Deputy Principal (Academic) at The Central School of Speech and Drama, University of London. Recent publications include *Drama/Theatre/Performance*, with Mick Wallis (2004) and *Theatre, Body and Pleasure* (2006). Forthcoming books include *The Cambridge Introduction to Modern British Theatre* and *ORLAN: A hybrid body of artworks*, edited with Simon Donger and ORLAN.

CONTRIBUTORS

Cariad Astles works at the Central School of Speech and Drama as Puppetry Tutor for the Theatre Practice (Puppetry) BA. She trained at Exeter and London Universities and before CSSD worked at Plymouth University. She is a professional puppeteer and performs in Catalonia for several months each year.

Bojana Bauer is a PhD candidate at the EDESTA doctoral school at Paris 8 University with the full scholarship from FCT (Fundação para a Ciência e a Tecnologia, Portugal). As a dramaturg she currently collaborates with Mário Afonso and Pedro Gomez-Egaña, and she worked with Vera Mantero, Brynjar Bandlien and the Alkantara Festival (Lisbon). She publishes her writing in *Repères*, *Mouvement.net* and *Dance Zone*.

Frank Camilleri is Artistic Director of Icarus Performance Project and Lecturer in Drama and Theatre Studies at the University of Kent. He was Academic Coordinator of Theatre Studies at the University of Malta from 2004 to 2008. He is a co-founder of Icarus Publishing Enterprise (Holstebro, Malta, Wrocław).

Véronique Chance is an artist who works predominantly in photography, video, installation and performance. She is currently completing a practice-led PhD in the Department of Art at Goldsmiths, University of London and is also an Associate Lecturer of the University of the Arts, London, teaching at Camberwell and Wimbledon Colleges of Art.

Joan L. Duda is Professor of Sports Psychology in the School of Sport and Exercise Sciences, University of Birmingham, UK. She has over 200 scientific publications concerning motivational processes in physical activity settings. As a practising consultant she has worked with coaches, athletes, dancers and musicians.

Wolf-Dieter Ernst is Professor of Theatre and Media at Ludwig-Maximilians-Universität in Munich. He has published widely on postdramatic theatre, performance and media art. He is review editor of the journal *Forum Modernes Theater*, principal investigator of the DFG-funded project 'Vorschrift und Affekt' and his books include **Performance der Schnittstelle** (Passagen Verlag, 2003) and, with Meike Wagner, *Performing the Matrix: Mediating cultural performance*. Forthcoming book projects include the 'Discourse of Actor Training 1870–1930' and 'Image and Imagination: Critical readings in visual studies and acting theory'. Professor Ernst has also contributed substantially to the development of the IFTR Intermediality, Theatre and Performance research group.

Josette Féral is a full professor at the Université du Québec in Montréal. Her published books include *Voies de Femmes* (2007), *Teatro, Teoria y Practica: Mas alla de las fronteras* (Buenos Aires, Galerna, 2004), *Trajectoires du Soleil* (Paris, 1999) and *Rencontres avec Ariane Mnouchkine* (Paris, 1995, reprinted in 2001). She has edited books on the theory of the theatre, the most recent being *The Creative Processes* (Theatre Research International, 2008), *The Transparency of the Text: Contemporary writing for the stage*, co-edited with Donia Mounsef (Yale French Studies, 2007), *Mnouchkine und das Théâtre du Soleil* (Berlin, 2003), *L'Ecole du Jeu: Former ou transmettre* (L'Entretemps, France, 2003), 'Theatricality' (special issue of *Substance*, 2002) and *Les Chemins de l'Acteur* (Montréal, 2001). See <www.josette-feral.org>.

Ulf Henrik Göhle is a junior lecturer at the Hochschule für Musik und Darstellende Kunst in Frankfurt am Main, Department of Dance, and is undertaking postgraduate research in Motologie at the University of Marburg. He previously studied music in London and sport science in Frankfurt am Main.

John Matthews, PhD (Surrey), is Co-ordinator for Contextual Studies at Rose Bruford College. He received the *University of London Award for Excellence*. Formally editor of HUB, he is co-editor of *Ethics and Performance* (Cambridge Scholars, 2010). He has performed in BBC Film Drama and in theatre in the UK nationally and has exhibited work at South Bank Centre, London.

Dick McCaw co-founded the Actors Touring Company in 1978 and the Medieval Players in 1981. He was the Director of the International Workshop Festival from 1993 to 2001. He is a qualified Feldenkrais Practitioner, is working on *The Routledge Sourcebook for Rudolf Laban* and is a Senior Lecturer at Royal Holloway, University of London.

Guillermo Gómez-Peña is a performance artist, writer and director of La Pocha Nostra. Using performance, multilingual poetry, journalism, video, radio and installation art, his work has contributed to the debates on cultural diversity, identity, and US-Mexico relations. He is a MacArthur Fellow, American Book Award winner and contributing editor of *The Drama Review* (NYU-MIT).

Kimberlee Pérez is an Instructor of Intercultural Communication in The College of Communication at DePaul University, Chicago. Her teaching, writing and solo and collaborative performance address queer Chicana politics and identity, queer intimacies, transnational feminism and globalization, and the cultural and resistive work of performance.

Jonathan Pitches is Professor of Theatre and Performance in the School of Performance and Cultural Industries at Leeds University. He has written two books on Russian actor-training: *Vsevolod Meyerhold* and *Science and the Stanislavsky Tradition of Acting* and is co-editor of the new Routledge journal *Theatre Dance and Performance Training*.

Eleanor Quested is a research fellow in the School of Sport and Exercise Sciences, University of Birmingham, UK. Her research focuses on social-environmental and motivational predictors of well- and ill-being among athletes and dancers. Eleanor has also lectured in dance psychology at Laban, London, for five years.

Roberto Sifuentes is a performance artist and founder member of performance collective La Pocha Nostra. His work fuses charged cultural issues with a wild pop culture aesthetic, combining live performance with interactive technologies. He has exhibited work in several hundred venues throughout the United States, Europe, Canada and Latin America. Sifuentes is full-time faculty at the School of the Art Institute of Chicago.

Peta Tait is Chair in Theatre and Drama at LaTrobe University and publishes on the practice and theory of theatre, performance and circus. She writes for performance and her most recent books are *Circus Bodies: Cultural Identity in Aerial Performance* (Routledge, 2005) and *Performing Emotions* (Ashgate, 2002).

David Williams has taught and made performance in Australia and England, working as writer, dramaturg, performer, director, editor, translator. After twelve years at Dartington College of Arts, he has recently joined the Theatre and Drama Department at Royal Holloway, University of London. He is currently dramaturg for Lone Twin Theatre.

Piotr Woycicki is a doctoral student in Theatre Studies at the Lancaster Institute of Contemporary Arts, Lancaster University. His work focuses on post-cinematic performance and 'intermedial' theatre.

Credits for Pages from a Lost and Found Family Album

Page 3 : *left page of album, top left* - RAT Theatre training 1972, courtesy of Mike Pearson; *top right* - Grotowski's Theatr Laboratorium training 1967 courtesy of the Grotowski Institute; *bottom* - Alfred Court, courtesy of Yves Kohl

Page 3 : *right page of album, top left and right* - Lisa Ullmann teaching students at the Art of Movement Studio, Manchester, 1947. Photographer: Roland Watkins courtesy of Laban Library and Archive; *middle and bottom* - Cardiff Laboratory Theatre Peking Opera Explorations 1986-87, courtesy of CPR Archive

Page 4 : Meyerhold Biomechanic exercises 1934 courtesy of Maria Valenti and CPR Archive

Page 35 : *top* - Cardiff Laboratory Theatre Peking Opera Explorations 1986-87, courtesy of CPR Archive; *middle* - Dancing Men in a training exercise, 1910. (Photo by Hulton Archive/Getty Images); *bottom* - Meyerhold Biomechanic exercises 1934 courtesy of Maria Valenti and CPR Archive

Page 53 : *top left* - Alfred Court, courtesy of Yves Kohl; *top right* - Cardiff Laboratory Theatre Peking Opera Explorations 1986-87, courtesy of CPR Archive; *bottom* - CPR Summer Shift training session courtesy of CPR Archive

Page 66 : *top* - Mirror Dance. 1932: Margaret Morris dancers rehearsing and training in Chelsea. (Photo by Topical Press Agency/Getty Images). *Bottom left and right* - Meyerhold Biomechanic exercises 1934, Kustov and Zlobin, courtesy of Maria Valenti and CPR Archive

Page 113 : *top* - Cardiff Laboratory Theatre Peking Opera Explorations 1986-87, courtesy of CPR Archive; *middle left* - Cardiff Laboratory Theatre Peking Opera Explorations 1986-87, courtesy of CPR Archive; *middle right* - Ballet mistress Ninette de Valois training the Sadler's Wells company (Photo by Kurt Hutton/Getty Images); *bottom right* - Grotowski's Theatr Laboratorium training 1967 courtesy of the Grotowski Institute

Page 129 : *top left* - Alfred Court courtesy of Yves Kohl; *top right* - Litz Pisk conducting a class in 1962 courtesy of Central School of Speech and Drama; *middle left* - Warren Lamb, Valerie Preston and another student at the Art of Movement Studio, Manchester, 1947. Photographer: Roland Watkins courtesy of Laban Library and Archive; *middle right* - RAT Theatre training 1972, courtesy of Mike Pearson; *bottom left* - Grotowski's Theatr Laboratorium training 1967 courtesy of the Grotowski Institute; *bottom right* - Cardiff Laboratory Theatre Peking Opera Explorations 1986-87, courtesy of CPR Archive

Page 134 : *top* - Alfred Court courtesy of Yves Kohl; *bottom* - Body conditioning being taught to students at Jacobs Pillow Summer Ballet School. (Photo by Lisa Larsen//Time Life Pictures/Getty Images)

Editorial Statement

Performance Research is a specialist journal that aims to promote a dynamic interchange between scholarship and practice in the expanding field of performance. Interdisciplinary in vision and international in scope, its emphasis is on contemporary performance arts within changing cultures.

It is a condition of publication that authors assign copyright or license the publication rights in their articles, including abstracts, to Taylor & Francis. This enables us to ensure full copyright protection and to disseminate the article, and of course the Journal, to the widest possible readership in print and electronic formats as appropriate.

Authors retain many rights under the Taylor & Francis rights policies, which can be found at www.informaworld.com/authors_journals_copyright_position. Authors are themselves responsible for obtaining permission to reproduce copyright material from other sources.

© Taylor & Francis Ltd 2009